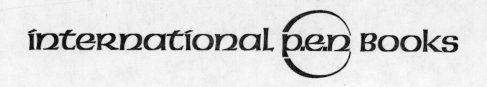

international p.e.n Books

ANTHOLOGIES - I

D1713773

AN ANTHOLOGY
OF
MODERN
YIDDISH LITERATURE

Compiled and edited by

JOSEPH LEFTWICH

1974
MOUTON
THE HAGUE – PARIS

LIBRARY OF CONGRESS CATALOG CARD NUMBER 74-82386

Printed in The Netherlands.

Acknowledgement

Grateful acknowledgement is made to Mr. Thomas Yoseloff of Thomas
Yoseloff Inc., Publishers, and A. S. Barnes Inc., Publishers, Cranbury, New
Jersey, U.S.A., for his kind and ready Permission to use in this volume
material from my three Anthologies published by his Firm:
'Yisroel' — short stories — *'The Golden Peacock'* — poetry — and *'The Way
We Think'* — essays.

Joseph Leftwich

Contents

Contents

Contents

Foreword

It is fitting that this Anthology of Yiddish Literature appears under the auspices of International PEN, which includes a Yiddish Centre based in New York, whose representative I have been for over thirty years at PEN Congresses and on the PEN International Executive. For it was PEN through which I came to do my first Anthology, 'Yisroel', a collection of short stories by Jewish authors, of whom twenty-two were Yiddish, published in 1933. The poet Hugh McDiarmid who at that time was connected with the London publishers John Heritage and Unicorn Press, the publishers of his 'First Hymn to Lenin', had at a PEN Congress met some Yiddish writers, and with Hitler inveighing against Jewish Literature and everything Jewish, culminating in the burning of Jewish books and then of millions of Jews, he conceived the idea of an Anthology of Jewish authors. The publishers called me in to produce the book. The Yiddish PEN, then in Warsaw, helped me with the permissions, as acknowledged in the book. And the publishers gave recognition to the book's provenance by dedicating it to 'The Past and Present Members of the PEN'.

It would take more pages than is possible in a volume most of which should be devoted to actual examples of Yiddish literature, to trace the development of Yiddish literature from its earliest days in the 15th. and 16th. centuries, with its outstanding writer Elijah Levita and his Bovo Book, and such figures as Glueckel of Hamelin (Heine's ancestress) in the 17th. century, and Rabbi Nachman Bratzlaver, in the 18th. The number of pages in a book is inexorable. Denis Saurat, an early friend in PEN, faced this problem in an anthology of French stories he edited in 1947. He found some things he wanted wouldn't go in into his space. 'So let no one blame me overmuch', he said, 'if this and that good thing has been omitted'. Those wishing to follow up the subject may find interest in my articles on Yiddish Literature in the 1970 Encyclopedia Britannica and in Chambers' Encyclopedia, and in some of the other works listed in the Bibliography.

I should say a word about the sort of thing one finds in, for instance, Fowler's 'Modern English Usage', that 'Yiddish is not a kind of Hebrew, but a kind of German'. It is much less a kind of German than Dutch, or for its Anglo-Saxon elements, even English. Yiddish is not a kind of German any more than it is a kind of Hebrew. It is a language that has evolved from Middle High German and Hebrew, in almost equal halves, and has gone its own separate way for centuries. I recently came upon a review of one of Bashevis Singer's books by Anthony Burgess, who found it 'pleasingly ironic that a once despised German dialect is producing an important modern international literature'.

For reasons of space I have had to omit the so-called classics of Yiddish Literature, Mendele, Peretz and Sholem Aleichem and other writers of their period, the 19th. century. They would have alone filled the book. I felt that the purpose of the book would be better fulfilled by devoting it to more or less contemporary writers.

Certainly, the older writers would have had nothing in their work about the vast tragedy of the Hitler extermination, which came after their time. Though in my book of Peretz stories I did draw attention to an astonishing prophecy in his work: 'It is possible that in a number of years Grzybowska (the Jewish Community building in Warsaw) will be ruins, not a stone left standing. And in another place there will stand a huge palace with a great chimneystack like in a vast factory, and flames will shoot from the windows, from a furnace, and the chimney will belch smoke from human flesh burning, bones and blood and brains — a tremendous crematorium'. An inspired prophecy! Foretelling Auschwitz!

When Eliezer Greenberg addressed the 1953 PEN Congress in Dublin on behalf of the Yiddish PEN he regretted that 'with the exception of one or two writers Yiddish literature is hardly known to the non-Yiddish public'. But our three giants, Mendele, Peretz and Sholem Aleichem, and also the later Sholem Asch and Bashevis Singer exist in good measure in English translation, as the Bibliography will show. I have myself contributed a volume of Peretz's short stories. And I have made frequent obeisances in English to Mendele, as on his centenary in 1935, and to Sholem Aleichem, on his centenary (in 'The Unesco Courier' in 1960). I am not sure that Sholem Aleichem would have approved of what was done with his Tevye stories in 'Fiddler on the Roof', but the musical did make Sholem Aleichem and his Tevye something of a cult. I was glad when my translation of Sholem Aleichem's 'Little People' was produced in 1966 at the Edinburgh Festival, that the 'mere Gentile' who wrote the notice in the 'Glasgow Herald' decided that it made 'Jewish daily life come gloriously alive'. In an essay on Bashevis Singer in the Jewish Book Annual in New York in 1970, I suggested that in the same way as Hazlitt claimed that 'the four greatest names in English poetry are almost the four first we come to — Chaucer, Spenser, Shakespeare and Milton', so 'the three greatest names in modern Yiddish literature are Mendele, Peretz and Sholem Aleichem. I would add Sholem Asch, the most important of Peretz's disciples'. Of course there are others among the later writers, and one of them, Shlomo Rosenberg, enumerating the Yiddish writers of to-day made a list: 'Together with Mendele, Peretz, Sholem Aleichem — Sholem Asch, Weissenberg, Bashevis, Demblin, Mendel Mann, Leivick, Mani Leib, M. L. Halpern, Almi and scores of others. All of them together make up our contemporary Yiddish literature'.

I am sorry I had to omit a number of the Yiddish writers who 'all together make up our contemporary Yiddish literature'. Maybe there will be another chance to add examples of their work. I have in mind something Ludwig Lewisohn wrote about Yiddish poetry, about the poets Leivick, Glatstein, Sutzkever, Boreisho and Segalowitch, that 'had so powerful and fruitful a movement arisen in Denmark or Venezuela or Bengal the world would have heard of it and its chief representatives would have been parts of at least the vocabulary of a few cultivated people'. I think of a score or more of really important writers; among them four Soviet Yiddish writers, Israel Kipnis, Meir Wiener (who fell in battle in the Soviet-Hitler war), Eli Shechtman and Nathan Zabore. Their major works are too long for this book. But they are major writers, and these are major works. It has bearing on Soviet conditions that both Shechtman and Zabore chose for the period of their novels not present-day Soviet life, but Shechtman the recent past, the heroic period of struggle in Czarist Russia for the coming Revolution, the period of Czarist oppression, the knout, Siberia, pogroms; and Zabore the distant golden era of Spanish and Provencal Jewry, before the Inquisition, the days of great scholars and poets and thinkers, the age of Rambam, whom the world knows as Maimonides. We have heard that Eli Shechtman recently arrived in Israel as one of the new Soviet immigrants. I hope that we shall soon read further chapters of his 'Erev', which has been appearing in the Moscow Yiddish journal 'Sovietish Heimland'. Again on this question of length — I had meant to include Mendel Mann's long story 'Glushino'. I am glad that when I suggested to him instead his 'Black Oak' he agreed, writing to me, 'It is quite representative of my work'. Yet 'Glushino' is the more important.

It seems unpardonable for a book of contemporary Yiddish literature not to include such poets as Avrom Reisen, Yehoash and Moishe Leib Halperin. Or in prose to omit Bashevis's brother I. J. Singer, Joseph Opotoshu, A. M. Fuchs, Katzisne, Ozer Warszawski, and a dozen others of like importance. There is only the consolation that some of their work is otherwise available in English translation.

Agnon was a Hebrew writer. But it is to the point that when he was given the Testimonial Dinner in London after receiving the Nobel Prize, Ifor Evans, as I heard him at the dinner, reminded Agnon that he had started writing in Yiddish. 'His earliest work was in Yiddish, and I hope he will never forget his Yiddish, and that Jews will never forget their Yiddish'. There is nothing surprising in this affinity of Hebrew and Yiddish. Those two great Hebrew writers, Bialik and Shneour, were also Yiddish writers. And Yiddish pervaded also the thought and the work of Kafka and Babel. Kafka knew and studied both Hebrew and Yiddish. He was interested in a Yiddish theatre company, and there is his famous address at one of its performances, 'Ladies and Gentlemen, I would tell you how much better you understand Yiddish than you suppose'. As for Babel, he grew up in a Yiddish-speaking home, and had friends and colleagues among Yiddish writers, and in the 1920's he compiled a Russian translation of Sholem Aleichem's stories.

Yiddish literature has been fortunate in recent years in the number of works translated and published in English. But (not much otherwise in other literatures) it suffers from being presented more or less haphazard, without a system. I spoke of it in the Foreword to my first 'Golden Peacock' which appeared in 1939. I quoted from the Yiddish writer Melech Ravitch (who was the Secretary of the Yiddish PEN in Warsaw, who helped me with my Permissions for the Yiddish writers in 'Yisroel') — one of his essays where he described a dream — that a millionaire had placed all his wealth at Ravitch's disposal, to serve Yiddish Literature. With this money, said Ravitch, 'I would rent a villa in a quiet village in a neutral country, and call in three objective Yiddish critics. I would get for them all the Yiddish books that have appeared since the beginning of Yiddish literature, and tell them to edit a Library to be called 'The Great Storehouse of Yiddish Literature'. The Library will be in 100 volumes. Then I shall have these 100 volumes translated into all the great languages of civilisation. Because it is only in the mirror of other languages that the real sense and meaning of Yiddish Literature can become apparent; because Yiddish Literature must not be turned in upon itself, but must be regarded as an integral part of the world literature'.

When I spoke at the PEN Congress in London in 1941, during the war, I dwelt on the death and destruction Hitler was dealing out in Poland and all Eastern Europe: 'In this present moment Yiddish literature and Yiddish writers (except for those in America), in that central and eastern Europe which was the cradle and has been the home of Yiddish literature and of the millions of Yiddish-speaking and Yiddish-writing and reading Jews, are being destroyed by Hitler. There is death and slavery there. What literature do they produce in the Lublin reservation? In the Warsaw Ghetto?'

But Yiddish literature *was* being produced in the Warsaw Ghetto. And elsewhere, in the camps. And some Yiddish writers survived. Hillel Seidman survived the Warsaw Ghetto. Sutzkever survived the Vilna Ghetto. Rachmiel Bryks, whom I first met soon after the Liberation, at the PEN Congress in 1946 in Stockholm, survived the Lodz Ghetto. So did Chava Rosenfarb who has written a wonderful trilogy about the Lodz Ghetto. And those who died did not die mute. Emanuel Ringelblum, who died, left a mass of material about the life and struggle in the Warsaw Ghetto, which after the Liberation was published in Warsaw in Yiddish. It became source material for John Hersey's 'The Wall'. Isaac Katznelson, who was murdered in the Warsaw Ghetto, left his great poem 'The Song of the Slaughtered Jewish People', as well as other poetry illuminating the holocaust, like 'Shlomo Jelichovsky'. Hirsh Glick was killed fighting in a Partisan band in the Vilna woods. But his poem 'Never Say This Is the Last Road, the End of the Way' survives. No collection of Jewish literature could leave out such work, the literature of one of the most barbaric devastations in human history.

Life has made adjustments, and to-day's Germany has tried to atone for the crimes of the Hitler Germans, though a poet like Isaac Katznelson who met death at their hands could not imagine a time when Jews would ever forgive Germans — 'We shall stand at every road, silent like the grass. And we shall ask you, "Why did you murder us?" '

To-day Jews are preoccupied with a present problem, the treatment of Jews in Russia and other Soviet countries. It was at the PEN Congress in Copenhagen in 1948 and again at the Edinburgh Congress in 1950 that I brought up on behalf of the Yiddish PEN the disappearance in Russia, later revealed as the murder of the leading Soviet Yiddish writers, among them personal friends of mine, like the poet Itzik Feffer, and the actor Mikhoels, the head of the Yiddish State Theatre in Moscow. In 1943 when they were in London on a goodwill mission during the war, PEN had entertained them at a dinner, with H. G. Wells in the chair, and Sir Lewis Casson and I as the welcoming speakers. I remember how about that time at a meeting at which they spoke in the Albert Hall, Joseph MacLeod read out my translation of Feffer's poem 'I Am a Jew'. Now Stalin had decided to purge Yiddish literature and Yiddish writers.

My questions were resented. Friends of the Soviets here and elsewhere denied that any harm had come to the Yiddish writers. It was said that they were all alive and well, on a sort of group holiday. Feffer in Latvia, others in Turkestan. I was publicly accused of spreading 'cold war' propaganda; I found myself involved in a libel action turning on the truth or falsehood of my charges. I recall with gratitude that on Paul Tabori's initiative the International Writers Fund of PEN helped me by launching an appeal on my behalf.

When Stalin died and Krushchev revealed the facts of the murders of the Soviet Yiddish writers, Sutzkever who in Moscow during the war after his escape from the Vilna Ghetto had been a close friend of Mikhoels and Bergelson and Markish, wrote in 1956 in his journal 'Goldene Keit', which appears in Israel: 'This should have been a joyful occasion — our twenty-fifth issue. But our joy is shamed and disturbed by the pogrom now openly admitted against the Yiddish writers in the Soviet Union'.

The irony is that many of the Soviet Yiddish writers who were purged and slain, Bergelson, Markish, The Nistor, and Mikhoels too, had been living abroad, and went to Russia with a sense of exhilaration, a sense of mission, to take their part in the building of Socialism, and to use the wonderfully favourable opportunities being given there for the development of Yiddish literature, in line with all the other minority literatures. Vendroff, who was one of the survivors of Stalin's concentration camps, wrote to me in 1923 about those favourable conditions for Yiddish writers in the Soviet Union. They had no worries about making a living or getting their work published. All they had to do was write. The State saw to the publication. The State paid them. And their work sold in thousands. Bergelson while visiting Warsaw in the '30's boasted in an interview about the mass readership he had. Neither Bergelson nor Vendroff said anything of course about the Party censorship, having to write so as not to overstep the Party line, which Sholem Asch at the Edinburgh PEN Congress in 1950 called the line on which humanity is hanged.

There was another motive which had won for the Soviet Union the admiration and gratitude not only of the Yiddish writers in the Soviet Union and Soviet Jewry generally, but of Yiddish writers and of masses of Jews throughout the world. Most of these Yiddish writers in many countries had spent their early years in Czarist Russia, and had suffered from antisemitism, from discrimination and pogroms. Sholem Aliechem had fled to London in 1905 from a pogrom in which his home had been destroyed. Some of the Yiddish writers had been revolutionaries, and had been in Russian prisons. Leivick escaped from Siberia to America, and never forgot his Siberian experience. Whatever else, Soviet Russia had in its early years, till Stalin reintroduced it, abolished antisemitism. Leivick, who afterwards brought out with Opotoshu a volume 'Dedicated to All the Slain or Silenced Yiddish Writers in the Soviet Union' speaking in 1937 at a Conference of Yiddish writers in Paris, declared 'My love for the Soviet Union', because faced with Hitler, Jews had to look to Russia. That was before the Hitler-Stalin Pact. But the memory of that Pact too was wiped out when Russia came into the war against Nazi Germany. It was the time when the whole Free World acclaimed the Red Army. Certainly the Jews in Soviet Russia did. 'I am not alone', Feffer said. 'The Slavs are my brothers too. I am a Jew!' And 'I am a Jew who has drunk up Happiness from Stalin's cup'. The same Stalin who then had him and his colleagues killed.

It is all understandable if we bear in mind what life was like for the Jews, and for the mass of the Russian people, under the Czars. That old Russia — the Russian poet Nekrasov wrote a book about it — and he died a hundred years ago — which he called, 'Who Can Be Happy and Free in Russia?' This year is the centenary of the birth of the great Hebrew and Yiddish poet Bialik. He leapt to fame with his poem 'In the Slaughter Town', inspired by the pogrom in Kishinev in 1903. It shook the Jewish world. It shook the Zionist Congress, so that when Herzl, who founded the Zionist movement, stood up and uttered his first word 'Kishinev', a shudder ran through the assembly.

Bialik wrote:

'Your brothers' heads, blood from their throats.
Go wander about among the ruins,
Through broken walls, through doors torn from their hinges.
Where fire and axe and iron yesterday
Danced at the blood-orgy, at their wild play'.

It is against such a background that we must judge the pathetic wishfulness of Jews to believe for so long in the abolition of antisemitism in Russia.

Yet no one will suggest, even after the disillusionment, that Jews in the Soviet Union are being massacred by the million, as Jews were in Nazi-Germany and Nazi-occupied Poland. The President of the World Jewish Congress, Dr. Nahum Goldman, speaking in London in January 1973 at a Conference of Jewish Communities, pointed out that 'there are three and a half million Jews living in Communist countries, and their future', he said, 'is naturally of the greatest importance for us. A large part of them want to leave and settle in Israel; but nobody can foresee whether the majority of these three and a half million Jews want to leave their countries'.

From 1948 to 1961 Yiddish publication was forbidden in Soviet Russia. But there had been some rehabilitation. I have a photograph of a monument put up to Mikhoels in Moscow in 1959. A Markish Museum was opened in his birth-town, Polange, in 1963. His poems were published in 1960 in

Russian translation. I have a batch of Yiddish books published in Moscow in 1959 and later, including the works of Mendele, Peretz, Sholem Aleichem and Bergelson. There is a 500 page anthology of Soviet Yiddish poetry, published in 1965. Some of the poets in that volume have since left Russia, and live in Israel. In 1961 the first issue appeared in Moscow of the Yiddish monthly 'Sovietish Heimland', which has been appearing regularly since. In one issue, in 1963, the Editor, Aaron Vergelis, a considerable Yiddish poet, published a poem of his own, 'Dedicated to Peretz Markish, Victim of Stalin's Cruel Ferocity'.

When Vergelis was in New York in 1963 he was asked how he had remained alive in the Stalin era. 'If Beria had the means', he answered, 'he would have arrested us all. It almost happened'. Dr. Levenberg, the Jewish Agency representative in London, and himself a Yiddish writer, welcomed the appearance of 'Sovietish Heimland'. 'It is better', he said, 'to hear a Jewish voice in the Soviet Union, however distorted, than for this large and historic community to be completely silent'. The Yiddish poet Sutzkever in Israel wrote: 'I turn the pages with tears in my eyes. Its Yiddish characters are grave grass, over the graves of Markish, Bergelson, The Nistor. I knew many of the present contributors; here and there someone escaped the claws of Soviet Justice. Three names gave me special satisfaction — Jacob Shternberg, Hirsh Osherowitch and Shlomo Roitman'. 'I have made a discovery', the American Yiddish poet Glatstein wrote, 'Shlomo Roitman. Remember the name. He writes fine poetry. I feel a thrill of joy reading him, that a poet of such magnitude has come into Yiddish poetry'.

'Sovietish Heimland' (it means 'Soviet Homeland') in the twelve years it has been appearing, since 1961, is not unmindful of its links with Yiddish literature as a whole, and with world literature. For instance, an article on 'Soviet Yiddish Literature and the Classic Legacy'. It links on to Mendele, Peretz and Sholem Aleichem, and continues: 'We have confined ourselves to the three masters, but the time has come to connect ourselves also with such great writers as Bergelson, Markish, Sholem Asch, Bialik, Reisen, The Nistor, Leivick and others who belong to our classical heritage'.

Vergelis, the Editor, who has emerged as a kind of demon figure, alleged in the Jewish world to be not only a Soviet apologist but a Soviet informer, has made several journeys abroad, including London and both North and South America to explain himself and his journal. He is, as I said, a considerable Yiddish poet, and on the publication in Moscow of his book of Yiddish poems in 1970 he sent me a copy with an inscription hoping that I would make some of his poems available in English translation. His songs of Biro-Bidjan are interesting. When he was in London

Agnon happened to be here, and Vergelis made a point of going to see him. When he was in France he went to see Chagall in Vence, and wrote several poems about his talks with Chagall.

At one time the Jews in Israel in order to re-establish Hebrew tried to force out Yiddish, which was predominant in the Diaspora, the countries outside Israel, at that time Palestine. I see in a news report as I write, that 700,000 Jews in New York State have returned Yiddish as their mother tongue; nearly 500,000 were American born. I had another reminder these days of the extent of the Jewish tragedy in Poland during the Nazi occupation in a Press report recalling that in the Polish census of 1937, when there were nearly three million Jews in Poland, 2,732,573, 88%, returned Yiddish as their mother tongue. To-day the number of Jews in Poland is said to be ten to twelve thousand. Many, as I know from my visits there, still speak and read Yiddish. But the great sea of Yiddish is no longer there.

There is however a considerable sea of Yiddish now in Israel. Hebrew has established itself, and no longer needs to struggle with a rival. The Yiddish poet Sutzkever, who lives in Israel, has said of this language problem, 'Yiddish and Hebrew are the two eyes of Jewish life. Take either out, and we are blind'. 'To-day', he claims, 'there is more Yiddish read and spoken in Israel than in many non-Hebrew countries'. The President of the State of Israel, Zalman Shazar, recently published a volume of his poems in Yiddish, which I have translated for him into English. There are Chairs in Yiddish at the Hebrew University and in Tel Aviv University. And the former President of the Jerusalem University, Eliahu Elath, who was Israeli Ambassador in London, spoke of the Chair in Yiddish as something 'our University is proud to have'. The Yiddish poet Itzik Manger, who died in 1969 in Israel, has become a cult in Israel, especially among the young people. I saw something of it when they were playing his 'Megillah' in a Tel Aviv Theatre. But let me quote Mendel Kohansky in the London 'Jewish Chronicle': 'A veritable Itzik Manger cult has developed in Israel. The young generation of Israel has come to realise the presence of a rich flowering culture which must inevitably become part of the culture of the new Israel'. Significantly the Israeli Government has established an annual Manger Prize for new Yiddish works of literature. To those who say Yiddish is dying, Sutzkever has given the answer in one of his poems: 'In a hundred years from now we shall still be discussing it by the banks of the Jordan'. I didn't go as far as a hundred years, but I did dedicate my 'Golden Peacock' in 1961 'To the Yiddish Poets who will be writing Yiddish Poetry fifty years hence'.

I no longer have to show my credentials as a translator; but it is pleasing to pass on something one Yiddish writer, Leo Kenig in Israel has written: 'I loved reading your translation. I hear my voice in it. If I had translated it myself I would use these same words'. Or to have Aaron Zeitlin in New York write: 'I still relish on my tongue your translation of my "De Haan" '.

The pages I was able to give to Yiddish Drama are of course inadequate. I contributed the article on Yiddish Theatre to the Encyclopedia Judaica, so that I could have extended the number of samples. But one whole play like An-sky's 'Dybbuk', which in the '20's took not only the Jewish world by storm, would have taken all my space. So it is helpful that the play exists complete in English translation in Joseph Landis' 350 page Bantam Book, together with four other full-length plays — Sholem Asch's 'God of Vengeance', Peretz Hirshbein's 'Green Fields', David Pinski's 'King David and His Wives', and Leivick's 'Golem'. Sholem Asch has other powerful plays, but 'God of Vengeance' is a good example of his work, though it is one of his earliest. It has had the distinction of a German production by Reinhardt, and a Russian production by Vera Komisarjevsky, and a Mikhoels production in the Moscow Yiddish State Theatre. I could not give full-length his 'String of Pearls', but it seemed to me that the Prologue and Epilogue could stand by themselves to illustrate his constant theme, Jewish Messianism. 'I was captivated by this Jewish Messianism', Asch has written. 'And where I found it I sang it, whether in the figure of the Psalm Jew or the fallen people of "The God of Vengeance". The Messianic faith is the mother of hope'. The opening in Rome at the Arch of Titus with Messiah in chains waiting for God's word that his work of Redemption may begin, is part of Jewish Tradition. And Asch uses the epilogue to make his powerful protest against War, against brother fighting brother, someone's brother, 'for the Moloch called the Fatherland'.

Pinski, whose play 'King David and His Wives' is in Landis' book, is a dramatist of note, whose plays have been produced also in English and other languages. Lawrence Langner in his book on the New York Theatre Guild, where he was Director, refers to the Guild's production of Pinski's 'Treasure', and remarks 'His admirers included Martin Buber, Franz Werfel, Rabindranath Tagore, Max Reinhardt, Stanislavsky'. His plays 'The Eternal Jew', which went into the repertoire of Habimah and the Moscow Yiddish State Theatre, and 'The Dumb Messiah', produced in German by Emanuel Reicher, also turn on the Messiah theme.

Many of the Yiddish poets have also written plays, mostly dramatic poems — among them Aaron Zeitlin, I. J. Singer, Broderson, Manger, Weichert, Veiter, Katzisne and Leyeless. Leyeless' play 'Shlomo Molko' is written round the Pseudo-Messiah of that name, who was burned at the stake. 'Our destiny is salvation', his Shlomo Molko proclaims, 'not only for ourselves but for the whole world'.

The Moscow Yiddish State Theatre while it existed produced under Mikhoels' direction a number of Sholem Aleichem plays dramatised from his stories, among them a very different Tevye from the Fiddler on the Roof. It also produced Peretz's 'The Old Market at Night', and Mendele's 'Benjamin the Third'. And of course, like all Yiddish theatres, the great favourites by Goldfaden, the founder of the modern Yiddish stage, and its principal playwright Jacob Gordin. And naturally plays by Soviet Yiddish writers — Bergelson's 'Prince Reubeni', Halkin's 'Bar Kochba', Markish's 'Family Ovadis'.

A great favourite is Itzik Manger's 'Hotzmach Play', also known as 'The Goldfaden Dream'. He started it as a reworking of one of Goldfaden's plays, and 'the reworking', he explained, 'became a work of my own. Hotzmach found a purpose, and a dream. The clown grew wings. It became a dream play. This stage-play has given much pleasure to Yiddish audiences, and I found my way through it to the Yiddish Theatre'.

The Vilna Troupe created a stir in London, Paris and other centres when it came out of Poland in the early '20's with 'The Dybbuk', Peretz Hirshbein's 'Green Fields' and 'The Empty Inn', and Andreyev's 'Seven Who Were Hanged'. So did Maurice Schwartz's Yiddish Art Theatre of New York, which included the young Paul Muni — with dramatisations of Sholem Asch's 'Three Cities' and 'Mottke the Thief', I. J. Singer's 'Yoshe Kalb', Opotoshu's 'Polish Woods', Shneour's 'Song of the Dniester'. There is also the Yiddish State Theatre of Poland, till recently under the direction of Ida Kaminska, now playing in Israel and America. I have seen some excellent very impressive performances there of 'The Dybbuk', Goldfaden's 'Witch' and 'Two Kune Lemels', Manger's 'Hotzmach Play', Gordin's 'Mirele Efros', and 'The Lonely Ship', by Dluzlnovsky, about a shipload of refugees from Nazi-occupied France, drifting from port to port, nowhere allowed to land.

Leivick's 'Golem' which is included in Landis' 'Great Yiddish Plays' is a great play, but it belongs to a cycle of plays on the same theme, of which the 'Golem' is the first. They derive from the same theme that Asch used, the chained Messiah at the Titus Arch — 'I dream the dream', wrote Leivick, 'of freeing Messiah from the chain', and the legend of the Golem, a clay figure infused with life to do its creator's bidding, supposed to have been made by the medieval Rabbi Loew of Prague. The second play is 'The Redemption Vision', and the third, the completion, the most powerful of the Trilogy, is 'The Wedding in Fernwald', with which I have a personal link. Leivick who was then President of the Yiddish PEN in New York and I had been appointed to represent it at the 1946 PEN Congress in Stockholm. Leivick went first to Europe to visit the D.P. Camps, where the survivors of the Hitler extermination were waiting for opportunities to leave for other countries, to rebuild their lives. He got stuck there. He wrote to me: 'I can't come (to Stockholm). I am weighed down by the Jewish sufferings. I go from camp to camp. I find it hard to write about it yet'. Out of that experience grew 'The Wedding in Fernwald'.

Leivick went to a wedding in the Fernwald Camp, the first wedding among the survivors, on the spot where the death factory had been. Abraham the bridegroom's wife and child had been killed there by the Nazis. Sarah the bride's husband had also been killed there by the Nazis. The wedding is symbolic of Jewish determination to live. Leivick watched, and among the wedding guests he saw the Patriarchs, Abraham and Isaac and Jacob, and the Matriarchs, Sarah, Rebecca, Rachel and Leah. He saw the Prophet Elijah and the Messiah stand beside the bride and bridegroom, the bridegroom's murdered wife and child and the bride's murdered husband. And he saw there the spirits of the six million Jews murdered in the holocaust. All come to the wedding.

'See again', says Leivick in the play, 'what others do not see. Penetrate deeper into to-morrow'.

The vision haunted Leivick. And in his play Messiah came not to save but to share the sufferings of the people. Messiah too was cast into the oven. But the flames leapt away from him, as once in the legend where Father Abraham was cast into the flames. It made Messiah angry with the fire. He wanted to be consumed in the flames like all the Jews burned in the Nazi ovens. It haunted Leivick; he had the feeling of guilt that he had escaped the extermination.

I was not in Treblinka.
And in Maidanek I was not.
But I stand on their threshold.
I stand near to the spot.
I stand waiting my turn,
In Treblinka's fires to burn.

It haunts Jewish literature to-day. It is the inescapable theme. Only some put it another way, like the Yiddish poetess Rochel Korn, who was with me, taking Leivick's place at the Stockholm PEN Congress:

We are coming back from far places,
From Ghettos, bunkers, crematorium fire,
The heirs of six million graves.
And we shall rise high, if not higher.

Joseph Leftwich

STORIES

SHOLEM ASCH

Kola Road

I

Between Greater Poland and Mazowsze stretches a triangular tract. It is bounded on one side by the sandy hills along the River Vistula, that extend close to the silvery stream around Plock and Wloclawek. On the other side, towards Leczyca, it has as neighbour the Province of Kajawy, which is full of dark mysteries, and to the left it has the rich and colourful principality of Lowicz.

This area, which includes the towns of Kutno, Zychlin, Gostynin, Gombin and several smaller towns, is rugged and monotonous like the peasant who lives in it. Poor in water, poor in forest, and the horizon stretches far and wide. The eye finds nothing to rest on. Long, monotonous fields, mostly covered with poor grain, wander away for miles. Sometimes the endless, unvarying, cultivated fields are intersected by a white cart road, scantily planted with weeping willows, that leads from one small town to another.

The area has not the mysterious glamour of its neighbour Kajawy, about which so many legends are told, that the souls of the dead walk along its black lanes, that twist and turn around the fields, and decoy people into the marshes. Nor has it the richness and the colour of its other neighbour the 'Princess of Lowicz,' which produced the greatest Polish musician, the creator of the Polish folk-mazurka—Chopin. The field is rugged and monotonous, and the peasant who works in the field simple as the potato it yields. The peasant here does not trick himself out in white smock and gaily-coloured trousers, nor adorn his hat with ribbons and corals, as the peasant of Lowicz does. And he does not dabble in witchcraft like the peasant of the 'tall poplars,' which is in Kajawy. The peasant of the field here is like a clod of earth, into which God has breathed a soul, like a walking lime that grows outside his house.... He sticks to his reed, fluting away half through the night, tunes that have no theme, that do not begin and do not end, like his long, rolling, green-covered fields.... He is a man without subtleties—'This is the way God made me.' If he is in a good mood, he will give you the very shirt off his back. But if he is angered, he is ready to pay for it with his life, but he will have his revenge. He loves his cow, which lives with him, and he will never kill it for his own use. But most of all he loves his horse. He would never dream of using it for toil. In ploughing he prefers to yoke his cow and his wife, but not his horse. He saves his horse for his cart on Sunday, to drive to church, or into the next village, to visit his friends, to show off his horse to them.

The Jew who is born on this soil has more of the field and the orchard in him than of the Religious House of Study and the Ritual Baths. The land is rich in pasture. The peasant breeds cows and oxen and sheep. Jews buy them up from him and take them to Lodz or across the frontier, which is not far away. You find among the Jews there the renowned fishermen of the Lonsk Lakes, who supply fish for Lodz and for the whole surrounding district in the Provinces of Kalisz and Plock. Where there is no railway, there are great strapping fiacre-drivers, who take the Litvaks to the frontier. The peasant breeds his horse, and looks after it well, so there are big Jewish horse-dealers, who supply the Germans, who come down from Thorn and Berlin. The poor Jews rent the orchard from the peasant for the summer. In winter they wash his pelts in the lake, and take them to market in Lowicz, or Gombin. The Jew is in the village all the week long, lives there with the peasant. For the Sabbath he comes into town, to the Three F's Congregation (fishermen, fleshers and fiacre-drivers) to attend service. They divide the honours among themselves, and tell each other stories about what has been happening all through the week. After the Saturday mid-day meal they go into the field, where the horses are feeding, and the youngsters play ball. And at night they sit about on benches outside their houses, and watch the servant-girls go for a walk, and they tell more stories.

In one of these towns there was a street known as the Kola Road. Kola is a small town near by, and the street lies on the route from Zychlin that passes through Krosniewice to Kola. The Three F's Congregation was in the Kola Road. The Kola Road was not in the Exile. No Jews were beaten there. If recruits passing through the town in the autumn got out of hand they were soon dealt with. The shafts were taken out of the carts, iron bars were wrested off the shop-fronts, trees growing in front of the doors were torn up, and the recruits were taught who was the better man.

The Synagogue Street, where the Rabbi and the ritual slaughterers and the Hebrew teachers all lived, and where the poultry-slaughtering yard and the Ritual Baths are situated, felt thoroughly ashamed of the Kola Road. 'A lot of boors, butchers and fishmongers!' And though the Synagogue Street lived entirely on the 'offerings and Festival moneys' that the Kola Road used to send along, and though no matter what happened in the Synagogue Street—if a shepherd set his dog on, or a drunken Gentile started beating Jews—everybody, old and young, ran screaming into the Kola Street: 'Help, they're beating us!' yet at the bottom of their hearts they disparaged them: 'Not like Jews at all,' they said to each other. 'And when the Messiah comes they will have to ask us to intervene for them.' The 'best people,' of the Broad Street, like Reb Berachiah, the moneylender, for instance, did not think anything of them. 'Wild brutes! Speak to everybody as if we were brought up together. But we need them sometimes, for the sake of peace, when the recruits pass here, so that they don't go smashing windows.'

It is true that the Kola Road didn't have much to do with the gentry in the other streets. They used to call them 'wishy-washy Jews.' But if anything happened that required intervention with Heaven, like writing a petition to the Rabbi to pray for a sick child, or to read a Psalm (they were no adepts at that), they had to apply to the Synagogue Street. And when the Solemn Days approached, the Kola Road went in awe of the Synagogue Street. They showed deference to the least of the inhabitants of the Synagogue Street. 'One of Moses' bodyguard,' they used to say. And on the eve of the Day of Atonement a big strapping Jew, a hulking cabby or a burly fisherman, would lie down on the threshold of the Synagogue, and the Synagogue Street would for God and Heaven inflict stripes on the Kola Road.

In the Kola Road stood a house, built of timber, one storey high, and with long benches in front of the door. It was known as 'The Benches,' because the crowd used to meet there, and sit in front of the door. Reb Israel Szochlin lived in that house.

Reb Israel was the oldest and most respected inhabitant of the Kola Road. He was an old man—seventy or so, but he walked without the aid of a stick, and he did not wear glasses—a relic of those bygone days when you could get a quart of brandy for a couple of pence. When Reb Israel had chased around for a couple of hours after a bull that had broken loose from his rope, and had caught hold of him at last by the horns, so that the bull had to bow his great neck, he used to groan with a gurgling little laugh—'Not as strong as I used to be!'

He was a big cattle-dealer, who sold to the Germans, thousands at a time. He bought up all the cattle for miles around. And since he was a man who would let the other fellow earn a couple of coppers, everybody, Jew and Gentile, held him in great respect. They entrusted to him their money, they came to him to borrow money, they came to him for advice, to adjust their differences, and whatever Reb Israel said went. Reb Israel could box the ears of the biggest and strongest tough (when there was need). No one would dream of contradicting Reb Israel. If anyone dared, the Kola Road would probably have killed him on the spot.

All the 'boys,' as well as the Gentile fellows of the Kola Road, stayed in Reb Israel's house—they drove his oxen to Lodz, or to the frontier. And they spent the night in the stables, with the horses, oxen and sheep. Food was always there for anybody who wanted it; bread and butter always on the table; anybody could come in, cut off a slice, and go. A house full of plenty—cows, oxen, horses, goats, sheep, geese, and Jewish and Gentile 'boys.' Reb Israel did not keep anything in his house locked away. Nobody would steal anything. It would mean getting killed on the spot. If anyone was wronged in the town, he came running to Reb Israel to complain, and Reb Israel went out and boxed the ears of the offender.

Once the Hassidic Jew who had the tavern rights from the landowner of the town had the home of a Jewish widow raided on a Friday evening. They found brandy there, and she was put in jail. So they came to tell Reb Israel. Reb Israel took his stick and went to see the Hassid.

'Let the woman go!'

'But Reb Israel. You must admit that she is robbing me of my living.'

Reb Israel said no more. He came home and two of the 'boys' went into the tavern, armed with cudgels, took two barrels of brandy, twisted the taps out, and put them outside the door. Anyone might take as much as he wanted. Jews had brandy galore that Sabbath. They rolled along the streets drunk, and the licensee got his eyes blacked in the bargain, and was told that he would get some more next week, and he couldn't even complain to anyone.

A lout comes into Reb Israel's house, and stands there at the side of the big cupboard.

'What do you want, tailor-nob?' demanded Reb Israel, going up to him, and smacking him across the face. 'You beat your mother, they tell me, you scally-wag, you. Who's been feeding you till now? And if somebody else says a word to her, you whip a knife out!'

'Reb Israel, it's my mother. I may. It's my mother. But anybody else I'll rip his guts out! Isn't that right, Reb Israel?'

'And what do you want, Zirel?'

'That twister, the Hassid, who owns the oil and paraffin store, wants to give me a gold thick 'un if I crawl over the fence to his competitor, Yoske's son-in-law, and start a fireworks display among his barrels of petrol.'

'I'll break your head for you if you do. You take the gold thick 'un, and smash his ribs for him.'

'He won't hand over the thick 'un before I've done the trick.'

'Tell him to deposit it with me. Then you go to Yoske's son-in-law and get him to kick up a row to-morrow that he has found his barrels opened. I'll give you the thick 'un, and if the twister says anything to you, knock his teeth out.'

When a Jew like Reb Israel came home from his business on the road on a Friday evening, he used to sit down on the bench in front of the door, with his pockets full of small coins, and pray to God in his heart: Father, send me some Jews who haven't enough money for the Sabbath, and he didn't go into the house till he had distributed every penny of it among the poor. Then he washed himself, put on his Sabbath coat, and went to the Three F's Congregation to welcome the Sabbath Queen.

Beggars or wayfarers tramping the countryside made a point of stopping in the town for the Sabbath because of Reb Israel. The taste of his Sabbath meal lingered for the rest of the year. The congregation was always packed with them. Reb Israel used to take his stand at the door with all the applicants for a meal next to him, and wait—there are no Jews who love having a poor man with them for the Sabbath meal as much as butchers and fishers do—and as many as were left over, Reb Israel took home with him. The Shamash of the Three F's Congregation often had to sing out 'Three gulden for a guest,' holding them up to auction like the Portions of the Law, because there was so much competition for the honour of taking a wayfarer home to the Sabbath table.

On the Sabbath morning after the service the Rabbi of the congregation stood up and expounded the Midrash. The tears stood in Reb Israel's eyes. And afterwards he invited the whole congregation to his home for a glass of brandy for benediction. And while they toasted each other, Reb Israel kept banging his fist on the table, and shouting: 'Drink Jews! Our Father Jacob! Our Teacher Moses!'

The house shook with the force of his blows on the table.

Reb Israel could read the Portion of the Law, and he was at home with Rashi as long as he did not drag in any Aramaic words. Reb Israel loved Rashi. It seemed to him as if he were a near relative, one of the family to every Jew. There was another Jew whom Reb Israel loved—King David. His Psalms diffused sweetness in every nerve—and he was a Jew, King David. You might go out in the street and meet him there, and exchange greetings.

'How do you do, King David?'

'How are things with you?'

And the conversation veers round to the latest about the market.

When Reb Israel's daughter grew up, he went to the Rabbi, and said:

'Rabbi, choose a son-in-law for me, to marry my child, from among your pupils.'

He took his son-in-law, and gave him a home in his house for the rest of his days. 'Here is your food, your drink, your Sabbath raiment, and your pocket-money, and you sit and study Holy Lore.'

He had such respect for his sons-in-law, with their volumes of the Talmud, that he would go on tip-toe when he approached them. He put aside for them the best and most costly things he could get. When he heard the voice of the Law in his house this old Jew wept like a child for joy.

Reb Israel's sons were giants. 'Szochlinski's Guardsmen,' they were called. They were no students. And the one who surpassed them all was the son of his old age. Nat. Nat was a lad who went out in the morning with Borek, his dog, Bashke his sheep, and his whistle. And a dove stood on his shoulder. The street went in fear of him. He took his stand at the door, with his straw hat set on a rakish angle on the tip of his forelock, and his leaded whip in his hand, and started whistling to his doves, who wheeled over his head. Josephine led his horse out of the stable. If it wasn't well groomed, or the mane was not properly combed and twisted round the straw, his whip whistled over her body, so that the young blood in her spurted on to his hand.

Josephine was a maid in Reb Israel's employ, a Gentile girl, who had been brought from the village, and had remained in the house for ever. As strong as iron. She fitted into the family. She was one of themselves, joined in conversation, gave her counsel, and lost her temper when she didn't like things. Nat walloped her, dreadfully sometimes, but she was never angry about that. She tossed her head and stood her ground:

'Wallop away, if you feel like it!'

And half-an-hour later, when she caught sight of him on his horse, she ran out and stood in front of the door, with arms akimbo, and her eyes smiled through the black and blue marks which he had left on her face. 'There's a horseman for you!'

When he came back, he beckoned to her. At first she pretended not to notice. Then she went up sullenly, and lazily took the reins. He winked at her, and went up on the left to the dove-cote.

She quietly led the horse away to the stable. On the way she met the caretaker of the house, who asked her:

'Who's been decorating your face like that?'

'Whoever wanted to, and you go to the devil!' And she snapped her fingers at him, and scrambled hurriedly up to the dove-cote after Nat.

Nat had a dove-cote. It was traditional to have a dove-cote in the loft, where they kept the oats for the horses. No matter where they took the doves to and let them loose, they always found their way back to the loft and stood on the roof. At the other end of the town there was a Gentile baker who also had a dove-cote. Nat and the baker waged perpetual warfare. Nat released his doves. The baker released his. Sometimes it happened that one side won a dove from the other. A hen belonging to one side came along and started flirting with a cock, and lured him away to her dove-cote.

That was where the gang came in. Nat had his gang of boys, Jewish and Gentile, who spent the night with him. The baker had his gang of bakehouse boys. If one side got hold of a dove belonging to the other side there was jubilation, as if the world had been conquered, while the other side went about dejected, plotting revenge. That led to constant fights between Nat's gang and the baker's gang, something awful.

II

It was a Friday afternoon in summer. Reb Israel had just come home from the road. Casimir, the groom, had led the horses to the pump to drink. Josephine was taking the things off the cart. Among the rest she unloaded a goose, a turkey, a sackful of fish that Reb Israel had bought on the road and brought home for the Sabbath. Suddenly one of the 'boys' jumped into the courtyard, thrust two fingers between his lips, and emitted a shrill whistle that made your ears throb.

'What's the matter, you bastard!' asked Nat, coming into the courtyard with Bashke.

'The baker has let out his doves. The dove-cote is standing on the roof near the City Hall.'

In two leaps Nat was up in the loft, had opened his dove-cote, and released his doves.

Holding his whip and surrounded by his gang, Nat rushed into the street. On the other side of the market square, high in the clouds sailed the doves, with fluttering wings, in two separate flocks. Sometimes one flock flew into the other. They merged for a moment, but soon separated. Sometimes they swooped down towards the market-square, and sometimes they flew up on high. Then, after wheeling round several times on high, the doves settled on the roofs.

High on one of the roofs stood one dove, all alone, as if cast out by the rest. A hen dove belonging to Nat's flock presently flew up to him and started a conversation. Nat's gang watched it with beating hearts, waiting for the two doves to reach an understanding, and together fly into Nat's flock. One of the boys in the baker's gang suddenly threw a stone up on to the roof, and the doves flew off.

That started it. One of Nat's gang went up to him, and slashed him across the legs with his stick. The fellow went down on the ground and started bellowing for all he was worth. The baker's gang rushed up with their cudgels, and the battle was on. There was nothing else to be seen but cudgels whirling about and crashing down on heads. Here was a Jewish boy, there a Gentile fellow stretched on the ground with blood streaming from his face. Blind Leib came running out of the slaughterhouse with a shaft in his hand, whirling it over everybody's heads. Nat got hold of the baker by the lapels; with one hand he held him fast by the lapels, so that he couldn't get away, and with the other he punched him in the face, in the sides, under the belt. Every blow went home with a thud, and in the end the baker lay down on the ground. And above them the doves kept flying, one flock sailing into the other, as if they knew that the fight was on their account. They flapped their wings as they flew low, almost touching the combatants' heads, and then they soared up high into the sky.

When they saw the baker was done, that he couldn't even get up, the gangs separated to see what would happen next. The two doves managed to reach an understanding; the hen lured the cock into Nat's dove-cote. Nat's gang went mad with joy. And the baker's gang plotted revenge.

That Friday night the baker stole up into Reb Israel's loft, where Nat had his dove-cote, and wrung the necks of one dove after the other. It was a risky job, however. The doves sensed the stranger among them, and began to flap their wings, and flew, clucking, from one end of the dove-cote to the other. Josephine, who slept in the room beneath the dove-cote, quickly ran to wake Nat, tugging at his hair.

'Young master, there's someone in your dove-cote.'

Nat seized a bar of iron, that always lay beside his bed, and went up into the loft.

As he rushed into the loft, he got a blow with something on his skull, so that he saw stars. But he took no notice of that. He grappled with the fellow, stuffed his mouth, so that he shouldn't be able to shout, and then he set about giving him a hiding. He thwacked him over the head, he pummelled him in the sides, until he himself felt that he had given him enough. Then he took him by the head, dragged him down from the loft, and deposited him outside his own door.

A couple of days after that they clapped Nat in jail. They didn't bring it off immediately, of course. The sergeant of the local police came to fetch him, but Josephine decoyed him into the stable (she said she had something to tell him). He went with her very willingly. There were some lads waiting there for him in the dark, and they dealt with him so efficiently that he couldn't come a second time to fetch Nat. The town started feeling afraid. All sorts of rumours began to fly round. Nat was said to be going about the streets with his leaded whip, and his Bashke at his heels. But three jail warders and two policemen who were stationed in the town fell on him and carried him off to jail.

Meanwhile the baker died. The town was in a state of terror. Queer tales were told. The peasants were gathering here, they were mustering there. Yechiel, who went peddling through the villages, told them in the House of Learning that a peasant woman in one of the villages had asked him to look into a mirror and he had seen the Rabbi's head there, and the peasant woman had said that she had put a spell on him. They went on to talk of blood libels. Reports came from the adjoining villages of attacks being made on the dairy-men, who were despoiled of everything. The town met in the Rabbi's house. A day of fasting was proclaimed. The wealthier Jews left the town. The Synagogue Street looked as if Death were parading up and down, with his black wings outspread. Candles were burnt all day in the House of Learning, and Jews kept reading Psalms. Mothers suddenly started kissing and slobbering over their children when they came home from Hebrew School. Betrothals and weddings were all put off till 'after,' when things would be more calm. Jewish patrols were out in the streets at night, armed with cudgels. Psalm-readers were up all night in the House of Learning reading Psalms.

Nat stared through the tiny bars of his cell that looked out on the market-place. Each morning Josephine carried the dove-cote past the cell window, and showed him that it had been cleaned. Bashke and the dog Borek lay all day in front of the window, and their master spoke to them through the bars. And his gang had to drive the doves every day past the window, and he stood there, issuing orders, telling them what to do.

In the town, people kept getting more frightened. They went about looking like shadows. The Gentiles of the town, who lived amicably with the Jews all the year round, began to fill them with dread now. The water-carrier, who delivered water all the year round to Jewish houses, was said to have told a Jew that when St. John's market day came, he would go for Moshkowski's house. The candle-lighter in the synagogue would be appointed supervisor over the Jews, and the Gentile who helped with the burials in the cemetery would be an official, and the Jews would have to pay him tribute. Jews listened to these tales and went about in fear. Girls were sent away from home. People hunted up distant uncles and aunts, and sent their children to stay with them. The Synagogue Street prepared for whatever might happen: 'Lord God, we are in Your Hand. Your Will be done!' The Kola Road kept calm. As if nothing was happening. If one of them met a Jew from the Synagogue Street wearing a long and dismal face, he would say to him: 'Hi, you blighter! Have you got your funk-hole ready at home?'

They said that the day of reckoning would be on St. John's market day. That was one of the most important market days in the town. The peasant comes into the town for the first time after the harvest. The barns are bursting with corn. The fields are crammed full of potatoes and cabbages. The peasant comes into the town with his wife and children to buy them gifts. He sells the full-grown cattle, and buys young ones to crop his reaped fields. He meets his cronies at the fair, finds out what sort of a harvest they've had this year, and they go off together for a drink.

35

The Jews looked forward each year to this day, hoping to earn something; but this year it filled them with foreboding. They only hoped it would pass without trouble.

When the day arrived, Jews hurried off to the synagogue, and started to pray. The Rabbi stood at the reading-desk, and there was an outburst of weeping, as at the concluding service on the Day of Atonement. After the service, the Rabbi mounted the stairs, and stood by the Ark, and the whole congregation recited with one voice the Death Bed Confession of Faith. The Rabbi said the first verse, and then the congregation said the next. Before they dispersed to their homes, everybody wished each other that they might live to meet again to-morrow. . . .

Meanwhile peasant carts were heard rumbling over the town bridge. Carts arrived in the market place. Every sound of a cart filled Jewish hearts with the fear of death. It seemed as if the carts were being driven differently this time, as if the peasants and their women were walking differently.

For the present, things went as usual. The peasants sold what they had to sell, haggled about the price, and in the end bought what they needed.

At first, the Jewish shops were closed. A peasant wanted to buy some herrings, so a herring-woman opened her herring shop for a minute to sell him his herrings. Another peasant came up, and a third. When the shopkeeper across the road saw this shop open, he opened his shop as well. Gradually all the shops opened. The day seemed to be going like any ordinary market day. Jews began to pluck up courage, and started bargaining with the peasants. Suddenly a youth came running from the horse market, shouting: 'They're hitting Jews!'

In one minute all the shops were shut. The shutters were pulled down over the windows, and the doors of the houses were barred. Women and men snatched what they could under their arms—a child, a lamp, a table, a cover—and fled as if from a fire. But they soon stopped, not knowing where to run. They crawled under the beds. . . . Lay there for a minute . . . crawled out again. . . . Pushed aside the wardrobe, and got under it. . . . Out again. . . . Up into the garret; some crept down into the cellars; some scrambled up on the top of the stove. Children cried. Their mothers stuffed pillows into their mouths so that they should not be heard outside. Somebody was beating at the door outside, begging them to let him in. People found themselves in strange houses. They ran into the first house they came across. Fathers in other people's houses groaned, wondering where their children were. And pressed other people's children to their breasts.

The Kola Road had also heard that Jews were being beaten. Hershale Cossack ran out of the slaughtering-yard, snatched up a sack as he ran, flung into it three ten-pound weights, tied it up, and slung it over his shoulder. Come along, brothers! The entire Kola Road followed him—the butchers carrying their choppers and knives. The cabbies tore the shafts out of their carts. The fishmongers caught up the hooks with which they pull their boxes of fish out of the water. The horse-dealers got on their horses, and with their whips in their hands clattered along to the horse market.

The big square, out of which two roads run, was crammed with carts, carts, carts, that were swamped however, submerged with horses, oxen, people and pigs. It was a multi-coloured picture, and there was a confusion of sounds. Drunken peasants with cudgels in their hands were chasing Jews in long gaberdines, who were leaping like frightened hares over carts, horses and people. The terrified cry of someone jumping for his life over a cart, and shouting frantically for help was merged with a burst of wild, drunken laughter. Horses kicked and plunged, and people were lying under their hoofs, and pigs were squealing. Sticks, stone pots and hats went flying over people's heads. Frightened geese and fowls rushed squawking past the carts. Feathers came off their straggling wings and flew up in the air. Jews in black gaberdines went rushing all over the place, screaming terribly.

Then the Kola Street plunged into the panic like a stream of glowing steel into the deep cold sea. They were soon at each other's throats. Lumps of steel and iron thudded on human flesh, blood coursed down eyes, gaberdines, carts and wheels. It was impossible to see whom or what. Everything was mixed up, horses and people, people and horses. A peasant woman, covered with blood, dragged along her injured husband, and he kept hitting her in the belly, and trying to break away from her. Little children trailing at their mothers' skirts. Fathers pushing their children away from them and pressing with set lips and bloodshot eyes into the mêlée. And the mêlée was not a battle in which one tried to overcome the other. It was a mix-up. A plague came upon them. One dashed his fist into somebody's jaw, caught hold of his tongue and pulled at it, throttled him. Two fell upon each other, got jammed together against a cart, and pounded away at each other's chest with his fist and bit at him with his teeth. It was not a battle in which one sought to be victor. The slumbering beast in man was roused. It was a welter of confusion. Everybody was out to eat up alive the next man in the sight of heaven and God.

III

Nat looked all day out of the jail-window. He was not sorry for the affair he had started—he was not the sort to regret. He had waited for the minute for it to begin. He had no plan how to get out of here. He hadn't thought about it.

He was not the kind of man to make plans. When it comes, it flares up, crashes and bursts like thunder.

Then he saw people start running across the market from the horse-square. A youth ran by with bleeding head. Women were rushing all over the market collecting the children. Shops were being closed. He felt that something was going to happen. A stream of blood ran down from his heart and filled his hands and feet. He bit his lips. His eyes were suddenly bloodshot. He hurled himself against the door. But the door—though it was only the door of a small town lock-up—was strong enough to withstand a man's hand. So he caught hold of the bars at the window. They bent in his grip, but they were too firmly built into the wall. He seized his plank bed, and banged it against the stove, and in a minute boards and bricks were all mixed up. Like a thunder locked into the room, he hurled himself against the walls. Finally he dug his teeth into his hands, bent his head between his knees, and started groaning, so that the groans rose to the ceiling and beat against the bars, and went out of the window.

He lay like that a long time, till a voice called to him from the window:

'Young master! Young master!'

He looked out of the window, and saw Josephine with her hair flying loose.

'At your father's,' she screamed, and handed him an iron bar through the window.

He hurled himself at the door, prised the iron bar between the door-handles, leaned his heart against it, and pushed with all his soul—one, two, three—and the door broke open with a bang. The policeman who tried to stop him got a punch on the jaw that felled him, and lay in a pool of blood. Nat rushed home to his father.

The peasants of the horse-market made for Reb Israel's house.

'To Szochlinski's, whose son killed a peasant!' they shouted, rushing into Reb Israel's house with spades and pickaxes.

They poured into the courtyard, and stood outside the house, and the cry went down the Kola Road: 'They're at Reb Israel's.' And the whole of the Kola Road went into battle, little and big. Blind Leib (who could snap a bar of iron) laid his hand on a pitch-fork in the stable. The Kola Road surrounded the courtyard.

'What is this!' cried Reb Israel, coming out and standing all by himself in the midst of the peasants, clutching the iron bar that he sometimes had to use on the Lodz Road against the Lodz thieves.

'Whom have you come here to attack! Me? I have worked all my life for you, dogs that you are, bought up your cattle, paid you good cash, and exported them for you somewhere abroad. Worked hard for you, in the heat of summer, in the cold of winter, and stuffed your pockets with hundreds. Come here, you dogs! Here I am! Which of you will dare touch me?'

The peasants were silent. Then one of them cried:

'We have nothing against you, Szochlinski. It is your son we want, the one who killed the peasant.'

'Here I am!' cried Nat, throwing open the door into the courtyard, and coming up at a run. He caught up the first peasant he could lay his hand on, lifted him by the hips up in the air, and then flung him down on the ground, so that one heard his legs crack as he fell. The peasants hurled themselves on him like a whirlwind. Nat seized another of them by the head, lifted him up, and used him as a battering ram against the rest. Then the Kola Road plunged into the fray, right among the peasants.

But Reb Israel's voice stopped them.

'Stay! I tell you to keep off! He has killed a man! Let him fight his own fight!'

And Nat fought his own fight. Using the peasant as a battering ram, he laid about him on all sides. They fell before him like corn before the scythe. A peasant hit him over the head with a spade, and blood poured down and ran over his face. He didn't let go of the peasant whom he was using as a battering ram. He fought his way deeper into the midst of the peasants. He snatched a spade out of the hands of a peasant, and lunged about him with superhuman strength. His great arms filled with blood, till the veins stood out as if they were going to burst. Another peasant caught him a blow in the side from behind with an iron bar. He bent down, and stayed like that for a minute. Then he was at it again. His hands were seized from behind. He kicked, bit— then he bent down again and held his side.

'You dirty dogs!' Josephine cried, appearing suddenly as if from under the earth, with a rake in her hand. 'You have killed the young master!' She banged her rake over the head of the peasant who was holding on to one of Nat's hands, and then she went for the other.

'I'll show you,' she shouted. And wielding her rake, she pushed the peasants away from Nat, who was now bent low to the ground, holding one hand to his side; in the other he held the spade, hitting out at anyone who tried to come close to him, till Josephine helped him into the house and put him down on the bed.

The peasants wanted to make another move, but they saw the Kola Road standing by with their weapons, and they retreated, one with a bleeding head, another with a smashed hand, leaving the courtyard spattered with blood, and about seven or eight of their company lying about the courtyard, groaning. One said to the other: 'That scum isn't a Jewess!'

The market day was over, and the Synagogue Street crawled out from behind the stoves and cupboards, from the lofts and cellars where they had hidden. When they came into the synagogue next morning, they greeted each other and sang aloud: 'Give thanks unto the Lord.' After prayers thev sent for cake and brandy, and the congregation decided to have a party that night. Kasriel and Ozer, Reb Israel's sons-in-law, promised to get their father-in-law to give them Nat's doves. Nat was at death's door, so he would not be able to object. And it was only right that Jews should, in celebrating their deliverance, eat of the doves that had endangered the entire Jewish community, and thus get rid of this whole business of doves, which brought such danger and affliction on Jews.

That is what happened. The two young men came home from synagogue and talked it over with their father-in-law. They went up into the loft, and took all the doves and sent them to the slaughterer to be killed.

Nat lay on his bed, deathly pale. His head was bandaged, and he had ice on it, his lips were still set tight, and he breathed heavily. At his side sat Josephine, handing him whatever he wanted. He heard someone moving in the loft. He sensed the doves beating their wings. It lifted him out of his bed, but he was helpless. He kicked off the blanket, and lay there, listening.

The doves beat their wings. Nat looked at Josephine and pointed up to the ceiling. Josephine went out, went up to the loft, and brought down to him in her arms a couple of fledglings, whose mothers had just been taken away and sent to the slaughterers to be killed. They had hardly any feathers yet on their wings, and they flapped their wings, seeking something. They tucked their thin necks, which had a thin, warm little skin stretched over a delicate little bone which would snap under a finger, beneath their wings, and their wings were seeking something.

He took them in his hand, clenched his teeth, and with his leg pushed away the chair that stood beside the bed. The doves quivered in his hand, and searched for something pathetically. He put them under his shirt, and snuggled them against his breast, and warmed them.

The doves quivered tenderly against his breast, seeking som thing, pleading for something, flapping their wings.

His face became more pale. His eyes grew glazed and retreated behind his forehead, his nose stretched out, became elongated, paler, thinner, and his lips seemed to crumple up.

The room became silent. A slight wind trembled upon the windowpanes.

Everybody moved out of the room, and left the house to the thunder that was about to burst and destroy everything. He lay there, and felt the young, weak fledglings quiver upon his breast. His eyes started out of his face like fists, and filled up entirely with blood. And he kept silent.

He sat up in bed and looked round. He saw some grains of wheat. He ground them with his teeth into flour. He pushed the fledglings' bills into his mouth and fed them with his tongue. The fledglings' thin little necks quivered between his fingers and their wings pleaded. . . .

'God!' he suddenly cried out—seized the first dove and wrung its neck. The dove cried out once, and a thin stream of blood spurted into his face. He wrung the neck of the second dove, and hurled it away from him. Then he got out of bed, seized the mirror and banged it down on the floor. He went up to the wardrobe—one blow, and it was lying smashed to smithereens. Over to the bed. Ripped up the bedclothes with his teeth, and the feathers scattered. Another blow shattered the table. He caught up a chair and hammered away at the stove, and the stove caved in and crashed to the ground. He tore his shirt to threads, and bit his hands. Finally he collapsed on the floor, and dug his face into the wreckage, down on the floor, and fell asleep, and slept long—long. . . .

No one dared to enter the room to wake the sleeping thunder. . . .

ZALMAN SHNEOUR

The Immortal Orange

I

Two boxes of oranges going across the blue ocean. The oranges are Algerian, globular, juicy, heavy, with a glowing red peel—the colour of African dawns.

The oranges in the first box boast: 'We are going to Warsaw, the ancient Polish capital. Oh, what white teeth will bite into us, what fine aristocratic tongues will relish us!'

The oranges in the second box keep silent; snuggle one against the other, and blush for shame. They know—thanks to God—that their destination is a little village somewhere in Lithuania, and God knows into what beggarly hands they will fall. No, it was not worth drinking in so thirstily the warmth of the African sun, the cool dews of the Algerian nights, the perfumes of the blossoming French orange groves. Nimble brown hands of young Arab girls cut them down off the trees, and flung them into bamboo baskets. Was it worth while?

But we shall see who came off best: the oranges that went to Warsaw, or those that arrived later at Shklov—a remote place in Lithuania. And we shall draw the moral.

So the first lot of oranges arrived at Warsaw and the fruit merchant set them out in pyramids. They glowed like balls of fire out of the window. But that did not last long. They were sold the same day. The tumultuous, thirsty street soon swallowed them up. Tired folk thrust them into their pockets, pulled off their juicy, golden peel with dirty fingers, and flung it on the slush-covered pavements. They swallowed the oranges as they walked along, like dogs, without saying grace. The refreshing juice bespattered dusty beards, greasy coats. Their place in the shop is already taken by other fruits and even vegetables. No feeling for birth and breeding! Only bits of their beautiful peel still lay about in the streets, like the cold rays of a far-off, glowing sun. But no one understood that these were greetings from distant sunny lands, from eternally-blue skies. They were trampled underfoot, horses stamped on them, and the street sweeper came with his broom, and swept them, ruthlessly, into the rubbish box. That was the end of the oranges! The end of something that had flourished somewhere, and drawn sustenance between perfumed leaves, and fell into bamboo baskets under a hot, luxuriant sky.

The second box of oranges arrived a few days later at Shklov. They were dragged along in little peasant wagons, and jolted in Jewish carts, until they had the honour of being shown into their new surroundings.

The wife of the spice-merchant of Shklov called over her husband:

'Come on, my smart fellow. Open the oranges for the *Purim* presents.'

Eli, the spice-merchant, despite his wife's sarcasm, was an expert at unpacking. He worked at the box of oranges for a couple of hours. Patiently, carefully he worked around the lid with his chisel, like a goldsmith at a precious case of jewels. His wife stood beside him, giving advice. At last the box was opened, and out of the bits of blue tissue paper gleamed the little cheeks of the oranges, and there was a burst of heavy, festive fragrance.

In a little while, the oranges lay set out in the little shop window, peeping out on the muddy market-place, the grey, lowering sky, the little heaps of snow in the gutters, the fur-clad, White Russian peasants in their yellow-patched, sheepskin jerkins. Everything around them was so strange, northern, chilly, half-decayed. And the oranges with their festive perfume and their bright colour were so rich and strange and new in such an unfamiliar, poor *milieu*, like a royal garment in a beggar's tavern.

Aunt Feiga arrives with her woollen shawl about her head, and a basket in her hand. She sees the freshly-unpacked fruit, and goes in to buy. *Purim* gifts. And here begins the *immortality* of the orange!

Poor and grey is Lithuanian life. And the little natural wealth that sometimes falls into this place is used up a little at a time, reasonably, and with all the five senses. Not a drop goes to waste of the beautiful fruit that has strayed in here. No, if the orange had been no more than the wandering spirit of a sinful soul it would have found salvation at the home of Aunt Feiga.

II

'Then you won't take eight *kopecks* either? Good day!'

The spice-merchant's wife knows full well that Aunt Feiga has no other place where she can buy; yet she pulls her back by the shawl:

'May all Jews have a pleasant *Purim* as surely as I am selling you golden fruit . . . I only want to make a start.'

'We only want to make a start!' repeats Eli, the spice-merchant, the experienced opener of orange boxes.

A *rouble* more or a *rouble* less. Aunt Feiga selects the best, the heaviest orange, wraps it up, and drops it carefully into the basket, between eggs, onions, goodies for *Purim*, and all sorts. Aunt Feiga comes home, and the little ones clamour round her, from the eleven-year-old *Gemarrah* student to the littlest one who is just learning the alphabet, and who have all been given a holiday from school for the eve of *Purim*. They immediately start turning out their mother's basket.

'Mother, what have you brought? What have you brought?'

The mother silences them. One gets a smack in the face, because of the holiday; another a thump; and a third a tweak of the ear.

'What has happened here! Look at the locusts swarming around me!'

Yet, she shows them what she has brought.

'There! Look, you devils, scamps!'

Among the small town Lithuanian goodies, *the orange* glows like a harbinger of wealth and happiness. The children are taken aback. They still remember last *Purim*, a shadow of the fragrance of such a fruit. Now it has come back to life with the same fragrance and roundness. Here it is! They will not see the like of it again till this time next year.

They snatch at it with thin little hands; they smell it; they marvel at it.

'Oh, how delicious!' cries the youngest child. 'Oh, how it smells!'

'It grows in Palestine,' puts in the *Gemarrah* student, and somehow feels proud and grave.

Aunt Feiga locks it into the drawer. But the round, fragrant, flaming fruit lives in the imagination of the children, like a sweet dream. It shines rich and new among the hard green apples and pickled cucumbers that the children have been seeing all the winter.

When the *Purim* feast begins, the orange sits at the head of the table, among a host of little tarts and jellies, and figs and sweets, and shines like a huge coral bead in a multi-coloured mosaic.

Aunt Feiga covers it with a cloth, and gives it to the *Purim* giftbearer to take away. The orange sticks the top of its head out of the cloth, as one might say: 'Here I am. I am whole. A pleasant festival, children!' The children follow him on his travels with longing eyes. They know that it will have to pass through many transmigrations, poor thing, until it is brought back to them by the beadle.

And so it was. One aunt exchanges the orange for a lemon, and sends it to another relative. And Aunt Feiga has the lemon. So she sends the lemon to another relative, and there it again meets the orange, and they change places. And Aunt Feiga gets her precious orange back.

The cloth is removed. The orange, the cunning devil, sits in his former place, like the King of Bagdad, and rules over little cakes and sweets and raisins. The cold of the Purim night lies on him like a dew. He seems to be smiling wearily, a little chilled after his journeyings in so strange a snow-covered, unfamiliar night:

'You see, children, I've come back! You needn't have feared.'

III

When *Purim* is over, the orange lies in the drawer, still whole, and feels happy. If relatives call, and sabbath dainties are served up, the orange has first place on the table, like a prince among plebeian apples and walnuts. People turn him over, ask how much he cost, and give their opinion about him, like wealthy folk who are used to such fruits, and he is put back on his plate. The apples and the nuts disappear one by one, and the orange always escapes from the hands of the relatives, and remains whole. Relatives in Shklov are no gluttons —God forbid! They know what must be left for good manners.

'When the month of *Adar* comes we have jollifications . . .' About ten days after *Purim* there is a betrothal contract drawn up in Aunt Feiga's home. Aunt Feiga has betrothed her eldest daughter to a respectable young man. And again the orange lies on top, right under the hanging lamp, just as if he were the object of the whole party. True, one cheek is a bit withered by now, like that of an old general, but for all that, he still looks majestic. He lights up the table with his luxuriant, exotic strangeness. The youngsters, from the ABC boy to the eleven-year-old *Gemarrah* student, have already hinted repeatedly to their father and their mother that it is high time they had a taste of the orange. . . . Say the blessing for a new sort of fruit—that was all they wanted, only to say the blessing for a new sort of fruit. . . . But Aunt Feiga gave them a good scolding: 'Idlers, gluttons! When the time comes to say the blessing over new fruit, we shall send a special messenger to notify you. . . . Your father and mother won't eat it up themselves. You needn't be afraid of that.'

The youngsters were all atremble at the betrothal party lest the bridegroom should want to say the blessing for new fruit. Who can say what a bridegroom might want at his betrothal party? Mother always gives him the best portions.

But the bridegroom belongs to Shklov. He knows that an orange has not been made for a bridegroom to eat at his betrothal party, but only to decorate the table. So he holds it in his hand just for a minute, and his Adam's apple runs into his chin and runs out again. And the orange again is left intact.

But at last the longed-for Friday evening arrives. The orange is no longer so globular as it had been, nor so fragrant. His youth has gone. But it does not matter. It is still an orange. After the Sabbath meal the mood is exalted. No notification has been sent by special messenger; but the youngsters know instinctively that this time *the blessing over the new fruit will be said*. But they pretend to know nothing. One might think there was no such thing as an orange in this world.

Said Aunt Feiga to Uncle Uri:

'Uri, share out the orange among the children. How long is it to lie here?'

Uncle Uri, a bearded Jew with crooked eyes, an experienced orange-eater who has probably eaten half a dozen oranges, or more, in the course of his life, sat down at the head of the table, opened up the big blade of his pocket-knife —an old 'wreck'—and started the operation. The children stand round the table watching their father with reverent awe, as one watches a rare magic-maker, though they would love to see the inside of the orange and taste it as well. They are only human beings, after all, with desires. . . . But Uncle Uri has lots of time. Carefully and calmly he cuts straight lines across the fruit, from 'pole' to 'pole.' First he cuts four such lines, then eight, one exactly like the other. (You must admit that he is a master at that sort of thing!) And then he begins to peel the orange.

Everybody listens to the crackling of the fleshy, elastic peel. Slowly the geometrically-true pieces of red peel come off. But, here and there, the orange has become slightly wilted, and little bits of the juicy 'flesh' come away with the peel. Uncle Uri says 'Phut!' just as if it hurt him, thrusts the blade of his knife into the orange, and operates on the danger spot. The orange rolls out of its yellowish-white, fragrant swaddling-clothes, and is artistically divided up by the Uncle into equal half-moons, piece by piece.

'Children,' cries the newly-engaged girl, placing a big glass on the table, 'don't forget the pips. Throw them in here. They will be soaked and planted . . .'

She addresses her little brothers, but she means her father as well.

The youngsters undertake to assist their sister in her housekeeping enthu-siasm, which seems to hold out a promising prospect. And they turn their eyes on the tender, rosy half-moons on the plate.

The first blessing is the prerogative of Uncle Uri himself. He chews one bite, and swallows it with enthusiasm, closing one crooked eye, and lifting the other to the ceiling, and shaking his head:

'A *tasty* orange! Children, come over here . . .'

The youngest-born goes first. This is his privilege. Whenever there is any-thing nice going, he is always first after his father. He says the blessing at the top of his voice, with a little squeak, flings the half-moon into his mouth, and gulps it down.

'Don't gulp! . .' says Uncle Uri very patiently. 'No one is going to take it away from you.'

'And where is the pip?' asks his betrothed sister, pushing forward the glass.

'Yes, that's right. Where is the pip?' Uncle Uri backs her up.

'Swallowed it . . .' says the youngster, frightened, and flushes to his ears.

'Swallowed it?'

'Ye-e-s.'

And the tears come into the little one's eyes. He looks round at his older brothers. . . . They keep quiet.

But it is too late. . . . He knows. . . . No father can help him now. They will tease the life out of him. From this day on he has a new nickname: 'Little pip.'

Then the remaining portions of the orange are shared out in order, from the bottom upwards, till it comes to the turn of the *Gemarrah* student. He takes his portion, toys with it a while, and bites into it, feeling that it tastes nice, and also that it is a sweet greeting from Palestine, of which he has dreamed often at Chedar. Oranges surely grow only in Palestine. . . .

'And a blessing?' says Uncle Uri, catching him out, and fixing him with his crooked eyes.

'Blessed art Thou . . .' the *Gemarrah* student murmurs, abashed; and the bit of orange sticks in his throat. His greeting from Palestine has had all the joy taken out of it.

But Uncle Uri was not yet satisfied. No. He lectured the *Gemarrah* student to the effect that he might go and learn from his youngest brother how to say a blessing. Yes, he might take a lesson from him. He could assure him that he would one day light the stove for his youngest brother. Yes, that he would, light his stove for him. And . . .

But he suddenly remembered: 'Feiga, why don't you taste a bit of orange?'

It was a good thing that he remembered; otherwise, who knows when he would have finished his lecture.

'It doesn't matter,' Aunt Feiga replied. Nevertheless, she came up, said the blessing, and enjoyed it: 'Oh, oh, what lovely things there are in the world!' And then they started a discussion about oranges.

Aunt Feiga said that if she were rich, she would eat every day—half an orange. A whole orange was beyond her comprehension. How could anyone go and eat up a whole orange costing eight and a half *kopeks*?—But Uncle Uri did things on a bigger scale. He had after all been once to the Fair at Nijni-Novgorod. So he smiled out of his crooked eyes: No, if he were rich he would have the juice squeezed out of—three oranges at once, and drink it out of a glass. There!

His wife and children were astounded at the richness of his imagination, and pictured to themselves a full glass of rosy, thick orange juice, with a white froth on top, and a pip floating about in the froth. . . .

They all sat round the table in silence for a while, gazing with dreamy eyes at the yellow moist pips which the betrothed girl had collected from all those who had a share of the orange. She poured water over them, and counted them through the glass, one, two, three, four . . . She had nine in all. Yes. Next week she would plant them in the flower-pots; and after her wedding, she would take them with her to her own home. She would place them in her windows, and would let them grow under inverted glasses. . . .

You no doubt think that this is the end. Well, you have forgotten that an orange also has a peel. . . .

I V

One of the youngsters made a discovery—when you squeeze a bit of orange peel over against the lamp, a whole fountain of transparent, thin little fragrant drops squirts out, and when you squirt these into the eyes of one of your brothers, he starts to squint. . . . But before he had time to develop his discovery, he got a smack on his hand. And all the bits of peel vanished into Aunt Feiga's apron.

'There is no trick too small for them to play, the devils. Just as if it were potato-peelings. . . . If she could only get a little more, she could make preserves. . . . Yes, preserves . . .'

But that was only talk. By the time she could collect enough orange peel to make preserves the Messiah would have come.

So she placed the peel overnight in the warm stove to dry. The golden red bits of peel, that only yesterday had looked so fresh and juicy, were now wilted, blackish-brown, curled up and hard, like old parchment. Aunt Feiga took her sharp kitchen-knife, and cut the peel into long strips, then into small oblongs. . . . She put them into a bottle, poured brandy on them, strewed them with soft sugar, and put it away to stand. The brandy revived the dried-up bits of orange peel, they swelled out, blossomed forth, took on again their one-time bloom. You pour out a tiny glassful, sip it, and taste the genuine flavour and bouquet of orange peel.

Relatives come to pay you a visit, they pronounce a blessing, take a sip, and feel refreshed, and it is agreed unanimously that it is very good for the stomach. And the women question Aunt Feiga how she came to think of such a clever thing. . . .

'Look,' said Uncle Zhama to Michla his wife, 'you let everything go to waste. Surely you had an orange as well for *Purim*! Where is the peel? Nothing. Thrown it away.'

Uncle Uri interrupts him: 'Don't worry, Zhama, let us have another sip.'

And he smiles out of his crooked eyes at his 'virtuous woman,' Aunt Feiga.

The bottle is tied up again with a piece of white cloth about the cork, so that it should not evaporate. And it is put away in the cupboard so that it should draw for a long time. And the bottle stands there, all alone, like a pious woman, a deserted wife, in a hood. . . .

Passover comes, and Jews go through the formality of selling their leaven to Alexieka the water-carrier, with the dirty, flaxen hair; so the bottle of orange-brandy-water too falls into Gentile hands. All that week it stands there, sold, a forbidden thing, and scarcely lives to see the day when it is once more redeemed, so that Jews with grey beards and Jewish women in pious wigs should pronounce the blessing over it, and tell each other about Aunt Feiga's amazing capacity.

Sometimes a bottle like that stands for years. From time to time you add fresh brandy, and it is tasted very rarely, until the bits of orange peel at the bottom of the bottle begin to lose their strength, become sodden and pale. Then Uncle Uri knocks them out on a plate.

This is always done on a Saturday night, after the blessing at the termination of the Sabbath, when the spirit of exaltation has vanished, and the week-day drabness creeps out of every little corner. Then Uncle Uri looks for something of a pick-me-up, and remembers the faded, brandy-soaked, sugared bits of orange peel.

He turns the wide, respectable bottle bottom up—begging your pardon, and smacks it firmly but gently on the bottom.

'Phut, phut, phu-ut . . .' the bottle resounds complainingly, penetrating with hollow dullness all over the room, into the week-day, post-Sabbath shadows.

There is a sound, like a deep, frightened sigh, an echo from a dried-up ancient well. The bottle seems to cry aloud that the soul is being knocked out of it, its last breath. . . . And at the same time, sticky, golden-yellow, appetising bits of peel fall out of the neck.

Then all is silent. Uncle Uri pronounces the blessing over the leavings, tastes, and then hands them round.

The children agree that though they are a little harsh, one still detects the taste of the one-time *Purim* orange, peace unto it.

But at the very moment that the last vestige of the famous orange is disappearing from Uncle Uri's house, the heirs of the orange—the sodden, swollen-up little pips—have long since shot up in the flower-pots at the home of Uncle Uri's married daughter. Three or four spiky, sticky little leaves have sprouted out from each little pip.

The overturned, perspiring glasses were removed long ago. They are getting accustomed quite nicely to the climate of Shklov, and are sprouting slowly, with the reserved, green little smile that they had brought with them and secreted within themselves.

The young wife looks after them, waters them daily. And *God knows what may grow out of them one day.*

It Had To Be

He lived in the south—his wife in the north. It had been like that for years. She and the children lived in the northern town, where he and she were both born, had married and brought five children into the world. He, in a distant southern town, to which the bitter struggle for existence had banished him. It was to have been for a short time. For a few months. But it came to be years.

So they wrote letters. Yearning letters, often stained with tears. And at the end of each the wish that God might soon bring them together again.

A big river flowed past the town in the north, on to the town in the south. Hundreds of miles long. But to them it was a link, something that joined them together. It conveyed a constant greeting.

She could stand on the bridge in the north, look down at the waters flowing away from her, and accompany them with yearning glances, send her heart with them. For they were flowing south.

He could stand on the bridge in the south, watching the waters flowing down, with questioning eyes. For they came from the north.

One summer she wrote to him:

'I bathed yesterday. The waters went over my body and passed on to you in the south. Catch them and bathe in them.'

That was a strange letter for a woman of forty to write. Yearning makes ordinary people seers and poets.

She was a pious woman. When she had finished the letter she felt abashed. She blushed and looked round guiltily, lest the walls had seen what she had written.

But the words pleased her. They had come from the depths within her. She looked at them, and lived them over again and again. She felt the contact. She saw the contact.

Great is the distance. The waters that flow out between the banks in the north have many things to tell when they pass between the banks of the south. Ships, big and small, have gone over them. Lovers have rowed their boats on them. People have bathed in them, men, women, children. Some have been drowned, and some have drowned themselves.

Yet the waters that had passed over her, caressed her, kissed her, would reach the distant south untouched, would bring her husband the impress of her nude form.

In her later letters she only hinted shyly:

'I bathed yesterday,' or 'I am going bathing to-day.'

No more. She had created a secret understanding between them, and it buoyed her up.

And he prayed even more ardently and piously at the close of his letters that God in His mercy might reunite them.

He did so with even greater fervour in the letter that he sent her by the hand of a friend of his. He told her there about the bearer of the letter. A Hebrew teacher, from their own district, near their own town. He had tried his luck in the southern town, but without success. Now he was going back to try his luck in their northern town.

He proceeded to describe him—a great scholar, who ought to be more than a teacher. And a very observant Jew, a veritable saint.

He proposed that his friend should live in their house. His room was empty anyhow. The room behind the kitchen. It would be a good thing to have him there. He would be a teacher and an example to the two younger children. Till God took pity on them, and so forth.

His pious moan as he wrote those last lines lay on the words, shrieked, wept, sobbed out of them.

It evoked from her just such another moan. And bitter, scalding tears. That he should have to be far away, and a stranger be the example to their children! When would God have compassion on them?

The teacher came to live there. Moved into the room behind the kitchen. A room that was separated from the rest, as if it had nothing to do with any other part of the house. A dwelling on its own.

And besides, she had a grown-up son, in addition to the younger ones, a grown man, who was about to be married. And two grown-up daughters, of marriageable age.

So there was no liability in the stranger—a teacher, and an observant Jew, a veritable saint—occupying the room that stood empty.

Ah, they had forgotten the long winter nights, when the grown-up daughters and the grown-up son would go to their friends or to the theatre, to dances and parties, and the younger boys would be asleep in their room, sleeping the sound sleep of youth.

It happened presently. One long, cold winter night. The older children were not at home. The younger were asleep. The teacher had just come in from the Beth Hamedrash where he had been studying the Gemarah. He had eaten supper and said grace. Was sitting quietly for a while on the couch beside the dining-table in the warm, well-heated dining-room. Exchanged a few words with her, while she cleared the table. Talked about her husband in the distant southern town. Both spoke with a heavy heart, joylessly.

51

They talked for only a little while. It soon became quiet. Only the cricket on the hearth did not cease chirping, and from one of the bedrooms came the sound of the heavy breathing of the sleeping boys.

Suddenly they realised that were alone. Alone with the silence which pressed on them from all sides, and with the cricket and the breathing of the sleeping children. And with their piety. Yet, they both lost themselves. Became uneasy. The heat in the room grew unbearable. Almost as if their only course would be to fling open door and windows and let in the frost. They forgot what they had been saying when they had grown silent. They found no words for restarting a conversation.

She stood at the door of the larger room which they called hall, and which led to her bedroom. She slipped through the door, stole out. Shut it behind her. Even locked the bedroom door behind her. Undressed in a state of trepidation; crawled under the blankets as if to hide from something.

And he rose up terrified from his place beside the table. Rushed as if he were hunted through the dining-room and the kitchen, into his room. Put all his piety into saying the prayer before going to sleep. Talked down, shouted down something inside him. Was afraid to stop saying his prayers.

Both found it hard to fall asleep.

After that, there were evenings when she begged the grown-up daughters to stay at home, not to go away. Several times she ordered them not to leave the house. It was not proper for girls to be out at night.

The older son was beyond her. It was no use pleading with him to stay or ordering him not to go out.

She did not always succeed with the girls, either. And there were evenings when they had to work late. They were dressmakers, and people got married. Nor could she always beg or ban. The children might ask—'What new thing is this?' Why should they suddenly be told that they should not or must not go out of the house? They might even begin to understand!

Often on such lonesome nights the teacher would put on his worn fur, and leave his warm, well-lit room, with a groan, and a wry face. And go stumbling through heavy snow, in black night and biting frost. Take refuge in the dark, cold Beth Hamedrash.

But when he stayed at home, an atmosphere of disquiet hung over the house, of heart-beating and looming dread. Though he kept to his room, studying the Gemarrah.

One such night, as she lay in bed, restless, distraught, afraid of herself, she remembered that she had left her oldest son's blanket over the stove. She had accidentally upset a jug of water over it, and had put it there to dry. When he came home, he would look for it, get annoyed, and wake her. So she got out ot bed, and went to the stove. Walked, wrapped in the heavy folds of the darkness in the rooms. She did not kindle a light, because in the light she would have seen the disquiet and the looming dread.

The teacher had long finished his page of Gemarah, extinguished his lamp, and got into bed; but he was shivering, his teeth chattered in his head. So he decided to get up and go to the stove to warm himself.

At the stove they knocked into each other in the dark. Two almost naked bodies, a man and a woman. Terror. Almost a shriek. Then groping in fear and blackness. The groping became an embrace. The groan of a released, long-suppressed longing. And forgetfulness.

After forgetfulness came dread and despair. The next day the teacher left the town. Probably to suffer and expiate his sin. The reason given was that he had been called home by bad news.

But she had to conceal her fear and despair. She would have wept for days, but tears betray. She did not dare to be pale. Did not dare to lose countenance. Lest the older children observe, question, look at her in surprise.

So her face became a mask. When she was alone, she tore her hair, beat her head, tormented herself, fiercely, brutally. But she did not weep. And she met her children with her customary calm.

If only God did not see as her children did not see! She did not cease to speak to God. In her heart, quietly, without moving her lips. That He should forget what He had seen in the darkness that night. That He should forgive. Should not punish her. That it should remain in the dark. She counted the days, and lived in hope.

But when she had counted a certain number of days, a shudder passed through her body. Her hair seemed on fire at the roots. Day passed into day, and the horror increased.

She tried, in the days that followed, to lift up the heavy commode—several times—it almost killed her. One day she nearly fainted, after a dose of scrambling on to chairs and table and jumping off.

That day the children noticed that she looked ill. Something was wrong. What had happened?

But it was shortly before Passover. She had a lot to do. She was fagged.

The children only wondered why she was doing more that pre-Passover time than any other. And the younger daughter incautiously said:

'Father isn't coming!'

Those words saved her. They gave her an excuse to cry out. She became hysterical. She sobbed for a long time, bitterly. The children thought they had touched her raw wound, and wept with her, helped their mother to bemoan her parting from their father.

53

After that, they often saw her with tears in her eyes. But they asked no questions. Spoke no word. They were afraid lest they open the wound again.

And when she had counted six months, it was midsummer, and very hot. So she went to bathe.

The river was young in the northern town. Not far from its source. But broad and deep and dangerous. Mainly because it was full of whirlpools, abysses that swallowed people who came near. There were many such whirlpools. Especially near the places where they bathed the horses. And where the best swimmers bathed.

So she went to bathe where the strongest swimmers bathe. For she was an excellent swimmer. She walked into the water slowly. Hands clasped over her abdomen. As if trying to hide it. She walked, listening to what was underfoot, feeling for something with her feet. But she was, all of her, with her husband in the distant south. She breathed heavily, and tears blinded her eyes, rolled down her cheeks, fell like raindrops into the river. And all she was, cried:

'I am going to bathe, my husband!'

Another step, and she felt the ground had vanished under her feet. Her heart beat rapidly. She was almost turning back. Was on the verge of unclasping her hands, tearing them away from her abdomen, and flinging them out and swimming. She still wanted to speak to her husband, to tell him about the waters that would go over her naked body, and flow on to him. But she pressed her arms more tightly to her abdomen, shut her eyes, took another step, and disappeared. She sank as if she were forced down. As if there were a heavy weight inside her.

DAVID BERGELSON

The Witness

In the wide-open gap of what had been the entrance to a house that had remained whole, though terribly battered, stood a Jew, a man of about sixty.
All he wore simply begged to be changed to something else. Over his head
hung an obliterated signboard with nothing more legible on it than one word,
mach ...

The man didn't move a muscle, just as the word *mach* didn't, and for a
moment, seen from the side, it seemed that he wasn't a living thing—only something painted on in the dark aperture where the door had been, and there was
something missing to his face, as there was something missing to the word
mach on the signboard over his head.

All around him, in the not long liberated republican capital, everything
had just become lit up by a wintry sun that had appeared some hours after its
rising. Under its shine the snow that had been falling during the night got
whiter and whiter, and the many gleaming ice-crystals in it dazzled the eyes
of those who passed.

A white wall in the jumble of houses opposite stood jutting out, bright
with the sun, and seemed to give more stridency than usual to the meaningless
words left written on the wall:

'Hannah was taken out of the Ghetto very early on the 27th.'

It is about two o'clock in the afternoon, the time of the midday meal break
in all the central institutions. The street is coming to life, but the Jew in
the doorway without a door shows no sign of even contemplating making
a move.

Of all the many people hurrying by one stops, a woman no longer young,
wearing a light, almost summery coat, with an ancient brown fox fur round
her neck. Her smoothly combed fair hair beginning to turn grey shows from
under the white woollen beret on her head.

'Me?' she asks the Jew. 'You want me?'

She had thought he had called her. And now, looking at him it occurred
to her that he must be blind, and wanted her to take him across the street.

'What?' he asked dully.

Unhurriedly he removed his numbed gaze from the wall and the inscription there, and rested it for a moment on the young woman.

'Perhaps I do need you.'

He was debating something in his mind, but in doing so he was no longer looking at the young woman, but down at the crazily twisted laces on his shapeless boots. A few white hairs roughly cut as with a sickle straggled out from his thin little beard, and through many furrows, like deep gutters, ran a deathly darkness over his whole longish face and into the black hollows under his narrowed eyes.

'If it's about clothing,' said the young woman, 'come to see me in the Town Hall. I work there. Ask for Dora Aronstein.'

Suddenly she felt that she was too hasty with her words. The Jew was standing there, she saw, colder than before.

'No,' he finally shook his head—'clothes?'

Indicating slowly the signboard with the word mach left on it, he added sadly:

'I have just arranged about a job. I'm a tinsmith. I come from West Ukraine.'

He still spoke unhurriedly, and disconnectedly.

'They'll give me something to wear.'

He asked himself a question:

'Eh?'

And as though answering himself:

'They promised me.'

Then he sighed: 'It isn't that.'

For the first time he now looked at the young woman.

Slowly, very slowly his eyes shifted under his brows, that twitched from time to time, and not his lips but his cheeks angrily flung out the words:

'I am a witness!'

A pause.

'A witness?'

The young woman wanted to get his meaning. Her eyes narrowed, as if with pain throbbing at her temples; she had nice blue eyes, a little dulled, and too kindly to pierce into a human soul. There were dark blotches under her nostrils, evidence of her vanishing youth.

'The only remaining witness,' she heard the Jew repeat. 'That's me.'

'So that's what you mean?'

She thought that now she knew what the man was talking about.

'My God!' she wanted to comfort him and herself at the same time.

'Who isn't a witness nowadays? And who isn't nowadays a survivor? Aren't I? Of a family of eight.'

'Listen to what I'm telling you!' the man suddenly burst out angrily.

He spoke of a death camp somewhere outside Lvov. He took a step forward, and caught hold of the young woman's coat, as though to shake her. He had remained, he said, one out of over a million. He thought it all had to be written down, everything he had seen.

'And I,' he wailed, 'am so weak. Then what are you babbling about? I'm asking you: Will you write it down or not?'

Astonished, almost frightened, the young woman named Dora Aronstein, who was hurrying to get to her job at the Town Hall, stood facing him, and she thought how at her door in the corridor there were always more people waiting than at the other adjoining doors. She hardly heard the Jew speaking to her now. She only saw the useless meaningless inscription on the jutting white wall opposite, which the sun was illuminating brightly:

'Hannah was taken out of the Ghetto very early on the 27th.'

Since then the old Jew came every evening to Dora Aronstein at her home.

He spoke, and she wrote.

The home of the Aronsteins—a home for a family of eight in the halfruined building of the Chemtrust—was obstructed everywhere with debris. There wasn't anybody yet to clear a path. Nobody of the whole Aronstein family had been left alive except Dora, and everybody she knew had either perished here in the town, or had not returned from the evacuation. The furniture of all the rooms had been carried away. The first that had been recovered was the big circular old table round which a family of eight used to sit. It was on its last legs—hardly an article of furniture any more. Dora had worked hard and had sweated over it till she had restored it to life. Now the table already stood in its former place in the Aronstein's big dining room. Dora had covered it with the only remaining tablecloth, a woven cloth with a gold-yellow border and short but very thick fringes. It made the table look presentable again.

All round, on the battered, peeling walls, those places stood out where the oil-paint had remained intact. It was a very strong oil-paint, in a very fine apartment. The Chemtrust had once awarded a prize for it to the old chemist Mordecai Benzionovitch, the sire of the Aronstein family, a cheery, virile old man, whom the Germans took to the gibbet together with his neighbour living in the same house, the Russian Professor Birukov. It had seemed to the whole town that the entire achievement of the local Chemtrust was taken with them to the gibbet.

Of the old chandelier over the circular table only the skeleton was left. Dora had draped her coloured silk scarf over it. She had not spared her strength scrubbing the floor with hot water and soap. And in the wintry evenings the Aronstein rooms looked like home again.

A nagging sense of waiting spread endlessly round this circular table. The cleaner the room the more there was that sense of waiting for something, nagging at you. The Town Council had put a telephone into Dora's home. It stood in the far corner of the big otherwise empty dining room, and it had not yet started working. It was a cold permanently silent bit of mechanism. It seemed to be the source of the chill in this once noisy dwelling, where before the war the telephone had never stopped ringing.

Sometimes of a quiet evening the telephone made a sort of reluctant unclear trembling sound. Dora knew this meant the exchange was testing the line. So she sat where she was, with her heart dead in her, as though she had a call from that old noisy bustling life of before.

Since the war had started she had heard no word from her two youngest brothers, Genadi and Borach, who had lived together like partners both in one room in this apartment and had both worked together like partners for their student examinations, and had both gone away together like partners to the front. Hadn't a miracle perhaps happened to one of them?

Dora trembled, as though hearing a voice over the telephone—'He's alive!'

One evening—Dora and the old Jew had just sat down at the table, when there was a knock at the door and a young man came in, a very tall man, and very thin. The officer's uniform that he wore without the belt and shoulder straps added to his slimness. Dora and the young man stood for a moment or two frozen; then suddenly they fell on each other's neck. The old Jew watched, till the young man at last quietened Dora. It turned out that he was Professor Birukov's youngest son Cyril, returned from the war—he had graduated as a child prodigy nearly twenty years old, from both the Faculties of Philology and of Physics. Not Dora's brother. Not even one of her distant relatives. Only that Dora's father, Mordecai Benzionovitch, the old chemist, and Cyril's father, Professor Birukov, were both hanged by the Germans in this town for the same reason and on the same gibbet—so tell me these are not close to each other. It can't be closer!

The glow of the one electric lamp hardly manages to seep through the fine silk, and by its dim light scarcely illumining the surrounding cold emptiness Dora sits whole evenings long facing the old stranger, the Jewish tinsmith from Western Ukraine, writing down all he has to say about the death camp outside Lvov.

What she heard from the old Jew was much worse than destruction, more terrible than death. What those Germans had done in that camp! At their command Jews who had been brought there before—all people specially selected, people with fine features, men and women dressed as though for a wedding, met the trains with the new arrivals, and assured them:

'You can go easy now.'

'Thank God!'

'Here you will stay alive!'

'You may be sure of it!'

'You'll be all right now!'

Dora wrote it down exactly, unhurriedly, taking care that in putting into Russian what he told her in Yiddish there should be no errors creeping in, no barbarisation of the Russian language. Her back became hunched with whole hours of such writing, just as it became hunched with the days she spent sitting over her work in the Town Hall. She was by nature a hardworking person, with a love of work inherited and implanted in her by her scholarly father and her learned grandfather. Actually, she wasn't at all sure what purpose would be served by all this work, by what she was writing down from dictation from this old Jew sitting at her side. What would come out of it?

Only deep down she felt that it was all connected with the disappearance of her brothers, Genadi and Borach, with her father's death, and the destruction of her whole family and all her near ones in this town, where only few had managed to escape. Her father, as she was now told in the town, had been dealt with by the Germans in almost the same way as the Jews in the camp behind Lvov. The morning before they hanged him they had harnessed him to a small cart, as one harnesses a horse, with a collar and with reins, and had made him drag a barrel of water along the main street.

Dora's face and voice were grave when she read out to the old Jew some of his words translated into Russian, and wanted him to tell her if she had got them right.

'Yes,' he shook himself sadly, and after considering for a while, said: 'That's how it seems to have been.'

But once he had answered her: 'You ask me to judge? What can I tell you? Our sufferings were in Yiddish.'

His face was black, charred like a brand snatched from the fire. A smell of smouldering bones seemed to come from him. Dora had brought up a long bench to the table, so that he could half lie on it, to save him the strain of sitting up all the time. He could hardly talk; all that still lived in him was so worn out, so weak. And what he told was still only about one of the first parties of people that had been taken from the death camp to the gas chamber and the crematorium ovens. And there had been many such parties, ever so many, countless. And each party had its special association in his mind, some particular mark that would not let him forget it.

'In one party,' he said, 'there was a young woman, outstandingly beautiful, out of this world, impossible to describe. In that same party there was a young painter, also a Jew. The Germans made him sit down and paint her, completely nude, in colour. He painted her and wept, painted and wept. She got it into her head that they would let her live—because she was beautiful. The young painter thought so too; so did others. Yet in the end they took her to the gas chamber with the rest.'

Dora wrote it down, fast, very fast, completely forgetting that she must be careful not to let any grammatical errors get into her Russian translation of the old man's Yiddish.

Then he suddenly stopped. He seemed too weak, too exhausted to speak. Dora waited a while, not lifting her eyes from the freshly written lines. Then she heard a low sobbing, sighing, moaning. Like the faint buzzing of a fly banging all the time against the window, always hitting the glass. Dora found it strange—he had possessed enough strength to speak about the murderings; and now he wept. Tears were running down his longish face full of lines and furrows, and remained hanging on the few hairs left in his thin beard, hairs thick as straw cut by a scythe.

'What's the matter?' Dora cried. 'Why are you weeping?'

'I am weeping for her beauty which they burned. It makes my heart bleed.'

Dora suddenly buried her head in her arms and tried to stop herself weeping as well. Her shoulders heaved. She felt with all her senses that she was weeping over a disaster wide as the sea. She was weeping for murdered beauty. God in Heaven! How much beauty they had destroyed!

When Dora had composed herself and was quiet again she saw that the old Jew had dozed off. He had been too exhausted to stay awake.

Tears stood in her eyes as she looked round the room, staring into the distant desolation. All the time the words written on the wall went round and round in her mind. And her hand wrote the words down mechanically: 'Hannah was taken out of the Ghetto very early on the 27th.'

The old Jew was still asleep, half reclining on the long bench she had placed against the table. The numerous furrows on his forehead ran like channels down to the black hollows under his closed eyes, and in the light of the electric lamp seeping faintly through the silk scarf his face was like the waxen face of a dead man in his coffin. Dora remembered her father's face—the brick-red face of a well-built, broad-shouldered old man, one of those who remain vigorous to the last minute of their life—cheeks filled with wisdom in all the slits and crevices. Unconsciously she began to write:

'And mother, who spent a long life with him, was always looking after his health, as though it was her main occupation in life. She came from Bessarabia, a devoted woman, and physically very strong even in her later years. None of the children remembered a doctor ever coming to the house. And I was told here that the same morning when the Germans harnessed father to the water cart, she stole out of the Ghetto, hid her face in a peasant scarf, and went to help father push the cart along the main road. The Germans kept driving her away, but she always came back. The Germans beat her, knocked her down; she lay on the ground in a pool of blood. But soon she was up again, blood all over her, helping father to push the cart. That was her war against the Germans, for people fought the Germans not only with guns and bullets, but also with beauty, with plain, ordinary human beauty.'

Cyril came in sometimes while Dora was still sitting up late with the old Jew. He wasn't able to walk easily yet. He had a bullet wound in his right knee, and he limped. When he saw them busy he wanted to go out again, but Dora assured him that he would not be disturbing them, and made him stay.

Cyril had nowhere to go to. His entire family had perished. He had found his father's apartment—on the same floor as the Aronsteins'—boarded up, with cobwebs all over it, and littered with debris, just as Dora three weeks before had found her own rooms. He sat at the table, silent, his eyes on the old Jew. Cyril's young face, with his grey eyes, was strained the whole time with the effort to understand something that was not altogether clear to him. He had known many Jews in this town from his childhood. Some of them closely. This old Jew was different from them all, this one Jew who, as Dora told him, had remained alive, one out of a million. He was worn out, he was weak; he sang his words and swayed as he spoke. And because Cyril understood no Yiddish it seemed to him that his words about the death camp outside Lvov must be terribly significant, very powerful—words about a million destroyed lives. No small matter!

It made him regard the written pages lying on the table beside Dora with a special awe. He remembered how one evening about ten years ago, his father, Professor Birukov, had for the first time brought home Mordecai Benzionovitch, apparently from their work in the Chemtrust laboratory, where Professor Birukov was at that time making his experiments for converting something nasty smelling into something sweet smelling. When they came in from the street they were in the middle of an argument.

'All I know,' Mordecai Benzionovitch was saying, half banteringly, half seriously, 'is that just now there is an awful stink not only in the laboratory but all over the place—in the corridors as well. I can't stand it! It drives me out of the room. And I can't believe you that this can be made to smell sweet. What for? Enough that the world should not stop spreading nice smells, overpowering all that is naturally sweet-smelling.'

Cyril sat for a moment with his head bowed. Then he smiled, as if anticipating what he was going to say:

'Don't you think you might add something in those pages about our two old men, your father and mine? You get my meaning? The Communist Youth . . .'

He forgot his knee and started limping about. He spoke, as was his way, in short sentences and with long pauses in between, when his lips closed stiffly, as though they would never open again. Round his youthful mouth, where a soft dark-blond little beard was beginning to sprout, a charming naive shyness appeared. He spoke as though someone were prodding him after each sentence, to go on, to continue. His way of talking reminded one of a quiet sea gently lapping the shore, giving warning that it can also roar.

'Yes,' he said, 'Communist Youth over sixty.'

Then he told Dora all that he had learned in the town about his father and her father.

'Do you remember Valia?'

'Valia? I used to see you in the theatre and the cinema with a young girl, a beautiful young girl, quite young—about sixteen or seventeen.'

'That's her.'

Valia had been coming to Cyril's home to see his father, Professor Birukov. Early on, in the first days of the German occupation, Valia had entrusted a secret to the Professor:

'We have decided that you are to prepare hand grenades for us in your Chemtrust laboratory. We shall pass the hand grenades on to the partisans.'

'We?' the Professor had asked. 'Who are we?'

'The Communist Youth Underground.'

'Are you in touch with the older people?'

'You may set your mind at rest about that.'

Professor Birukov had talked to Mordecai Benzionovitch, and they had both, at the age of seventy, joined the local Young Communist organisation.

Cyril shrugged his shoulders.

'You see,' he said to Dora, 'when the Germans wanted to rejuvenate old Faust they had to bring down the dark, cynical spirit Mephistopheles. With us it was the bright believing spirit of the young Communist Valia. Doesn't that illustrate the difference between their people and ours?'

Dora didn't answer. She hadn't graduated in philology like Cyril, and she had to give a lot of thought to what he meant. She concentrated her gaze on Cyril, and from the strained look in her eyes it seemed as if the throbbing of her temples increased from minute to minute.

One evening, coming to the door of the Aronstein apartment, Cyril heard Dora inside shrieking hysterically: 'Help!'

One shrieks like that in the middle of the night, when one is attacked in an empty street. Cyril burst into the room, sure that something terrible was happening there. He was surprised when he saw that everything was just the same in this almost empty dining room, except for one thing—the old Jew was lying stretched full length on the bench alongside the big table. His hands were folded over his breast, and through the faint light coming from the coloured silk draping, there was a shine on the lids of his closed eyes. It seemed that someone had been pouring water over him. Dora, in tears, ran to the telephone and shouted into the mouthpiece. Cyril dragged her away:

'You know the phone isn't working!'

'Yes, but. . . .'

Dora roused herself as from a nightmare:

'My God, he is dying! He may be already dead. What shall I do?'

She flung her coat over her, and rushed out to find a telephone that would be working, to call the first-aid service, to get through to a doctor she knew, and make him come immediately.

She banged the door so violently as she ran out that the chandelier shook and the light in the shaded bulb flickered as though it were going out.

The old Jew's nose was tense and sharp under his closed eyes. Tense and sharp like the face of a man who has aimed at something with all his power and stopped in the middle—hadn't got there. On the table lay the sheets of paper with his unfinished story of a million people whom he had lost in the death camp outside Lvov.

The room was suddenly hushed, and Cyril felt that he was alone with a dying man.

Cyril sat down at the table and drew the sheets of paper towards him. He felt something strange and unknown about them, as when we see the last work a man did before his death, that he didn't finish. He expected to find in these pages something overpowering, such as no one had till now been able to express. But to his astonishment all the words and phrases were plain and ordinary.

One page described in words as dry as in protocol how a woman in childbirth died at the side of a mass grave together with an immense number of naked and half-naked people of all ages, of both sexes.

'And when one of the many bullets hit the woman in the head she had just given birth to the child. And when she was shoved into the grave the child went with her, still bound to the mother by the umbilical cord.'

Reading this Cyril screwed up his face, as though he was having a tooth pulled. On another page he found the details of Mordecai Benzionovitch's death, written down in Dora's hand. The name 'Professor Birukov' which occurred there several times roused in him a nagging desire for his father, a powerful, persistent craving.

Here, beside the old Jew, a memory came to him from his childhood, when he and some other children playing in the courtyard had made fun of a little Jewish boy. His father happened to come home just then and told him sternly to go indoors, as though he was going to deal with him. But no, his father had first gone to his own room and busied himself with his work; it was only in the evening that he spoke to him. He closed the door very carefully, and told him in a very serious voice that he, Professor Birukov, was really named Abrahamson. That was the true family name. He was a Jew.

His father had left Cyril thinking for a long time that he really was a Jew.

The more Cyril thought about his father the more intensely he longed for him. He didn't remember when he had picked up the pen on the table and started writing his own memories of his father, Professor Birukov, who had been exterminated.

Suddenly Cyril sensed that he was no longer the only living person in the room. He turned his head and saw the old Jew sitting up, supporting himself with both hands against the table, and through many wrinkles and furrows deep yearning ran over his dark longish face and poured into the black hollows under his half-closed eyes.

Becoming aware of Cyril's presence near him, he shivered.

'What has happened?' he asked wonderingly. 'You thought I had died?'

His eyes shifted under his quivering brows, and it was not his lips but his cheeks that seemed to fling out the words:

'How can I die? I am a witness!'

From My Estates

I don't know where it came flying from, but suddenly, in the midst of every-thing, I felt on my forehead a wet mud-patch. I looked round. Who could it be, and who had thrown it? Saw nobody. And at once removed the mud-patch with my hand, and lo, a coin.

And as I had long been going about penniless, had not eaten, nor had a decent lodging, I wanted to have a good time now. So I went to a fine restau-rant, had a meal, ate my fill, and then I went into the town for a stroll, with something still in my pocket for spending. And since a fine day it was, and I feeling pleased with myself, passing the splendid promenading place, and seeing tents and booths put up there, in which books were sold and many people, grown people and also children buying, because a cheap book-week had been proclaimed all over the country and books were being raffled in the booths, and each raffle, it was written down, must win, I also went up and drew a ticket, and when the salesman in the booth unfolded the ticket, he gave me a book.

The author, The Nistor!

The title—'The Writings of A Madman'. And on the cover the drawing of a pale lunatic wearing a strait-jacket.

I turned the pages and the book started like this.

The Nistor complained that he had ten bears boarding with him and eating his head off, eating him out of house and home. And when he had nothing left, not a cent, and he himself had to go begging in the houses, they still would not leave him alone. They kept coming to him, sat round his table, and everything he bought, that he had got together begging on the doorsteps of houses, they demanded, and he had to give it to them.

The last time he came home he found them round his table again—four on one side, and four on the other, and one at the head and one at the foot, the two oldest and most sedate. They were all silent, waiting, looking at him—and what they were waiting for was—food.

And when the Nistor showed them—let them see!—that there was nothing in the room, and he undid his wallet, and nothing there, and the only cupboard standing open, and the shelves bare, and on the walls no raiment, and in the corners of the walls only spiders, and the spiders, too, dead or faint with hunger—they still kept silent.

And the Nistor thought to himself—what more could he show them that they should see that he had nothing—except his ten fingers—maybe! And he said so to them: 'This is all I have and all I possess—no more. And do with me what you will.' And the bears looked at his fingers, and agreed. Fingers are fingers, and fingers are food.

So the Nistor went up to the first bear, a little bear, and offered his little finger to chew. And he bit it off. He offered the next finger to the second. And he did the same. And so from one to the other along one side of the table. The Nistor already had no fingers left on one hand—instead of fingers blood and chewed bones. And the others were famished, waiting their turn, and licking their jaws very respectably.

The Nistor went over to the other side of the table, and offered the little finger of his other hand, and then the next, till he had only two fingers left, and two more bears to feed, a young bear along the side of the table, and the oldest bear, at the head.

The young bear had no patience, seeing all the others busy eating, their mouths full of blood and gristle, and his appetite was roused, and he was full of desire. And when the Nistor went up to him and offered him his finger he snapped at it and in his haste bit off both fingers at once. And the oldest and last of the bears was left without food, without a finger, and he sat there very annoyed, and very sedate, and waited. Of course, the Nistor would not let him go without anything. Why was he worse than the rest? On the contrary, he was the senior and deserved more.

And the Nistor stood there with two bleeding hands now, holding them up, and the blood was running into his sleeves, and the pain was intense, and what could he do with the blood, since he could not even put on a bandage, or tie a towel round.

Then the Nistor went up to the oldest of the bears and said: 'Look, I haven't any more. And I can't do anything more. Even if I wanted to.'

And when the bear heard this, he silently and sedately laid his paw on the Nistor's breast, and asked: 'And this, what is this?'

'This!' answered the Nistor. 'It is nothing, a little watch, of no consequence. It goes wrong, and doesn't keep time properly.'

'A watch is a watch', answered the bear, and did not take his paw off the breast. And the Nistor realised that it was all up, that he would have to part now with his breast and his heart, and then the spiders in the room too, would have to die, and then he would not be able to go begging in the houses any more.

He stood for a while and looked at the bear, and here his finger-pain became more intense, suffering not to be endured, and a great cry broke from him, but he kept it back; he did not want to disturb the feast of the other bears. And then, when they had all finished eating, and the oldest of the bears still kept his paw on his breast, and he was hungry for his portion, and waited for the Nistor's breast, the Nistor lifted up his voice and said:

'My lord bears. You demand from me the last I have, and if I give it to you, neither I nor you will have any more, and we must now bid each other farewell. And since you have seen me in my poverty and in my bitter plight, and in my wealth never, I want to tell you about that now, so that you will see how being rich, one can become poor. So why not being poor again, again rich? And perhaps if you will now leave me this last that I have, who knows but you would have no cause for regret afterwards, and maybe by not eating this once you would afterwards be rewarded with many rich feasts?

'My fingers which you have chewed up hurt, and the bones which are now being digested in your bellies have left me blood-burning wounds, and there is a cry sticking in my throat, and it is only for the sake of your feast that I did not cry out, and a great cry is still in store for me, when my heart is taken out of me, and as much time as I am still destined to spend in company with it, I want to use in order to rejoice with it for the last time. So permit me this for the last time. And hear me speak of my riches.

'You must know that in the highest places I had my own ladder, and often I went up, and once I remained there for a long time. And up above as down below, there are places of different kinds, beautiful and eerie, and also ugly and muddy. And as usual, I sated myself first with the beautiful, and spent much time there, and then I left them, and I crossed the frontiers and a filthy, squalid, muddy place I found myself in.

'A town was there, and the town was more than half sunk in mud, and the walls sullied, and whiteness and something not filthy was a novelty there. And people trudged along up to their ankles in mud, and the houses were mud, and the roofs were covered with mud, and when it rained and the roof-mud got wet the filth ran into the houses, and what happened then in the houses can be guessed, and how the people looked inside these filthy houses can be imagined. And like the people, so were their means of earning their living. And they baked bread of mud, and with unwashed hands they ate.

'Anyone who came to them as a guest from outside suffered, of course, starved, couldn't put a thing in his mouth, but in the end he could not hold out any more. He had to eat. He gave in and willy-nilly had to join in their filth-feasts. And I, too, when I came there from the lovely places, suffered intensely at first from hunger and from cold, because their food I could not eat, and their couches revolted me. But after some time had elapsed, and all my fine things and everything I had brought with me from those other places gave out, I had no choice but to yield, and whether I wished it or didn't wish it (of course, I didn't), I had to break their filth-bread and dig my spoon into their dirt-plates.

'And I ate, and soon vomited it up, and I ate a second time, and I vomited again. And the filth-people were indignant. Why was I so fastidious—why could they eat it and others as well, even guests from outside got accustomed to it, and why was I better than everybody else!

'And they hated me. And when I became ill because of their food, and couldn't get up, nobody came to me, nobody brought me any different food, like for a sick person, nor even for one who is not sick. They forgot all about me, and did not bring me even their ordinary muck.

'And I became wasted, and nobody paid me the slightest attention. I just lay there and couldn't move. And when I asked in my room for a drink, and a child in the room, if its parents had gone out, or an aged person left behind, handed me sometimes on my plea a little of their water, and the water, like their food, was black and filthy, and I sipped it, wanting to still my hurt and quench my thirst, I vomited the water, too, and with the water everything I had left, the very gall in me, and I became green, and shrieked as I vomited, and when the child that had brought me the drink, or the old man who had been left behind grew frightened and ran to call the people of the house, their own or relatives or neighbours, these for the most part took no notice, would not even listen, and even if they did, and even if they sometimes came and found me green, belching and faint, they used to stand and look at me and spit and 'a nuisance' they would say, and 'who sent for him, who asked him to come here? Soon he will die and we shall have his body on our hands, and have to dig a grave for him—as if we hadn't anything else to do!'

'Help, of course, they did not give me. Nor did they have anything with which to help me, since it seemed to be all my fault, because my stomach and my guts appeared to be different, and I was a stranger besides, and what, after all, was I there, and what claim had I on them, and why should I be a burden on them.

'As for getting well, I saw that among these dirt and filth-folk I should never get well, because food and remedies of dirt are neither food nor remedies. And I did not want to die among them. The thought that even after I was dead filthy people would lay me out with their filthy paws—though life there was uninviting—did not make death any more pleasant.

'And I strengthened myself, pulled myself together and I got out of my muck-bed, put on my bemired garments, and as best I could, without saying a word to anyone, without a farewell to anyone, I dragged myself to the door, crossed the threshold and went outside.

'The very thought that I was already outside made me feel well, and the hope that perhaps by exerting all my strength I would somehow be able to get out of this filth, gave me increased powers, and I strode forward through the mud.

'And the people of the house saw that, and when I got out of bed, and quietly, without a word of farewell, left them, and went out into the fresh air, and the air agreed with me, and my eyes sparkled with health, they scoffed and jeered at me, and they believed, they were sure that I would not be able to get as far as their frontier. Also they were annoyed with me, as I have said, for being fastidious. They hated me. 'Look!' they shouted. 'He is going away. He is leaving us. Our country doesn't suit him. Our mud is not to his liking. He is looking for fresh lands, the perisher is leaving us!'

'And some of them accompanied me with curses and with reviling and others slung mud after me, first the children, and afterwards the fathers and the older folk. And the people got excited, and the people bent down to the ground, and picked up mud, and mud there was plenty, and how to handle mud these people knew well enough, and the people threw mud, and everything they threw stuck to me—first my back was plastered, then when I turned round to look at those who were slinging mud at me, I was covered with it in front, too, and my face as well, and my head, and the hair on my head, and I was wet and black all over, and heavy with the weight of the mud on me. And the mud kept flying at me, one lump after the other. The first I felt, but those that followed I ceased to feel, and muddied and besmirched, I just managed to get away from the pursuing, pelting mob.

'And with great difficulty and feeling very ill, I slogged for ever so long through the mud, and covered quite a distance, and many times I stopped in the midst of the mire to catch my breath, and many times I thought it was the end of me, that I should never get to my destination, and would leave my soul in the mud, till it was over, and I got out of there, and placed a wet foot on the dry frontier, and again came into a beautiful land.

'Soon the frontier people saw me, and they seemed very much surprised, and they stared at me, with awe, with their eyes wide open, and I understood, and I explained their wonderment to myself, thinking that they stared at me because I was an object to be stared at, like a corpse that had arrived in a living land, or someone filthy and bedraggled who had come into a clean country, for I was ill, and surely there must be signs of something deathly on my face, and I was covered with mud, and these two things together, ill and filthy, had no doubt provoked their amazement.

'But when I looked again, I saw that more than wonder, there was awe in their eyes, that they kept aloof from me with tremendous deference, not as if a sick man, poor and mud-coated, had appeared to them, but one who is very wealthy, overwhelming them with his opulence, and they, the frontier-folk, and the inhabitants of that land had never seen anything like it, as if he were walking on gold, and as if he were hung with gold from head to foot.

'And indeed, when I lifted up my hand and wanted to take the mud off my face, to get rid of some of the filth, and in this fair place make myself more fair, and I took off the first bit of dried caked mud, and held it in my hand, I saw in my hand not mud, but actually gold. Once I took off—a lump of gold, the second time—again gold. And when I looked at my mud-pelted garments and the whole of my body, I found myself all over shining, golden, as if encased in armour of gold.

'And clear it was to me why the frontier-folk paid me honour, and comprehensible also why they held aloof, full of deference and awe. And I saw myself terribly rich, and soon I felt myself strong, and since from the mud-folk I had come tired out by the journey, and ill, and famished, not having eaten for a long time, and as I looked round in that place, immediately on the frontier, and saw shops with fine raiment, and all sorts of luxuries, I went at once into the first shop, and owner and assistants ran up to me and gave me what I desired.

'And when I wanted to pay with the caked mud that in my hands immediately turned to gold, and I gave the proprietor a gold coin, and wanted to take the goods, he would not allow me to. 'No', he said to me, 'I must not do that.' His assistants would take everything home for me.

'And the proprietor asked me where I lived, the house where I stayed, and I could go, and soon I would have everything brought to me at home.

'And I was not living anywhere, and had no place at all, so I stood there for a time embarrassed, and could give the proprietor no street, no number and no house.

'The proprietor saw my embarrassment, and asked me the reason. And I said:

' 'I am a stranger, and I am not living anywhere yet, and perhaps you could be good enough to tell me where I could get a room.'

' 'Certainly,' the proprietor hastened to answer, showing me every sign of courtesy and honour. And he at once sent out one of his assistants, who ran and immediately ordered a room for me in a hotel. And he came straight back, and the proprietor ordered him to take me to the hotel, and to be at my service, if I wanted anything else on the way, that I would like to purchase in other shops, and he would go with me, point out everything for me, and carry home for me all the other things I would buy.

'I thanked him, and went out with the assistant, and wherever we went people stared after us, and wherever we turned people stopped their work, no matter what they were doing, and looked at us. And people came to the doors of the shops, and shopkeepers and assistants gazed at us with amazement, and from the houses too, and the windows, people looked out, and the whole town, all the streets through which we went, had one subject and one thing only to do—to admire me clad in gold, and not to take eyes off me or cease to talk about me.

'And the assistant went with me from shop to shop, and in all the shops we bought what I required and needed, and then the assistant took me to a hotel, the richest and cleanest, and the finest room was given to me, with all conveniences, with beautiful walls and great doors and tapestries and windows looking out into a lovely garden, and a strong, beautiful bed, and great comfort and excellent service. And many servants stood waiting to carry out my wishes, and everything I said was done at once.

'Presently I told everyone to go out and I got into bed and rested, and I had a doctor called, and the doctor came and examined me, and he found that there was no longer any illness in me. I was having good food, and the doctor prescribed in addition to the good food certain other good things, and his treatment was right, and in a few days I had forgotten all that had happened before, the muddy place and the bad treatment I had there, and the mud with which they had pelted me, and my illness there, and what was left me of the mud was gold, and I am rich and honoured and in a beautiful spot, and in the most beautiful house of this beautiful spot, and the owner of the house in which I am staying keeps hovering around me and servants walk on tiptoe in front of me, and what more could I desire?

'And, indeed, as soon as I felt well I dressed and went out into the town, and the town knew me from before, and the townsfolk stared after me more than previously. And many interested people I saw, merchants, agents, and others who wanted to do business, who kept following me, wanted to propose something to do, but did not yet venture to approach, stared after me, watched where I went in, but kept their distance, did not yet dare to come up to me.

'But after a time, first one, and then another, and then many others came up to me. And soon I was surrounded by a crowd of merchants, agents, and people with business schemes, and each of them proposed something to me, or had something to sell.

'They persuaded me that there was a shortage of money in the country at present, and if I want a house I can have a house, if I want a shop I can have a shop, if I want a forest, if I want a field, I can have it all, and for next to nothing, and I must not let the opportunity slip, but let myself be persuaded.

'I allowed myself to be persuaded, for without business there would be nothing to do, no way of passing the time, and what was the use of walking about with the gold? What would be the use of it to me? While if I trade I lose nothing, on the contrary, I add to my usefulness. For I had made enquiries, and saw that the businesses that were suggested to me were really advantageous, and the country really experienced a crisis, as they had told me, and it could be exploited, so why not, and why should I decline?

'And I bought. If a house was offered I bought a house. If it was a shop, then it was a shop, if something else, it was something else; and in a little while, when I looked round, and I went through the town, walking with my agents and business promoters, and they pointed out my possessions, the houses and the shops, I perceived that entire streets were already in my pocket. Also I had on me the contracts for a great number of shops, and I am the boss, and I give orders, and a large part of the town already belongs to me, and before long the whole town and everything in it will belong to me.

'And so it was. In a short time the man who was above everybody else in the town came to me himself, the man who owned the land, the site on which the town stood, and said that he had heard that I am buying, and that I am not short of money, so perhaps I would buy the town from him, the land and the titledeeds, and all the buildings, and the open spaces, and everything all around, and the whole of the revenue would be mine.

'And I bought. And I became master of the town. And for a little while I was content with that, had sated my buying-lust. Then when the town ceased to be sufficient for me, and sitting about doing nothing was tedious, I left that place, the town, with everything I had bought, and went to another place, and there I did the same as in the first place, and I did that too in a third place, and so on and so on; I bought up everything, and my breast-pocket was bursting with papers, and my case kept getting more full of contracts.

'And in all places my name was great, and everywhere I was known and respected, and whole countries were at my service, and entire districts waited for my orders. And merchants and agents stood in queues at my door, waiting to hear me speak a word, and revenue from the entire country came flowing into my pockets, and all my desires were fulfilled, and the loveliest daughters of the land were waiting for me to delight them. If I but nodded, the best of them were at my disposal. If I beckoned, the finest robes fell off the most ravishing bodies. And my banquets and balls that I arranged were talked about and remembered months and years afterwards. And the rich wished they had my wealth, and the poor dreamed of me on their couches at night, and in their dreams they looked up at me as from the earth to heaven, and I stood over their heads like a great sun, and their eyes were too small to see, and their heads were not big enough to imagine such great good as mine.

'And I was not sated, and all the good things I had were not enough for me, and already seemed little to me, and all that I had did not satisfy me, and I wanted to be the ruler over the whole country and the whole kingdom.

'And one fine day I achieved that. The Lord of all, the paramount ruler, whose word was law, once sent to me early in the morning one of his great officials, with his footstool for me, and the footstool looked like a crown, and it had a rest on which to place the feet, and the man offered it to me, and I placed my feet on it.

'And so there was nothing more to wish for, and no gold on my body was left, and the mud with which I had been pelted had by dint of long-in-riches-living and much washing been rubbed away, and left to me was only on my forehead a little gold, and a little mud-patch, which in spite of all the washings and soaps couldn't come off, and I picked at it with my fingers, and it was very hard—and then, when the man brought me the footstool, a little per-spiration broke out on my forehead—I was so excited and surprised, and I put my hand to my forehead, and a lump of gold came off, a hardened lump, and when I saw it in my hand, I felt very jolly, and that gold seemed to me the best gold of all, and it was indeed the best gold. And I said to the man:

' 'I am arranging a ball, and let the ruler come and see that his footstool has come to rest under deserving and worthy feet, and his crown—

'I did not finish, but I meant that his crown was on a head undeserving and little worthy.

'The man flushed red. But out of awe for me, and because his ruler had sent him on such an important mission to me, and the ruler himself had sent his footstool to me, he heard my insult to the crown and said nothing, but a little abashed for his lord, and also a little out of fear for me, he bowed his head.

'And the ball took place. The finest and largest halls were decorated, and all the loveliest flowers of the land were brought there, and all the most beautiful women filled the dance-halls and the tables. And servants handed round food on plates of gold—and there was plenty of everything, oysters from the sea, and birds from distant isles, and wines from the cellars of princes, and goblets from the biggest landowners, and the music was the most delight-ful, and birds and parrots with their cries helped to drown the music.

'And dresses were seen there such as no eye could have previously imagined, and the tables took away the breath of even old and former kings. And the guests marvelled and gaped, and no one was able to see all the wealth that was there, for wherever they looked they were unable to take their eyes off, they could not see enough of it. People walked about dazed. They looked at things without seeing them, and they did not know where to look first.

'The official had conveyed my wish, and the ruler came, and he, too, was amazed, and his eyes were lost. And the guests were so full of the splendours

73

there, and the servants also, that no one even noticed him, save I alone, and I called him to the head of the hall, and seated him at my side.

'There was a chair there for him, but he hesitated to sit down on it, because though he was a ruler, his eyes had never seen anything like it. When at last he obeyed me, and sat down, he soon jumped up again. The great joy and admiration all around him made him feel small and insignificant, and involuntarily his hands stretched up to his head, and he took off the crown, and placed it on my head, as the one truly entitled to it.

'And the rejoicing was intensified. And everybody was intoxicated and dizzy with happiness. And the music added to the noise, bodies soared on wings, and feet glided on air, and women did not feel their bodies, and men did not feel the women, the dance was so elevated and airy and joyous, that only music could keep time with it, and only women with young and beautifully-smelling blood could fit into the step.

'And here I started drinking. Without counting, and without any measure I drank, and a special servant stood at my right hand, and from a special flask he kept pouring out wine for me, and the wine, too, was of a special kind, and it knocked me on the head, and came down into my legs, and I felt hot all over. And the guests drank with me, and the eyes of all were full of wine, and my joy was above that of all of them, and of all the heads I was the crowned head, and all the women were for me.

'And there were many shut-off rooms in the halls, and if I ask and command, and the music plays, the most beautiful women would follow me submissively into the shut-off rooms, accompanied by the music and my riches. And I did not command, and I did not call any woman, because I could have them all, and call them all, and I only went on drinking, and the music deafened me, and the parrots shouted my head off.

'And then I shouted. And my shout rose above every other sound, the noise of the guests, and of the music, and of the parrots, and I cried:

' 'Let the Great Bear come down out of the star-constellation, and I shall dance a bear-dance with him.'

'And everybody was silent. And the music was hushed. And the parrots ceased their cries, and no one stirred, and the entire hall was petrified, and all eyes turned to the door, and all saw the Great Bear come in.

'And the Great Bear was very grave, as if he did not come willingly, and it seemed as if he had been called away from his work, or roused from sleep, and all the people who gazed at him were awed, and all stood silent, and all eyes were turned on him.

'That annoyed me. It made me feel a bit angry. Why were they all looking at him, not at me? I had called him, and he had come at my command. And my annoyance, and my haughtiness, and my pride and my superciliousness hurt my heart, and I cried out into the silence, in a loud voice to the Bear:

' 'Now, hear and see, Star-Bear, I have bought up the whole of your kingdom' (and I pulled out the title-deeds from my breastpocket, and brandished them in front of him). 'The ruler himself has abdicated his throne to me, and I have put on his crown. I am now the richest man in the land, and all the subjects of the land are here as my guests at this never-before-seen ball. I want to enjoy myself. I have exhausted and tired of all the joys this land can give me. One, one joy has been left—to dance with you here at my ball, in front of everybody, to the accompaniment of soft music.'

'And the Bear heard me out, and he came up submissively, and he entered silently into the centre of the ring formed by the people, and the ring was silent, and filled with awe, and I went up to him, into the centre. And we met there.

'And I told the music to be silent. Only one violin should speak. And the violin spoke. And I went up to the Bear and embraced him, and we both danced, silently, as one dances with a bear. He stood on his hind legs, and his front paws he held on my shoulders, and his head was a little averted, and a quiet star appeared on his forehead, and the lights in the hall began to go out, and the people were in darkness, only I and the Bear in the centre, and the little star shone on us, and I led, and the Bear followed, in time to the music, slowly, and I began to sing:

' "The Bear, the Bear. Oh, this is bliss. And I have nothing more than this. No place to which I now aspire. And nothing more that I desire.'

'And the Bear danced with me, and the music softly accompanied us. And the people stood in a dark, congested mass, and, faintly shone upon us, watched our steps.

'I felt happy. My head began to whirl with happiness, and I got happier as I danced. At first I led the Bear. But as we went on dancing, he took the lead. The people kept us in view, and the encircling darkness united us, and the little star shone on our union, and as I danced I shut my eyes, and my head fell on my shoulder, and soon I saw nothing. And as soon as I shut my eyes, I no longer knew what was happening to me, I only felt delirious joy, and there was supreme happiness in the dance.

'And suddenly the wine and my intoxicating megalomania rushed to my head, and I opened my eyes, and saw the star shine on me, and I dancing alone, arm-in-arm with the Bear, and I cried out again into the silence:

' "Bear, Bear, I have bought up the whole of your kingdom! And here I have the title-deeds!'

'And the Bear did not answer. He was as grave as before. And he went on leading me.

'Then suddenly the little star in the head of the Bear went out, and I could not see the Bear either, only I felt him holding me and I felt his fur, and suddenly, instead of the ring, there was a big opening in the floor, a pit, an abyss, and I was standing on the very edge of it.

'And the Bear bent his mouth to my ear, and said to me:

' 'You mad fool, with your vast riches: So you have bought up my kingdom, and you boast about the title-deeds in your pocket. Down with you, and see if you can feed ten of my children, my earth-bears. Here is the pit, and here is the abyss, and here is the ladder up which you came. And now I'm going to give you a shove. Catch hold of the ladder, so that you don't fall down. I don't want you to get hurt or killed.'

'And the Bear shoved me, and I flew. I didn't manage to catch hold of the ladder, my hands had no grip in them. I went bouncing down, hitting the ladder, rung by rung. My body bumped against the rungs of the ladder. Like a wind I flew down, and as I flew I lost my senses.

'How I escaped breaking my neck on my way down I don't know. I only know that I hit bottom, and lay for a long time on the ground, feeling as if every bone in my body was broken.

'Some time seems to have passed; it was day now, and I had rested and recovered a little from my flying and falling, and I arose and stood up.

'And I started to walk. It was my land and my town, but people who met me did not seem to know me. They turned away from me, and some stared after me, and some lifted up their eyebrows, and some actually laughed in my face.

'I did not understand. My mind was still full of recent events—my riches, and the ball, the Bear, and my fall. And I was full of doubts. I wanted to convince myself, to remember, to make sure whether it was true or whether I had dreamt it all, and I lifted up my hand, with a gesture of helplessness, and also because there was perspiration on my brow. And my hand encountered something soft, and I unstuck it, and I looked at it, and I found there was a bit of mud in my hand, a vestige of my gold.

'And I still believed myself rich, as I used to be, so I went into a shop, full of assurance, and I asked for soap and washing accessories, various little things I had need of immediately, and they gave them to me. And when I had to pay, and pointed to my forehead, meaning to indicate that there was gold there, and that they should recognise me, know who I am and where I come from, and they would naturally trust me, they laughed at me, and the shopkeeper looked at me with an odd expression, and the assistants surrounded me like a madman. And one of them very gently took the things I had bought and which had already been wrapped up, out of my hands.

'I resisted. And I shouted at him and at all of them who were in the shop: 'What does this mean? Don't you know me? Can't you recognise me?' And they went on laughing at me, and said that they knew me well enough, and they showed me the door, and told me not to waste their time, because time was money.

'I was furious. And I shouted at them: 'Idiots! Fools!' And I put my hands in my pocket, and pulled out a pack of papers, the title-deeds to my properties, and I showed them. 'See what a lot of property I own!'

'The shopkeeper and his assistants seemed indeed to have no time, for other customers had come into the shop and were waiting to be served, and my shouting caused a lot of people to collect outside the shop. I was really holding up the business. And one of the young men went up to the door, and out into the street, and called a policeman, and the policeman came into the shop, and took me by the arm, and put me outside. But I didn't want to go. I struggled and screamed, and a big crowd collected. And the policeman got hold of me by the scruff of the neck. And he was strong and I was weak, so I had no choice but to allow him to lead me away.

'He took me to the police station and I spent the night in the cell, and in the morning, when the police saw that I was quiet, they thought that I wouldn't behave like that any more, that I wouldn't pester any more shopkeepers, so they let me go.

'But since I had no home, nowhere to go to, no place to spend the night, and nothing else that human beings require, the same thing happened over again. I was again in a shop, and made my purchases again, and again I wanted to pay in the same way, and again I was treated like a madman, my coins were laughed at, and my assurances did not suffice.

' I flew into a temper, and the end of it was in the second shop as in the first, that a policeman came to assist the shopkeeper and his assistants, and I was taken away again to the police station.

'It happened several times like that. At first people did not know me sufficiently. I used to go into a shop, and they treated me at first like any other customer. But afterwards when this had happened two or three times, and crowds had collected, not only the owner of the particular shop in which I happened to be, and his assistants, but all the assistants in all the shops in the whole of the street rushed up and kicked me out; as soon as I showed myself at the door of any shop, they came up to me at once and drove me away.

'I was known not only to the shops, but also to the small boys, who used to collect round me as soon as they saw me in the street. 'Look!' they cried. 'There he goes, the man from heaven, the multi-millionaire.' And 'Hi!' they shouted. 'What have you been buying now? Show us your title-deeds.'

'Sometimes it annoyed me, and sometimes it didn't annoy me, and I pretended to take no notice. But sometimes I had to take refuge in a courtyard or hide in a passage, for if I didn't, after the shouting a stone sometimes came hurtling at me, and sometimes a lot of stones. And once I got a nasty knock, and I couldn't stand it any longer, and I jumped on the stone-thrower, and I nearly throttled him. And a crowd collected, and when they saw how I was avenging myself, mercilessly, some tried to rescue him, but they got something to remember me by as well; a great many of them got badly hurt, and the blood simply poured down them.

'And when people saw this they said one to another, and then they all shouted it to everybody else:

' 'Why do we allow this to go on? He's mad. He's capable of murdering somebody. We must have him put away.'

'And there were some daring spirits among them who took the risk and came up to me, pinned down my arms. I struggled, and I foamed at the mouth, and they got some rope and trussed me up, and one policeman and a second came running up, and they brought an ambulance, put me on it, and took me away where people like that are taken.

'They took me to a room, and slung me inside, trussed up as I was. And the floor of the room was of stone, the windows had bars, and the door was of iron. I was left there alone for a time and no one came to me. Then at last a man came in, a tall, burly fellow with a bull neck, and a red face. He carried some kind of garment in his hand, like a shirt, and he came up to me and undid the rope, and at first he tried to induce me with kindness to put on the shirt, speaking kindly to me, asking me who I was and where I came from. And I, seeing his size and his strength, wanted to answer him nastily, and I said: 'I come from above, and I have got a lot of estates up there, and in one of them I keep a dog like you.'

' 'Like who?'

' 'Like you,' I said, looking him straight in the eyes. And the man was, as I have said, very strong, and he drove his hefty fist into my face, and punched me on the nose, and bunged up my eyes, and I was knocked out.

'And then he did something else to me, but I wasn't aware of anything at all just then. I don't know whether he went on punching me, whether he kicked me, or whether he just left me alone. It was all one to me. I don't remember a thing. I only recollect that after a time I woke up as if from a severe illness, and I felt no anger, I had no estates, and I had no regrets that I had lost my estates.

'I found myself in a quiet place, all alone, in a house with other quiet people. I was provided with everything, with a shirt, a long, linen, patient's overall, and with food and drink, and plenty of rest, too much rest. And the other inmates of the house never disturbed anyone else. Nobody got into anyone else's way. Everybody lived a sequestered life, and retained of his past life only vague memories.

'And some, who, like me, remembered the blows we got from the keeper in the beginning, had already forgiven him, and bore him no grudge and no enmity. But others, whose anger lingered, and the keeper hit them often and long, they no longer remembered the blows, but they carried the marks, some on their faces, but mostly on their bodies. And if ever they saw a reflection of themselves in a window, or a glass door, they stopped surprised, looked at the reflection as if they did not recognise themselves, and asked others who passed—Did they know whose reflection it was, so terribly mutilated? And some had no answer and kept quiet. And those who did know said it was the keeper, and the mutilated people, looking at the reflection of their injuries, listened quietly, and they, too, were not angry with the keeper, and accepted the answer quietly, as if it were only natural, and of no special interest.

'So we lived, and in each of our heads it was quiet as after a storm. And our movements, too, were quiet, and none of us had any relations with the rest, and we did not form any association, nor any groups, but each was taken up with himself, segregated, only with his quietened head and his extinguished thoughts.

'I do not remember how long I stayed there like that, alone, extinguished, with those extinguished people. I only remember that once I found two of them sitting on my bed, and we got into conversation, and we discovered a close and common language, and the language opened us, and we had an understanding ear for each other's words.

'One of them was silent and a hoarder and grudged to use, and kept under his pillow food and all sorts of things, the hat off his head, the socks off his feet, the shirt off his back. And another, a poet apparently, also stuck everything under the pillow, for he was constantly fasting, and always kept something at hand to eat when the fast was over.

'The hoarder was unshorn, and the hair of his beard and on his head was hard, stiff and bristly, and the whites of his eyes were bigger than the pupils. And the poet, too, was unshorn, but his hair was soft, and blonde, and his beard was curled, and his pupils took up the whole of his eyes, leaving very little space for the whites.

'And when we got talking, they asked me why I had nothing under my pillow, and I answered that it was taken away from me, and as for saving, it was out of the question, because I gave away the very food out of my mouth, and often I didn't have enough to eat myself, and I had to buy additional food, and pawn the few things that were still left to me.

'And when they asked me how that was, who took it away from me, and whom did I give it to, I told them where I came from, and all the things that had happened to me, and about my fortune, and they listened to me, and sympathised with me, and they were very much interested in my tale.

'It was evening then, and on the window facing my bed the night had already descended, and I told them how I had grown rich out of mud and dirt, and how my riches had again become dirt, and at the end of my riches I had danced all by myself with the Great Bear out of the stellar system, and at the beginning of my poverty I was beaten in the madhouse by the keeper, and as a result of those blows my head is now empty, and I go about inside my head, as through immense chambers, and I am all alone there, and I light a lot of candles, and the chambers become kingdoms, and the kingdoms enormous, and everywhere lighted candles, set at great distances, all over the earth, all in candlesticks, and I keep going all round them, lighting and putting them out, serving them. Mostly I keep them all burning at the same time, and it is lovely and warm, a bright holiday, and the air is still, and the candlesticks stand up, and the candles splutter and flicker and I am the master and servant of both, and my cheeks are red with the glow of the candles, and I feel well and at peace, and very happy sauntering among all my bright lights.

'Once I went far away, ever so far, among avenues of lighted candles and I came to a palace, tall and turreted, and white stairs leading up to it, so I walked up to the door, and it seemed as if it were specially there for me, and the door opened by itself, and when I entered I found myself again in a huge room, and in the room there was a table, and sitting round the table ten bears on ten chairs, quiet and restful, as if they were waiting for me, and when I came in they greeted me very nicely, and then they waited a bit. There was nothing on the table, and no one serving there, the tablecloth was clean and nothing on it. And I felt that they were waiting for me to serve them and to put something on the table.

'And here I had nothing, and was far from home, and nowhere to bring anything from. So I said to the bears:

' 'You see, bears. I am indeed master here, and all the kingdoms are mine, but apart from candles and candlesticks I have nothing, so how can I offer you anything?'

'But the bears took no notice. The bears were hungry, and they went on waiting. And they looked at the walls, as much as to say: 'You have got a palace, and kingdoms of light. Sell the candles, sell the candlesticks, and buy bread for us bears to eat.'

'I was embarrassed, and did not know what to do, and what to reply to the bears. But after I had stood there for some time, and the bears still waiting, I had to go up to my candles and candlesticks, and I had to put out some of them, and I felt ashamed looking at the rest. But I took the candlesticks whose lights I had snuffed, and shoved them under my coat, and stole out. And I felt all the other candles and candlesticks staring at my back. And I went into a market-place, and approached people, and asked them to buy, or if they would not buy, at least lend me some money on them.

'And that, I told my bedfellows, is what I am doing ever so long—pawning them. A good many I have sold, and many more I have left as pledges, as hostages in alien and unworthy hands. And my avenues of light keep diminishing in number, and my kingdoms are growing dark. And everybody knows me by now. Everybody knows me and my candlesticks, in every street and every market-place. And people don't want any more. The market is flooded with them.

' 'And now I have come back from my bears, and I have got another couple of candlesticks with me, and I can't find a purchaser. And the bears are waiting. The bears are probably ravenous by now. Perhaps, friends, you will buy this time,' I said, turning to the two sitting with unshorn hair and beards on my bed.

'They both jumped up at once, both anxious to buy. 'Produce the goods,' they said, and they would look at them, and they would certainly buy. So I stretched my hand out towards the window, and pointed to the night outside, and there was a brass bit of moon in the sky, and I said:

' 'That is one brass candlestick. And there is one of silver. Only the moon has got the silver one hidden away under his coat.'

'And they were both agreeable, and both of them bought from me. One bought the moon, and went away and brought me from under his pillow stale bread and rolls. And the other bought the sun, the silver one, which the moon had hidden under his coat. And he brought me something as well. And (you probably remember it, bears) I brought it to you, and you ate it up, and you were satisfied. And so was I, because you were satisfied. And you went away. And then you came back again.

'And there was another sitting held on my bed, and I told my bedfellows again that the bears are now frequent visitors, and my avenues are half extinguished, and ever so many candlesticks are missing, and that I walk among them, and feel very sad, because I see that I am losing everything, that soon I shall cease to be master and even servant, because there are no more candles, and the candlesticks are disappearing, and soon there will be nothing left to light and extinguish, and the cold keeps blowing between the empty spaces, and my cheeks are chill always, and even near the light I freeze.

'And when I go walking sometimes in the avenues, I no longer come upon a palace, but a little wooden hut, and when I climb the wooden stairs, they give under my feet, and when I go inside I find an ordinary room, a rickety table, and a dirty table-cloth, and the bears sit and wait, but they no longer treat me with respect, and they look at me demandingly, and when I point to the walls, and show them that I have nothing, and I tell them that my road along the avenues this time was in darkness, that I have sold or pawned everything I had, and there is nothing more, and I can't get anything more, they won't listen, and they point to my head and the hair on my head, and it isn't their affair, they say. I've still got a head, so I can think of something, and, if not, I should give them my head and the hair on my head. Bears don't mind. They are not fastidious. Food is food.

'So I felt perplexed. I stood there and didn't know what to do. The best candlesticks are already sold, and those that have remained are only little ones, toy candlesticks, for children to play with. No one will buy them if I took such to market. But here—I said to my bedfellows—here I have brought them along for you, and since you know me, and we live together, and we have concluded a bond of comradeship, perhaps you will buy again, as you did the first time. I hope you will not refuse.

'And, indeed, my bedfellows did not refuse this time, either. Only they asked me to show them my little candlesticks, which I said were only toys, playthings for children. And since it was now night, like the first time we had discussed this matter, sitting together on my bed, and our window was already dark, and in the sky there were only little buttons to be seen, I extended my hand towards those buttons, and indicated that they were mine.

'And my bedfellows were agreeable this time, too, and they bought, and they went to their own beds, and gave me their leavings, bread, hard crusts, and I stuffed my coat full of it, and ran off to you bears, right away with the whole lot, and fed you. And I thought that would finish it. You see that I have no more and I possess no more, and my comrades have done me this last kindness, and more such favours I cannot demand from them—they have purchased from me the last paltry little candlesticks I had left, that nobody else would have bought from me. 'Look,' I said to you bears, 'it was very humiliating and annoying to have to worry my comrades to induce them to buy things they did not need (something entirely contrary to my character), and the result is that I have lost all my hair, and now I am quite bald. And if you come here again, I shall really not be able to do anything more for you. Unless, unless, my ten fingers. Perhaps that.

'And you bears devoured the crusts, and as you ate, you half heard me, and half didn't hear me, and you finished eating, and went away. And for a time you left me alone, and for a time I thought you would not come to worry me any more, so that I need not worry other people.

'I was poor, terribly poor at that time, and my bright kingdoms were in total darkness, and when I walked through them I felt like in a cemetery. There was no vestige left of my beautiful big candlesticks. And of the little puny ones, too, there were only a few left. And the candles which I had stuck in them were tiny, and the flames were paltry, and they gave very little light, they only flickered and spluttered.

'I felt like a gravedigger, walking around there, and dead sorrow rested on my head, and my avenues were in darkness, and the roads were black, and I stumbled as I went, and I probably looked daft. I no longer believed in my road, and I did not think to find a palace there.

'And, indeed, the last time I wandered around there I only knocked into a little ramshackle hovel, with a roof on top of my head, and the entrance three steps down underground, and I walked down, and came to a dark and filthy door.

'And when I went inside I couldn't see anything for some time. The ceiling was black, the walls sloping, oozing and black, and flies on the walls, a host of them, thin and dried up, and the spiders in the corners also thin and dead, because there were no flies crawling around for them to catch. And as I got accustomed to the dim light, I saw a table in the middle of the room, narrow and rather longish, and I saw you bears sitting round it, huddled against each other, and your eyes, too, gleamed with hunger.

'And you all turned your eyes on me, and demanded from me food. And I had nothing at all, not even any hair on my head, and you looked at my body, as much as to say—'If there isn't anything else you wouldn't make a bad meal yourself.'

'And I complained to you, and showed you the room and the walls and the spiders in the corners. 'Look,' I said, 'even the spiders are dead, and what can I do, and what is it in my power to do? My kingdom is extinguished, and my world is dark, and I myself am in a madhouse, and I don't get enough food, and the keeper is always in a temper. So what more can I do, and what more have I save only my fingers?'

'And you bears chewed up my fingers. My ten fingers would have sufficed for the ten of you, only the ninth of you snapped off the tenth finger as well, so there was nothing left for the tenth, and he saw my breast, and my heart, and he won't listen to reason, but insists that he is hungry, and I must give him my heart.

'And more than one I have not got, and then you will have nothing either. So remember, bears. I begged you to give me this hearing, and that is why I have told you this tale, so that you should realise that this is really the end. Only one hope is left to me—my bedfellows, and though they, too, are poor, and they have already given me all they had, yet I shall not hold back, I shall go to them again, and try once more, and perhaps they will dig up something else, or get something from somebody else, but let me go now, and trust me, and I shall speak to them, and you wait here a bit, and perhaps I shall be able to get some more from them.

'And if you are afraid, and if you think I shan't get anything from my friends, leave me for a while, and perhaps I shall in time get out of the mad-house, and who can say, perhaps I shall be lucky, and again find the ladder and climb up into the kingdom of mud and there become rich again, and again buy a lot of things, and we shall have banquets and balls, and I won't let myself be hurled from the heights any more. Perhaps—'

And here, the Nistor concludes, the bears were persuaded by his plan, and the tenth bear, the hungry one, forgave him that his belly was empty, and let him go to the madhouse, and quietly and furtively he called together his comrades, and told them the whole story, and asked them to advise him about the bears, what he should do if they came again. This time he had bought them off with a tale. But he would not be able to do that again.

And truly his comrades realised the Nistor's plight, and more help they could not give him, and more to sell the Nistor did not have, and the comrades had no more to buy with. And they consulted long, examined every possibility, and it was agreed (there was no other way out) that the Nistor should write it all down for the doctor of the madhouse, and complain to him about his uninvited visitors and their too-frequent visits. And that was the decision, and that was how it was left, and the Nistor wrote it down. And since he had no more fingers, he described the whole story to the doctor in great smears of blood. And he is waiting for an answer from the doctor.

Yes, and he still has his heart. As long as he keeps well—if only he keeps well. Till the doctor's answer comes he will probably have to wait a long time.

MOISHE KULBAK

Muni The Bird-Seller

Muni's father, a man with a thick tangled beard, walked about the room one of those dreary winter nights, thinking. He was thinking about that overgrown son of his, who had no legs, poor thing, and propelled himself along from daybreak on his behind over the cold clay floor, and—help!—he was making a beggar out of him!

Night after night he worried about it, and swore: that boy was eating him out of house and home!

Only when the Spring began, and the frost melted, this Jew with the thick tangled beard came home one day with a secret joy. He had brought a cage with birds; he set it down on the table, and from his bosom slowly produced Odessa doves—slowly and carefully, as if they had grown there under his armpits. Then Muni suddenly smelt a delicious warmth rising from the birds' bodies, a pleasant cooing and chirping that moved him to tears. He crawled down from the couch, startled and confused. He nearly fainted. And his creased and wrinkled father growled through his prickly beard:

'There you are, curse that has afflicted me, breed these, and earn your living!'

And after that Muni's father died.

Muni bred and dealt in birds. His rotting house which sprouted moss and slithery fungi began to look like a hencoop. The doves spattered all the walls, the shelves and the tables with a thin lime. The place smelt of mould and bird droppings. And through the small muddy window panes always came a thin cold leaden light. A twittering rose from all kinds of cages, and behind the wires there was a hopping about and a beating of beaks on tin lids and other things.

Muni propelled himself about on his leather seat, crawled into the cages with the doves, ran his fingers over them, blew into their feathers, and quietly paired the different kinds of birds.

There were small cages in which sang quiet canaries, yellow as lemons. Through the room stalked doves, thickly-feathered and strong as cockerels. And in the semi-dark there were always stubby snub-nosed peasants sitting about, bird-catchers, come from somewhere in the wet White Russian forests; they talked, they slept sitting there in the corners on sacks of potatoes, and puffed at old-fashioned pipes the size of steam-machines.

Deals were concluded in silence. Plump red-breasted finches were exchanged for broken cages; olive-green finches for mouse-traps, for old worn-out hats that had lain for years in the lofts. The dull eyes of simple folk peered out from under shaggy brows like waters overhung by heavy bushes. And if a lazy, husky word was uttered now and then, it sounded more like a cough or a groan or a moan.

Muni propelled himself all over the place, shook a cold hundred-year old hand, and it meant that to-morrow at dawn this silent peasant would make his way to some birchwood forest, and hang around there for several weeks, till he gradually lured a squirrel into his cage, or even a pure-feathered canary. There were probably songs sung about Muni in the marshlands and in all the remote forests of White Russia. Things went well with him.

Hot, clotted summer days. Trees, carved out of the clear brightness, stood shadowless. Not a branch stirred. A magpie on a plank held open its black bill in astonishment at the heat. Muni sat on his doorstep waiting for somebody to come along. Yet no one appeared on the scorching road. But towards dusk the woman Neche came to visit him.

She had a stall in the market, but she understood the affairs of young men. The birds hopped about and sang in their cages. Muni sat at the table and prepared to listen. The woman Neche spoke round and about, illustrating what she said with fine parables, hinting that a man must these days have a housewife to attend to the home. She also dealt with birds, she said. She sold poultry—so she knew what hard work it was.

Muni sat red-faced, not like a man but like a grey broken block of stone. He didn't blink an eyelid, but every pulse in his body beat like a hammer. And the woman Neche spoke round and about, with fine parables to point the moral of what she said. The windows which were coming closer let in a cool reflection of the poor distant sunset, which had no warmth or colour in it. Then Neche took a good look at Muni, moved nearer to him, and whispered in his ear something that opened him up, and poured fire into him, everywhere where there was room for it.

Muni was silent, but that night he crawled slowly into the cage with the doves, and sat there till dawn with open eyes. He was thinking.

In the morning the canaries sang more beautifully, and Muni washed himself in a bowl. He combed his black forelock, twirled his moustache, and sat at the open door. It was midday, and the woman Neche had not come. The clod-like peasants were already in the house, dozing, looking like wire-mended old pots, holding the cages on their knees, and chattering to the chirpy birds like senile fools. Muni too was feeling more relaxed, and he even started whistling like a bird, and then he opened his mouth and craned his neck and tried his bass voice in a song; but he couldn't sing.

At dusk heavy shadows stretched across the walls. A little peasant, old as the world, was spending the night with Muni. He had brought him from his distant village a raven that he himself had fed for fifty years. He was now standing and talking to the birds, leaning on his two sticks. Muni propelled himself through the room, feeling bewildered; he rubbed his forehead, for there were important thoughts passing through it now.

When the old peasant was quiet for a minute, Muni beckoned to him to come nearer, and he shouted into his dirty hairy ear:

'Is it possible for someone like me to take a woman into the house, eh?'

'It's possible! Why shouldn't it be possible?'

And then the little peasant wanted to laugh, but nothing came of it. He looked like an old broken barn, where the wind blows, and bangs about the dried boards and the roof-slates. The birds were now drowsy, and the peasant who was only twice as old as his raven, still wandered about the room, babbling away to himself, till he finally went off to sleep on a sack of potatoes. There were about five hundred living souls sleeping in the dark room.

The woman Neche arrived in the morning.

Because the birds can't be moved they wouldn't whitewash the house. But Muni must put up a sign-board. The young woman Malke must know whom she was going to marry.

And what have you got in the trunk, Muni? Neche went through the house, looking everywhere. She opened the windows. Then she rolled up her sleeves, and set about cleaning up the place. She scrubbed the benches, filled her mouth with water, and swilled them down. She beat the pillows into shape. Then she took her basket, and went off. She was gone. Like the wind.

Muni crawled over to the brass-bound green trunk, and with a long key that hung round his bare neck, opened the heavy oak lid. All Muni's possessions were there—dazzlingly white shirts with peasant embroidery at the neck, colourful flowered ties of all varieties, all sorts of coats and waistcoats, and right on top a pair of well-pressed trousers, and even a pair of new patent-leather boots. There was nobody in the room when he gently tapped the soles as one taps an earthenware pot. And nobody looked round afterwards to see Muni when he came away in the evening from the bath-house, with the shirt under his arm, looking rosy and steaming like a baked apple. Nobody turned round to look at Muni.

The woman Neche helped Muni to knot the red fiery tie. It was a white evening. Where the sun was to set there was an empty waste. Hollow cloudy passages, very much dilapidated, like scaffolding round a building that has never been built. The two small windows hung on the house like a pair of spectacles that can't see anything. But there was a lamp burning, and the woman Neche was helping Muni to knot the red fiery tie. A cool cloth like snow gleamed on the table. The samovar bubbled. Very clear glasses with brown fragrant tea gave a grey festivity to the house.

There was a stillness too in the freshly-washed cages. Muni twirled his black moustache. The woman Neche was busy about the house, going in and out. Wasn't the lovely bride Malke coming yet? The lamp burned a long time, and Muni's tie glowed with seven fires. Then Neche slowly, with a deep bow, opened the door to the bride. She entered slowly, and stood silent—silent. And is this the place for admiring the wisdom of the woman Neche, who at once started talking, very much concerned about the high cost of living in the town —for let this not be held up against her as anything to be ashamed of—the bride Malke was at first quite confused. She didn't even put her umbrella away in the corner, as people do everywhere. Muni coughed, in a man's way, stared and pulled up the belt round his belly, as though he were really wearing trousers.

But after that Malke started talking. As the woman Neche said, pearls poured from her mouth. And he, Muni, sat leaning on his hand, listened and beamed. Then she said:

'You won't regret it, Muni. For if Malke wants to things get done as fast as lightning.'

So it was clear to him that Malke would make a good housewife. He sat dumb, with a sharp joy in his heart, and waited. After a while the woman Neche left, and only then Malke spoke of the fine way people lived, and she chided Muni because he didn't take a glass of tea in the morning when his stomach was empty. Then she rose from her place and indicated with her finger how she would rearrange all the things in the house. And of course, she was right!

Day was breaking now. Malke sat down close to Muni, and suddenly she pinched him, her bridegroom, just under the armpits, and she said:

'Mark my words, Muni, I'll make a man of you yet.'

In this way it became clear to him that Malke was really devoted to him. His heart started quivering with ecstasy. He snuggled against her, and quietly, almost swooning, he began to dream:

'Malke, you'll boil potatoes for me, and make potato pancakes . . . You can buy shmaltz herring at Hannah Dvoires . . .'

And they already kissed, as well. The old finch was the first who woke in the semi-darkness, shook his warm olive-green feathers and slowly whistled to the sun, which had just, barely, barely splashed the window-panes with rose-ate dew. Then the cages became alive with cackling, and with a dim, dark rumbling of the doves in all the shady corners. The canary stood out from the rest with his golden whistle.

The rotting house ran damp with the persistent autumn rains. The roof slid down towards the ground like a lump of mud, and a crumbling swelling chimney smoked and stank to high heaven. The crooked door on one hinge creaked terribly. And on top, just under the roof, hung the sign on a blue board—a red-footed dove with an open green beak and a yellow eye, and beneath it in black lettering:

'We sell doves and other birds.'

The wind pushed and shoved against the swelling roof, plucked at the wet rag of a window-pane, and pawed the walls with long watery hands.

Malke stood at the burning stove. The room was stuffy. The birds were preening themselves, busy with their beaks under their wings. Peasants from all round the neighbourhood, with their sheepskin coats soaked by the rain, sat silently, pulling at their moustaches and drying themselves. A thrush had died that day, and lay rigid on the table, its yellow legs stretched out, and with one open, dull empty eye. Muni was already busy at the cage. A little peasant, all bones, with a scraggy neck, stood talking to him, clucking like a hen, and looked in his breeches like an autumn scarecrow on a pole. Muni was laughing heartily at the story he told him, wiping the tears with his sleeve, and actually shook under his leather seat.

The raven on the chimney-piece turned his backside sleepily to the room and shook his tail. Malke clutched at her face, and burst out in a fury:

'Take your raven away from here, Muni! It's making a mess on my hair!'

Peasants full of respect for Muni's wife rose from their seats and waved their hands: 'Shoo! Shoo!' And the raven, proud and sedate, moved away behind the stove, as much as to say:

'Go to hell, the lot of you!'

Malke sulked. She wouldn't say a word. And when she went to the table afterwards she took the dead thrush and flung it on the floor. Muni was em-barrassed. He crawled over to the dead bird and put it into his bosom. He shouldn't have done it. For Malke went white, ran up to him, snatched it from him and threw the poor crumpled thing out of the door.

'You stink of carcasses, dear husband!'

That's what she said. Muni raised his stark eyebrows and looked at her fatuously, but he didn't speak. Sheepish peasant eyes went wandering through the room, and then slowly went dead behind their bushy brows.

It was autumn. Overclouded light in Muni's room. The crooked autumn rains soaked away the last traces of happiness. Somewhere in a dismal field a brassy tree resounded. Dirty mists hung over the roofs like tattered bits of rag.

It was autumn. Down below the poorest evenings in the world dragged their course, meagre and mournful, without stars. Muni still sat at the table, peeling potatoes for his pancakes. The lamp smoked. Malke would in those long nights have sat darning, but now she sat with folded arms, dozing. A wet wind was having a game with loose waters, dragging them into the room in fine streams and splashing the walls with them.

It was autumn. Muni sitting there one long endless night suddenly heard a whistle on the other side of the window. Somebody had put his fingers in his mouth, and was whistling almost straight into Muni's ear. Malke woke and snatched her shawl.

'Who's whistling, Malke?' Muni asked.

'Look at him!' said Malke. 'Just look at him! It's Ziske Hannah Dobke's.'

Muni was annoyed that he hadn't known it was Ziske Hannah Dobke's by his whistle. And he asked:

'Who is Ziske Hannah Dobke's, Malke?'

'Look at him! Ziske of the gang!'

And out she went through the door. Muni scratched his head and swore. Then in the dark he beat his breast with his fists. It was quiet round the house —it meant Malke had gone away with Ziske the Thief.

Somewhere the rain dripped drop by drop into a bucket. Muni crawled into bed that night, drew the cover over himself, and lay with open eyes till daybreak. Just before dawn the door creaked. Malke came in, quickly flung off her clothes, crept quietly into bed and slept immediately.

Muni lay against the wall, not breathing, afraid to move a limb. It hurt him so much. But in the morning Malke was the busy housewife. The stove was lit, steaming potatoes on the table, the birds hopping about one over the other, sipping clear water, and Malke was singing lovely songs.

Then Muni thought cunningly—'Malke does get things done! But she still oughtn't to run around with other men, eh?'

Peasants with scraggy beards and sheepskin coats brought cold with them from the pine forests. The trade in the house was now in belated birds. Mad blue-birds pushed their heads through the wires of their cages, red-breast finches whose fat bellies looked like juicy strawberries smelt of damp swamps. The wind came blustering into the house, drunk with the winy aroma of grey apples in the orchards. Out of the mists stepped a strong blood-red autumn that set the whole neighbourhood alight with wine-odoriforous fires, and went roaring far and wide with its damp winds over each thin mirroring stretch of water.

What is Muni to do with himself this drunken autumn when his wife Malke leaves him and goes out almost every evening? He lies all through those re-sounding nights like a dog in his kennel, listening to the distant footsteps round his house, holding his breath under the bed-cover, waiting. And only in the frosty, silvery dawns he crawls out to the yard, to the well, pours cold water over himself, and slowly sobers up from his night of misery. That's the way Muni lived.

Then once Malke said to him:

'I'll tell you the truth, Muni. Ziske is too shy to come in.'

Muni dropped his eyes, thought, and answered:

'What is there to be shy about? I'm not a bear . . .'

Soon after she brought him home, this shy Ziske Hannah Dobke's. He swung his way in, wearing a pair of shiny highboots, a short fellow with a red neck. And standing there, swaying on his feet, he thrust a cold heavy butcher's hand into Muni's.

'How are you, Muni?'

Muni held this heavy hand which was like a whole porged rump, and slowly stammered:

'Not bad . . . One gets along . . .'

'And your birds?'

'Thank you for asking.'

Then Ziske sat down, stretched his legs comfortably, slapped himself on his strong neck, and from behind pushed his cap over his eyes, as though the sun was dazzling him. And soon he was talking only to Malke.

Muni went quietly away to his doves, for it had dawned on him that he was redundant here, just as the belated song of a bird in one of the side cages was redundant in this lilac autumn. The two little windows that always sifted through only a thin leaden light now admitted the meagre shine of the sunset over the fields. Or it was the afterglow of the red-veined autumn himself, who splashed and clanged about with his copper feet over all the roads.

That night Malke bedded Muni on the couch under the window. He felt ashamed when he went to sleep alone, like a bachelor. Afterwards he lay awake in the dark nights and listened intently. What did Malke mean to do? At that time nobody came at night.

Malke was sleeping restlessly, and once she cried out wildly in her sleep, so that Muni had to crawl down from his couch to wake her.

So night followed night, accursed and void, as though the pulse of the world had stopped. Muni started fretting. He went to bed late, when Ziske should have already left. But Ziske came when one didn't expect him. One midnight he burst in like a wild brute, made a hullabaloo, and with Malke on his knee they drank, laughed and even kissed. Muni kept quiet. Suddenly Ziske blew out the lamp and, laughing, the two of them tumbled into bed together. Muni was so frightened that he could hardly sit up on his couch, and speaking into the dark he asked in a choking, sobbing voice: 'What are you doing there, eh?'

The laughter stopped at once. Then after a while Ziske's sharp voice cut the silence like a blank slaughtering knife being drawn from the top of a boot:

'Keep quiet, brother! I shan't skim your cream off!'

And for a long time after a passionate whispering carried through the darkness, hissing like a serpent in the night that was lying coiled over the room, silent and glowing like a red-hot iron.

Muni pressed himself against the wall, stopped his ears, and lay for hours cold and stiff, like hardened clay. He prayed for the day. And only at day-break he crawled down from his couch.

A dirty light dripped from the windows and merged with the thin shadows round the walls. The raven on the stove flapped its hard wings and moved silently behind the chimney. The empty bottle lay on the floor. And in the bed, against the wall, lay Ziske, his arm under his head, snoring and whistling, and Malke was just waking; she sat up, rubbed her eyes, and then she saw Muni far in the corner. She yawned, and said:

'Please get me a drink of water.'

Muni brought the water. Malke drank thirstily, gave back the tin can, and turned over on the other side.

The windows were greying, like cold steel. There was a poor little dawn standing in the room. Muni propelled himself over to the big wire cage, slowly opened the door, and crawled inside to the warmth of the doves. The startled birds flapped their wings, rose, but soon dropped back on the boards and the wires, huddled together in pairs round him, and went to sleep again.

Muni sat down with his hands on the ground and stiffened like that, not like a man, but like a broken block of grey stone.

ISAAC BASHEVIS SINGER

The Bird

My apartment overlooks on one side Central Park. I can see from my window Fifth Avenue, the City Reservoir (a silent mirror by day, copper at sunset) and the skyscrapers down to the Empire State Building. On summer nights I see the lights of the Yankee Stadium. And on the other side, of Idlewild Airport. Planes landing and taking off all the time.

My study and bedroom look out on a tiny yard, hardly big enough to put up a Sukkah there. At night you can see right into the kitchens and bedrooms of the people living opposite—all eighteen storeys. There are Irish, Italians, Jews, Cubans, Porto Ricans, Negroes, even Chinese, Japanese, and Filipinos living there. Each kitchen has the same ice-box, and almost the same pattern linoleum on the floor. The housewives with curlers in their hair, Amazonian matriarchs, are scrubbing and mopping the floors, cooking in aluminium pots, ironing clothes with electric irons, drying their hair with electric driers. In between they glance at the serial in the magazine. I hear the radio blaring, and I catch a glimpse of the television screen in the kitchen. The menfolk come in, give their women a quick kiss, and snatch a hasty bite. I see it all, the whole eighteen storeys, like a huge panorama.

I find it particularly interesting when it is raining. The rain floods the yard, and it runs like a gutter. The black asphalt looks like a deep well, mirroring the lights of the city, and the lightning flashes in the sky.

If you shout down, the echo comes back as from a chasm. When it snows the snow lies there perfectly white for a long time. Nobody treads in the snow, because nobody has any business in that small space in our civilisation, which keeps climbing upward. You don't see even cats and dogs out there. These yards seem built specially for suicides.

I stand by the window, holding on so as not to lose my balance, my head tilted to the sky, which hangs like a dull metal lid glowing red with the city fires and lights, without moon or stars.

Though I have lived here in New York almost as long as I had lived previously in Warsaw, I still feel a stranger here. I am here by virtue of a visa that a kind-hearted Consul stamped into my foreign passport. My ears are full of a roar that never ceases, the underground trains, the overhead trains, the automobiles, the whirr of machinery, ambulances and fire engines rushing past, police sirens, shouting and laughing, the sound and bustle of many millions who are never silent for a moment. Sometimes I think I hear the voices of Chedar boys and Yeshiva students, and the songs of young workmen and young working girls. You can hear in this noise anything you wish.

My mind is saturated with memories of a town in ruins, of a people burned to ashes, of a language half-forgotten.

There is a woman busy in the next room with whom I speak in a foreign tongue. Somewhere between the bridges, the rivers, the towering buildings, behind the countless lighted windows rising to the clouds like flaming hiero-glyphics, people move about with whom I have in one way or another linked my mind-nerves, friends, relatives, dear ones, my readers—invisible threads stretch between them and me. We have our calculations. We converse through telepathy. We quarrel and are reconciled without a word. Who knows? Perhaps the spirits of the dead wander here in this dense atmosphere? I have a good share already in that sphere to which we go and break off all communication. I often have a feeling that the souls watch me, silently ap-praising me, scoffing at my lies and my temptations. The astral body of the woman with the dark eyes rests often at twilight on a chair or on the couch. She is silent with the silence of those whose lips are sealed.

The telephone rings in the next room; when I return I see something strange. A little bird on the window sill; not a sparrow nor a dove, but a brightly coloured bird, a parakeet.

One of the neighbours must have inadvertently left the cage open and the window open, and the bird flew out. A parakeet wouldn't know the way back. Nor could it survive long out of doors in the New York climate. Even if it could, other birds would kill it. But the bird doesn't know it is doomed. It hops about with an air of 'Lost my way! Could have happened to anyone.'

I have so far protected no one from death; but I am determined not to let this small creature perish. One false move and the bird will fly out into the cold night. A long-forgotten cunning of a hunter and trapper awakens in me. I stretch out my hand from behind, to bar its way, and hold the bird by its tail. It beats its wings, trying to fly, but now I have managed to close the window. The way out is blocked. Against your will, little bird, you will live! Your time has not yet come.

I let it go; and it flies zig-zag, to and fro, from wall to wall, corner to corner. It has banged into the furniture, against vases and other things. It has lost a few feathers. It is bewildered and frightened in this new cage into which it has blundered so unexpectedly. Then it stops still, perched on the frame of a picture. It is trembling all over with fear and exertion. A shuddering runs through its feathers. It flaps its wings in an effort to dislodge this evil visitation. Its tiny eyes, like black onyx beads set in blue, say: 'See what has come upon me! Who knows what I have been trapped into!'

94

I telephoned the superintendent of the block of apartments. I also hung a sign in the lift that I had found a parakeet; would the owner please claim it. There was no immediate response. It occurred to me that the parakeet might have come from another apartment block. Perhaps even from Fifth Avenue, from the other side of Central Park. Meanwhile I would have to feed it and look after it. And I didn't know a thing about birds.

I went into the kitchen and brought out a biscuit, and offered it to the bird. He looked at me with his bright beady eyes, but didn't budge. He seemed to say: 'I know your tricks. You think that by offering me food you can lure me down and catch me.' I could have chased him down with a stick, but I didn't like using force.

It was getting late, and I wanted to go to bed. I left the bird perched on the picture frame. I put a saucer of water on the table for it, and a few grains of barley. The room was warm, but I knew the central heating was turned off during the night and the radiator went cold. I told myself that even in the tropical jungles where parakeets came from there were sometimes cold nights; and there were other dangers—serpents that swallowed birds whole. I had done what I could. The rest must be left to God, who had created birds and flies and rats and all else that His Will had made, for His praise for all generations!

I went to bed, pulled the blanket over me, and switched off the light. Then I began to think about what had happened, and what had seemed in the light to be simple and natural took on in the dark a touch of the mystic. Why had the parakeet found his way just to my apartment? I remembered that a bird flying into your room through the window is regarded among the folk as a lucky sign. May be!

Perhaps the parakeet was the reincarnation of a near one. Perhaps the soul of the woman with the dark eyes sits in it, and has paid me a visit. Perhaps the bird has brought me a greeting from a being that can't get in touch otherwise with those who wander about on earth. The last dregs of sober commonsense that I possess when I am up and about were running out. I was back to the belief in demons and spirits, to say nothing of faith in God and God's Providence. What do we know about God's creatures? They may possess forces which man does not suspect.

I couldn't lie in bed any longer. I put on my dressing gown and slippers and went to have a look at the bird. I stood still for a moment in the dark, ready to hear the parakeet speak. Then I switched on the light. The bird was where I had left it, still perched on the picture frame. It hadn't touched the food or drink. It looked petrified, neither awake nor asleep, sunk in a kind of bird Nirvana. What a tiny creature it was! All feathers down! Would weigh half an ounce in all! Yet it had everything—heart, lungs, brain, stomach, bowels, a behind. Nature had made a *multum in parvo*. How had this bird got here to me? Millions of generations of parakeets had to busy themselves for this parakeet to perch there now on the picture frame. Countless mothers laid eggs, hatched them, attracted males, sang to them.

One saw plainly that this bird thought. What were its thoughts? One thing was certain—underlying everything there was submissiveness, the sacred submissiveness that leaves man as soon as he comes from the womb and returns only when he breathes his last.

I couldn't move from the spot. Suddenly the bird began to preen itself. Its beak was busy among its feathers, wings, tail, underbody, legs. If it had a bird-bath it would surely dip in. It seemed to say: 'Enough of this thinking! I must get to work now to rid myself of the dirt and the vermin attached to little birds.'

I stood watching for a long time, but the bird did not for one moment interrupt the process of cleaning itself. I don't know why, but it reminded me of the night of Yom Kippur, of the Priests bathing in the waters of purification. To a bird every day is Yom Kippur. A bird is a High Priest, engaged in the sacred service every day. When the morning star rises. When the face of the east lights up.

I was wakened by a song. I got out of bed, half asleep, weighed down by the dreams that crowd on me in the night. I went into the other room, and saw in the east a great sun, purple-red just come up bathed from the sea, the ancient sun that our Father Abraham had once thought was God. It lighted up the Park like a heavenly lamp, shone on the windows of the skyscrapers, reddened the freshly-fallen snow.

Against the glow I saw my bird with its yellow-green body, yellow-grey tail feathers, and two blue spots at the beak. That wasn't all. The Creator had put more colours and shades into robing this little bird than I have words for and my pen can describe. The yellow on the neck is a different yellow than that on the tail feathers. He has every shade of yellow—banana, saffron, lemon. He wears a coat of many colours, but wears it discreetly, not to excite the envy of his brothers. He still stood on the frame of the picture, but now he was singing a hymn of praise to the new day.

As I lack words to describe his colouring, so I lack words to describe his singing. He was doing everything at once—trilled, whistled, chirped, quavered, twittered, warbled, produced tones and semi-tones that only the ear knows what they mean. Now and again he started jabbering in a birdish slang that only King Solomon and perhaps Ashmedai too could understand. He sang as is fit for a singer by God's grace, without fee, without an audience, only for himself, purely out of the desire to thank God for the fresh beginning.

I pointed my finger to the water and the food on the table, to attract his attention. I said that singing on an empty stomach wasn't good even for a poet. I told him that God has hosts of angels singing in the celestial choir, praising Him each day, and one little bird less in the song wouldn't be noticed in Heaven. But no scoffing and no heretical ideas of mine stopped his singing, which burst from a heart the size of a pea, out of a throat thin as a thread. This was true ecstasy. It was flaming sacred devotion. This is how the Baal Shem prayed at sunrise in the forests of Podolia. I am no Cabbalist and I don't know what goes on in the heavenly spheres, but I would have sworn that angels and seraphs and cherubim were listening to this song and weaving from it crowns for the Shechina. Messiah himself heard this singing prayer where he sat waiting for the Redemption.

There was a ring at my door. A faint, timid ring, as though whoever it was didn't trust themselves to touch the bell, were hesitant, unwilling to intrude. It was so faint that I wondered if I had really heard it.

I went to open the door. The room was bright with sunlight. But the corridor was still dark. Here it was still night. Not yet to-day, but yesterday. My weariness of last night returned. My eye-lids grew heavy. I stumbled against a chair. Who could it be so early?

I opened cautiously. There was a woman there, a slight little woman of about thirty, apparently still wrapped in sleep as I was, unkempt, and probably not yet dressed under her coat. I could hardly make out the face. There were so many dark shadows about. She spoke English, but with an accent, and the uncertainty of a recent arrival. She was very apologetic:

'I am sorry to disturb you so early in the morning. But I've got to go to work soon, and I wouldn't be back till late this evening. I saw the notice about the bird, when I came home last night. I didn't connect it with my bird. I don't keep my bird in a cage. I couldn't put any living thing in a prison. When I got in I found he had managed to fly out through the slightly open window, open just enough to air the room. I hadn't imagined he could have squeezed through that small opening. I didn't sleep all night. I don't know how to apologise for disturbing you now. On the other hand, why should I leave you with the burden of looking after my bird?'

'You didn't disturb me,' I assured her. 'I was up before you rang. I was listening to your bird singing.'

'Singing?'

'Come in, and listen to him.'

'I have brought the cage, to take him away in.' She indicated a tall wicker cage that she had set down by the door.

97

'You said you don't keep your bird in a cage.'

'I don't! But I give him his food in the cage. Otherwise he would make a terrible mess all over the place.'

'Then come in, and take your bird.'

'I hope I am not disturbing your family.'

'No! My wife sleeps so that she can't be wakened. It would take much more than your coming here to waken her.'

'Thank you! You are very kind. The bird is the only living thing I have in the world.'

She followed me in with the cage, which was almost as big as she was herself. A spacious dwelling for her pet. I wanted to relieve her of the load, but she wouldn't let me. In the bright daylight of the room I saw her face clearly— younger than I had thought, dark eyes, pointed chin, sunken cheeks. I had been right about her having flung on her coat over her nightdress. Her bare feet were in slippers.

She noticed my gaze and apologised for her attire. She stood regarding the bird happily. But he had stopped singing. He stared at her, in apparent recognition. He opened his beak, but made no sound.

She saw the grains of barley and the water on the table. 'Thank you,' she said, 'for feeding him. I was afraid he would go hungry.'

'You're not long in America?' I asked.

'Eight years.'

'Where were you before?'

'In Germany. In the camps.'

'You're Jewish?'

'Yes.'

'You speak Yiddish?'

'It is my mother tongue.'

'Where do you come from?'

'Kovno.'

'Where were you in the Hitler years'

'In the Ghetto. In a bunker. Then I was working for the Germans.'

'Doing what?'

'Digging trenches, sawing timber, loading lorries.'

'Your family?'

'All killed.'

'What did you do before the war?'

'I was still at school. A Yiddish Secondary School.'

'I am a Yiddish author,' I told her, wondering at my own words, for I am not in the habit of parading myself in this way.

'What is your name?'

I told her.

'I know your work. I have read your stories. How strange!'

I looked at the tear-off calendar on my table. The date was December 16—the anniversary of the day the woman with the dark eyes died.

The Squire's Moustaches

This happened in a little Jewish town in Poland. It was recorded in the Jewish Community Register. But the Register was lost. Burned in a fire. I am the last person who remembers it. So I am telling you the story. Listen!

There was a Jew named Mottel Parnass living in this town. He was a barber by trade. He earned his bread by cutting the hair of Gentiles and shaving their chins.

Now there was a big fair in this town, and peasants came from all the surrounding villages, and some of them went to Jonah Singer's tavern, and some went to Mottel Parnass, to have their hair cut or to have a shave. The few copper coins that Mottel earned on such a fair day came most welcome. They went to buy what was needed to fill the mouths of his wife and children. But there were not many fair days in the year. And Mottel Parnass didn't make much of a living.

It is the general rule that where there is no bread there is no peace in the house. And that was true with Mottel Parnass. There was no peace in his house. His wife, Red Faiga, made his life a misery; she often hit him, and Mottel, though he was more than a head taller, swallowed it all quietly, because he was by nature a quiet man, with big frightened eyes, who only wanted to be left in peace.

Mottel went through hell, but did not complain. As though he accepted the onus of guilt, that it was all his fault that there was no bread in the house, as though he didn't want to work to earn a living.

His only revenge was when his wife was in childbirth. Then her cries of pain and anguish were like soothing balsam to him, sweeter than the singing at the Rebbe's table. But Mottel had never made the journey to the Rebbe to ask him for the blessing of children. He hadn't the money for the fare, or the money to leave a tribute to the Rebbe when he came to plead with him for his blessing. So God spared him the trouble so far as children were concerned. Red Faiga was continually in childbirth, so that Mottel often had the satisfaction of revenge for the blows that he got from her.

The years went by. The years ran. The years flew. Mottel Parnass and his wife both grew older, and his family increased, a new addition every year, another mouth to feed, more money needed. Then this happened.

The town and the whole district was ruled by a squire, a cruel man, a tyrant, with long Polish moustaches. He used to whip his peasants mercilessly for the slightest thing. As for Jews—he couldn't stand the sight of them!

This squire was a widower. The rumour was that he had got rid of his wife by poisoning her. She had been a very pious, devout woman. And he had hated the constant smell of incense in the house, the ikons she had put in every corner, and her frequent fast days, which made her all skin and bones.

'I want a wife in my bed,' he used to grumble to his friends, 'not a never-ending prayer.'

He could do nothing with her. She went on burning candles and keeping fast days and growing skinnier all the time—like a shadow with a cross between her breasts.

The squire found a way of satisfying his needs elsewhere. He was going through the woods near his great mansion one day when he came to a stream, and by the stream sat a beautiful young woman, Magda Walczynska, who owned the adjoining estate. She had also been walking through the forest. She was the widow of the squire who owned that estate. She was beautiful and she was tempting as his wife Maria had been before she had become a penitent. When the squire saw Magda he called himself an old fool, for not having sought her out sooner.

The first meeting was followed by a second and a third—all in secret, always by the stream in the forest, so that his wife, the 'prayer', should not get to know.

The 'prayer' did not get to know. She lived like a nun, showing no interest in anything that went on round her. She only fasted and prayed and crossed herself before the ikons and burned candles.

And in the forest birds sang, and the trees rustled. And the wind whispered mischievously—'The squire is coming!'

Indeed, the squire was coming. But now he came without his hounds and without his gun. He came to meet the beautiful Magda, who generally kept him waiting a very long time, before she appeared at last among the trees, laughing merrily.

There, at their trysting place, in the forest, beside the stream, they hatched their plan to send the 'prayer' to heaven, where she might go on praying for the beautiful young Magda and her elderly squire with the big Polish moustaches.

That was the talk of the peasants among themselves; but only in whispers, so that no word of it should come to the ears of the squire, for they went in fear and trembling of him.

But this is sure—one night, the squire's wife, the 'prayer', prayed before each of her ikons, and went to bed, and never rose again.

How did she die? Some said he poisoned her; others that she was strangled.

She certainly had been a barrier to his marriage with Magda.

It was a grand funeral. Three priests said masses for her soul. Peasant women walked behind the coffin, bearing holy images and holy pictures. The squire walked immediately after the coffin, his head bowed, looking very sad and mournful.

But when they came home he ordered all the windows to be opened, to drive out the smell of the incense from the rooms. And three weeks later he arranged a banquet for Magda, at which he was going to announce their engagement to their assembled friends and neighbours.

The banquet was fixed for the Sunday evening. He kept his servants busy at it all that Sunday, cooking and preparing the feast.

That same Sunday, about ten in the morning, the squire ordered Mottel Parnass, the barber, to be brought to him. Mottel had a great reputation in the town for his barbering skill. He had 'golden fingers', people said, though everybody knew that his 'golden fingers' didn't earn him a living.

Why the squire decided that particular Sunday morning not to be shaved by his valet, but to send for Mottel to shave him, is a mystery. Perhaps because he was feeling exceptionally well-disposed to everybody that Sunday, and he wanted the Jewish barber to earn a few coppers. For to-day his fair charmer of the forest would become officially his betrothed. Or it may have been just a whim of his, with no real reason at all.

However it may have been, when the squire's messenger strode into Mottel's room he found Mottel's wife, Red Faiga, busy pouring out a flood of curses at his head. Mottel always got a double portion on Sundays. Faiga would never profane the Sabbath by swearing and cursing. She kept the Sabbath holy; on that day she was pious and God-fearing, and sat over her Tze'enu Urenu, like every other Jewish woman in the town. But she made up for it on Sundays, when she gave him a double portion of abuse, specially barbed and pointed.

So the squire's messenger came to Mottel now as a blessed deliverer. Mottel took the opportunity to get out of the house as quickly as possible, with the tools of his trade, walking along at the side of the squire's messenger, on his way to the great mansion.

But as he came nearer to the great mansion Mottel felt his heart beginning to sink in him. For he knew the squire's reputation for cruelty. He felt like returning to face the inferno of Faiga's tongue rather than risk meeting the angry squire.

But the squire was not angry that Sunday. He was in the most affable mood, well-disposed to everybody. He had been going from room to room; he had been listening to the canaries singing in their cages. He had clapped his old chief gardener Andrei on the back; he had asked the groom Anton when he was going to marry his Maria. He felt very happy, and he stroked his long Polish moustaches.

Mottel's heart beat like a demented clock. The squire had no frown on his face. Mottel Parnass prayed to God that his work should succeed, that the squire should remain in a good mood, that everything should go smoothly, so that he could return safely to his wife and children.

'Good morning, Mottel,' the squire greeted him. But to Mottel the big Polish moustaches still looked aggressive and angry as always. And his hands trembled with fear.

All the same, God had heard his prayer, and his work went smoothly and well. Even the squire was satisfied with the way Mottel had done his work. He looked at himself in the mirror, and he said: 'Well done, Mottel! Thank you!'

The load lifted from Mottel's heart. The unbelievable had happened! The squire was pleased with his work. Mottel indeed had 'golden fingers'.

Yet it was not all over. Mottel was doomed to great misfortune. As he stood at the mirror, admiring himself, the squire suddenly said: 'I think, Mottel, that my left moustache is slightly longer than the right. You must snip off a bit from the left, to make them both equal.'

Mottel, who had already been packing up his tools, felt a cold shiver go right through him. He was afraid! He was sure that both moustaches were absolutely equal, but he dared not contradict the squire. He was so scared that he forgot to pray to God before he started work again on the squire's moustache. Suddenly he seemed to see his wife, Red Faiga, rise in front of him, and cry: 'Don't, Mottel!'

It unnerved Mottel. His hand slipped, ever so slightly. But a bit of the squire's moustache was snipped off, more than Mottel had intended, and it lay there on the floor. Beads of anxiety and fear covered Mottel's face.

The squire jumped up from his chair in a towering rage, his eyes flashing fire. His right moustache was as it should be, but his left, God help us! . . .

And this had happened to him this day of all days, when all his friends and neighbouring squires were coming to his feast, to the announcement of his betrothal.

'Jan!' 'Stefan!' he called. When the two servants entered: 'Take this Jew, and give him 150 lashes. No mercy!'

Jan and Stefan took the luckless Mottel, one by the head, the other by the feet, and carried him into the big courtyard, where they tied him up and started counting the lashes. Mottel shrieked and howled. By the time they got to thirty he had passed out, unconscious.

The squire standing at the window watching, ordered: 'Pour cold water over him! Then carry on!'

Mottel was brought home more dead than alive. He was in a high fever, in delirium. He thought he was in heaven, meeting his grandfathers, talking to them about his chances of being admitted to Paradise.

They took Mottel to the Jewish Hospital. A few hours later he died there, about ten o'clock at night. He had never been a strong man. He could never have survived 150 lashes.

When Red Faiga was told that Mottel was dead, she looked at her orphan children left fatherless, without a breadwinner. Then a curse broke from her heart: 'Over a piece of moustache he killed a husband, a father of children! May his moustaches grow and never stop growing, Father in Heaven!'

There are curses that fall on the wind; there are curses that fall in the water. And there are curses that are fulfilled. Faiga's curse was fulfilled.

The squire sat at the head of his table at the banquet. Magda sat at his side. The squires from all the surrounding estates were round the table. The candelabra were glorious with light. The wine sparkled in the glasses. There was a fragrance of roses and eau-de-cologne. Nothing was left of the old smell of incense and burning candles. The squire had himself cut off a bit of his right moustache to make it look equal with the left. It wasn't as workmanlike as Mottel would have done it, but it would do. The guests were already arriving for the feast, and he couldn't put them off.

The guests were in fact a little surprised at the untidy look of the squire's moustaches, and because they were much shorter than usual. But they didn't say anything. They asked no questions, when and why. But they all thought that it was very odd. It didn't stop them however from eating and drinking their fill.

But the squire knew that something was wrong. He knew that everybody felt it. He couldn't get it out of his mind. So when the whole company was well under the influence of the drink, he stood up and told them the whole sad story of the misfortune which had happened to his moustaches, how the Jew had ruined them, and how he had punished him.

'It's a pity, friends,' he said, 'but by the time I marry my moustaches will have grown back to normal.'

He bent down and kissed Magda. When he raised his face again she screamed, and the other guests gasped.

The squire couldn't understand it. 'What has happened?' But no one wanted to tell him. Everybody pointed at his face. The squire ran to the mirror—his moustaches had grown; they were growing longer every minute!

He rushed out of the banqueting room. When he came back his moustaches were again short, as at the beginning of the banquet. His valet had trimmed them.

'We must have imagined it!' said Count Edward Potocki, laughing the whole thing off.

'What happened to your moustaches, dear?' Magda asked him.

'Nothing! Nothing at all!'

'It was just our imagination,' said Count Edward Potocki.

But the next minute everybody sat up again and gasped. His moustaches had in those few moments grown longer and were growing, longer and longer.

'The devil has a hand in this!' cried Count Edward Potocki, and fled from the room.

The squire rushed out of the room again, and returned with his moustaches cut back to the old length. But the guests had not waited. They had fled.

Magda had fainted. He tried to revive her, whispering words of endearment to her:

'Evil spirits are making a mockery of me,' he said. 'Help me to overcome them! Let us pray together to Pan Jesus.'

But when Magda opened her eyes, she screamed: 'Devil! You are the Devil himself!' And she ran out.

The squire was left alone in his great mansion; he stood in front of the mirror, and watched his moustaches growing longer every minute.

After that night the squire no longer showed himself outside the house. He no longer went hunting. He avoided his friends, the squires of the surrounding estates. He kept thinking of Magda, his lost love, whom he had met in the forest and had planned to marry. And he wept and sighed. His valet was always at his side with his scissors, cutting short his moustaches that kept growing longer and longer all the time.

At night, when everybody slept, the squire took a lantern and went out to the grave of his wife, the 'prayer', to plead with her to forgive him. For he thought that she was punishing him for what he had done to her. But afterwards, when he heard that Mottel the barber had died after the lashes, he began to suspect that there was a connection between Mottel's death and the curse that lay upon him.

He stood at night by Mottel's grave, beat his fists against his breast, and begged the poor Jewish barber to forgive him. The squire even made the journey to the Rebbe, gave him a handsome sum as a gift, and asked him for a blessing. But the Rebbe's blessing didn't help. Faiga's curse was more powerful.

One morning, when the valet entered the squire's bedroom with his scissors, to cut short his moustaches, which had grown terribly long during the night, the squire chased him out. He didn't need him any more, he said.

For the first time since his wife, the 'prayer', had died, the squire lighted the lamps at the ikons. And at each ikon he prayed, and did penance. He stayed alone in the house all that day, with the holy images and the holy pictures.

At dusk, when the things in the room began to vanish, and only the big mirror was still bright in its golden frame, he stood in front of it and looked at his face, with the immensely long moustaches, which now reached to his knees.

'Now they're long enough,' he said, with a bitter laugh.

At midnight the squire hung himself by his long moustaches. There was heavy rain outside and a high wind.

MENDEL MANN

Black Oak

In Nasielsk the Black Oak suddenly decided not to stay the night there, and ordered the horse to be harnessed to the cart and to drive on to Bodsanova, because there was going to be the annual fair there. The circus folk didn't like it. What's the idea? A day's work done, and no time even for a proper rest, hardly got a glass or two of brandy down, and off we go! Where to? Bodsanova, which isn't even a town, only a big village, with a lot of goats, which goes to show that there are only a few poor Jews living there. What's the idea of driving the horse about twenty miles, passing towns on the way where they could have raked in the money? Just after harvesting time. When the peasants have got plenty of money, and are thirsting for brandy and entertainment. The best time for the circus folk.

Antek, who played the drum and cymbals, kept rubbing his forehead with all his fingers, spat and made an angry rumbling noise under his breath.

Mariusia, the acrobat, put on a pleasant smile and played with her string of beads. She thought that being nice to him would win the Black Oak from his decision. When she realised from the way his nostrils twitched that he wasn't going to budge, she turned away angrily, and her breasts heaved.

Juzef Granda, the clown, sat moodily over an empty beer tankard, and swore.

Voitek Biez, the fire-eater, was blazing with fury. As though any moment he would explode and all hell would be let loose. But it was enough for the Black Oak to appear suddenly in front of him and Biez's fury evaporated.

The only one who wouldn't give up was Mariusia. She found something suspicious in the way the Oak was so insistent on getting to Bodsanova. It could only be that he had a woman there. And she was burned up with jealousy. She had plenty of reasons. She couldn't rest.

And the Black Oak, the chief of this circus troupe, knew that losing his temper with her would not break down her resistance.

The tavern was packed with peasants. They didn't want to go away from the fair still sober. The Black Oak had drunk two full glasses of brandy. The third glass would make him drunk. And then anything could happen. They would have to tie him up with the reins and dump him in the cart on the bed of hay. Or else he would do something that the circus folk had seen him do before— pick on one of the biggest and strongest fellows in the town, start a friendly conversation with him, and as he still talked get hold of him by the lapels and drag him out into the market place to fight. In every town, when he got drunk, he always asked who was the strongest man in the town, somebody everybody was afraid of. He asked the tavern keepers, the horse dealers, and very often he knew who it was even before he came to the town, because he had asked some of the Jews from that town he had met on their way to or from the fairs.

The drummer-cymbalist harboured a suspicion that he always picked on Christian boys, never a Jew.

But here in Nasielsk it was all straight sailing. The Black Oak had suddenly come bursting into the tavern and called out: 'We're harnessing the cart! We're off to Bodsanova!'

They had never seen him in such a state before. Nothing they could do about it. They had to obey. Though each and every one of them was dead against the idea. But they all kept their mouths shut.

The cart moved along slowly, at the side of the stone road. On both sides of the road lay bare fields, cleared after the harvest. You saw wide flat distances, misty horizons, and bushes in the lower parts. The circus folk, covered over with fresh hay, dropped off one by one to sleep. You could hear them snore. The horse plodded along slowly.

It was a miserable night. No stars, and grotesque clouds everywhere, like a pack of huge water-rats with black paws and gaping jaws. Between the cloud-rats a phosphorescent shine.

When the cart passed through a darkened village two big black dogs flung themselves at the wheels, trying to bite into them. They leapt at the horse, in front and from both sides. They didn't bark. They didn't growl. They just tried with silent dogged fury to get at the horse's throat.

The Black Oak turned his whip round, and lashed out with the heavy handle at the dogs. But he failed to hit them.

'God in Heaven! They're demons!'

'Don't go on, Black! Turn back!' Mariusia cried out.

'Aren't you asleep, Maria?'

She sensed a warmth in his words, and that warmed her.

'Stop the horse! I want to tell you something.'

He tugged at the reins, and the horse stopped. Maria took his hand and put her head in his lap. She sobbed. The cart stood still. The dogs ran off, not back to the village, but further along the highway.

'Go back, Black! Those were not dogs. They were messengers from the skies to tell you not to go to Bodsanova. Something dreadful will happen if we go there. I feel it in my bones. Aren't you happy with me? Why do you go looking for other women? You think I am angry with you when you go to a woman? I am angry with myself. I curse myself as a failure. I say to myself—"Maria, Mariusia, you're no good! You can't even keep your man tied to you. You don't know how to love a man. You don't know how! You're right, Black Oak."

She sobbed quietly to herself, unbared her broken heart to him. She felt so low, such a failure.

'I must be in Bodsanova by the morning.'

Mariusia suddenly moved away from him, and she was no longer feeling low. Her voice rang firm and hard.

'For the last time, Black, I'm asking you—you're going there because of a woman?'

Her white teeth gleamed. So did the whites of her eyes.

'It is not because of a woman, Maria. I swear it!'

'Then why do you drive the guts out of us, rushing us away to Bodsanova?'

'I must be there, I tell you, Maria! Don't ask me why. To-morrow is going to be a very hard day for me. And I need you there. You won't leave me alone in Bodsanova. You will go everywhere with me, won't you? Please!'

Mariusia kissed his hands.

'I won't move from your side, Black!'

'If everybody leaves me, you will stay?'

'Yes, I will, Black! I swear it!'

'Cross yourself!'

She crossed herself. But she added: 'I'm afraid!'

'Afraid of what?'

'You're up to something, Black! I don't know what it is. But you're up to something that I don't know about. Something happened to you in that tavern to-day. Those young men with student caps. I saw you listening to every word they said. And you clenched your fists. I was sure you were going to start a fight with them. Thank God you didn't. I didn't know you when you came back to me afterwards. Your eyes were blazing. Your lips were trembling. I know you, Black! I know every twitch of your face. I can read everything you have in your mind by the way you look. I can even read your feeling of regret, your penitence when you come back to me after you've been with some other woman. I feel it in the way you kiss me, when you come back. Then I say to myself: 'Go to them, Black! Go to them! So long as you come back to me!' Because you will never find another Mariusia, who will jump through hoops of fire, who will fly through the air like a serpent, like an angel, like a fire-bird, like a flash of lightning, to lie quietly afterwards in your strong firm arms. But to-night you were not strong and firm. You were restless. Something has happened! What is it! What is driving you to Bod-sanova, a poor small heck of a place, where we've never stopped to play before? Why are we going there now? Why, Black!'

He listened to Mariusia without saying a word. Then he brought the whip down twice smartly on the horse's back.

'Gee up! Get a move on!'

One of the others woke, stuck out his head, looked round, lay back in the hay and snored again.

Black Oak wondered to himself if he should tell Mariusia why he was going to Bodsanova. Should he? No! Not yet. After the Fair was over. You could never be sure. She might let a word slip to Antek. Antek would get her drunk, and when Mariusia was drunk, there was no secret safe with her. Antek was after Mariusia. Black knew that. He was only waiting for something to happen to him, Black Oak, to get Mariusia. Black Oak knew that. And he was on guard. He could surprise one on a dark night, when he wasn't on the look out, and drive a knife into his heart. He had tried getting rid of Antek, but it was no go. Antek hung on. As long as Mariusia was there. And Mariusia was there only because he was there. She wouldn't leave the Black Oak!

Black Oak reckoned to reach Bodsanova around eight o'clock in the morning. That would give them three hours to rest. Meanwhile he would go looking round the town, to find out when the pogrom was set to start. By what the students in the tavern in Nasielsk had said it would start about four o'clock. Why four? To let the peasants have enough time to sell their produce and buy what they wanted. And the tills in the Jewish shops would by then be full of money.

What should he do? Tell the Jews there was going to be a pogrom? That some sinister people had arrived in Bodsanova from surrounding towns and villages? That there were policemen among them, dressed as peasants? Bodsanova was a Jewish town. All the peasants who came to market came from the sur-rounding villages. These Jews were simple Chassidic people, who wouldn't believe that their peasants were really going to harm them. If he told them what he had heard they wouldn't believe him. Why should they? Who was Black Oak to the Jews? What sort of a Jew was he? A circus-act, the chief of a band of strolling players, a mummer, a mountebank. No proper Jew. Some-one they would not want to be seen with. And that story of his about a pogrom —cock and bull story. Something he'd made up; having a game with them. Wanting to start a panic among them, and then laugh at them for being cowards.

What good will it do if I tell them that I'm a Jew? Will it make any difference to them? What sort of a Jew am I in their eyes? I don't know myself for sure if I really am a Jew. My mother told me she was Jewish, and that my father was a Jew. But then I lost sight of her. I was put in the circus. And I never saw her again.

What Black planned to do was to spread some mats on the stones in the middle of the market place, and let the troupe show what they could do. And he would keep them going at it. They would give a wonderful performance, their best things, to hold the attention of the peasants till after the time for the pogrom. That's what he would do! He would keep them riveted till the time for the pogrom was past! He would show them how to jump through hoops of fire, to swallow fire! He would show them acrobatics, conjuring tricks, juggling tricks. He would have them stand there goggling. They would forget all about the pogrom!

Four o'clock. That was the time fixed for the pogrom. If he could keep the peasants glued to his performance Bodsanova would be saved. Three hours. Till seven o'clock. Because it would be nightfall by seven, and the peasants would be wanting to put their horses back in the shafts round that time to drive home. Three hours! He would show them his feats of strength. He would show them! Not for nothing that he was called the Black Oak! He was like a black oak! Strong as an oak! No, he wouldn't tell the Jews! They wouldn't believe him!

Driving into Bodsanova Black immediately recognised one of the policemen as a man he had seen in plain clothes in the tavern in Nasielsk.

The cart drove into the yard of the inn. Mariusia went inside to see about breakfast. The others went on sleeping. The market place was already packed with carts, and there were more arriving all the time. Jews were opening their shops. Some were still on their way back home after the service in the Synagogue, with their Tallis under their arm. Little boys were going to chedar. It was a grey and misty morning. Clouds in the sky. A pig was squealing. A cow tied to a cart stretched its neck and stared dumbly towards the distant fields.

Black Oak walked about among the shops, looked the Jews in the face, raised the peak of his cap as if to show them the worried restless look in his eyes. But the Jews didn't see, couldn't understand. He stopped one Jew, and was going to say something to him, but the man looked at him with suspicion, and walked away. He approached another Jew, who was dressed like a European, and whispered in his ear, in Polish: 'They're organising a pogrom here. Get some sort of defence weapons ready!'

'A pogrom? Oh, they've been talking about pogroms for years. Hi,' he called to the policeman whom Black Oak had seen in Nasielsk. 'This chap here says there's going to be a pogrom!'

'That policeman is one of the organisers,' Black Oak whispered to the man. 'Don't trust him!'

The policeman looked Black Oak up and down.

'I've seen you somewhere before! Show me your papers!'

Black Oak unbuttoned his jacket and his vest, and produced his documents. His face was white with rage.

About noon the Church bell rang. The peasants in the market place took off their caps and crossed themselves. The iron gate of the Church was shut. The Church bell sounded grim and angry. The strokes chased each other, ran into each other, and became one great copper groan that drowned the neighing of the horses, the cries of the crowd, and the sound of Antek's drum and cymbals.

Black Oak was worried. Why was the Church bell ringing? Had someone died, and the bell was tolling for him? Or was this the signal for the pogrom?

Antek made the crowd of peasants open out into a wider ring. He twisted and turned and spun round like a top, with the drum on his back, and the cymbals to his chest. He spun round with such force that he did not touch the ground, but swung in the air as though a whirlwind had lifted him up at the crossroads. No stopping him now. He was swept along by his own force. Wider and wider round he spun, and the peasants gave way to him, moved out of his way, fearing that his drum might bang into them.

Black Oak moved around in a sailor's vest, with a spiked stick in his hand. His muscles rippled with strength.

'Back! Move back there! A little more! Make a bigger ring! Antek, play! Give us some music!'

He pushed the peasants back and back. He saw that some of them had cudgels. And some had sacks under their arms.

Suddenly the drum and the cymbals stopped. Several people in the crowd were trying to force their way into the middle of the circle in which the Black Oak was moving round.

'That's some of the students who were in Nasielsk,' the Black Oak said to himself. 'And there's that policeman. They want to break up our show, so that the peasants can get on with the pogrom. I won't let them!'

'Maria, the greatest acrobatic artist in the world! Performed in Warsaw, London and New York! The flying serpent! The bird of fire! See her jump through hoops of flame!'

He stopped. He was afraid that if he talked any more the students would succeed in breaking up the ring. So less talk! On with the show! 'Hold them, Maria! Go on till I give you the word! Maria! My dear!'

Such fond words from Black Oak won Maria absolutely.

She moved to the performing mat. She wore a long blue cloak down to her ankles. And she had a gilt crown on her head. When she let the cloak drop to the ground the peasants gasped. 'A Queen!' The words went running like an echo round the ring.

The clown lighted burning hoops, tossed them in the air, and Maria went through the flaming hoops. Into one and out again, into another and out on the Black Oak's shoulder, on to his head, then down to his outstretched palm, where she stood for a moment and made several rhythmic dance movements, finally jumping off and turning a double somersault on the mat.

'Good God,' the crowd muttered.

Instead of their usual practice of having the clown at this point go round with his shiny high hat for the collection, Black Oak now called Voitek Biez, the fire eater and sword swallower.

'The fire eater, the sword swallower, the wire walker. He could walk on the telephone wires all the way from here to Warsaw. Watch him!'

Biez came forward. A short thin man with furrowed forehead, a flat squashed nose, wearing a blue jacket, and started dancing about on naked swords. One sword, two, three, four swords. He picked them up and flung them in the air, and they fell back, on to his hands, his forehead, his nose, and there they stood. He juggled with them, took several steps forward and back. Then suddenly a flame shot out over his head like a crown of fire. He opened his mouth wide, and the flame vanished in his mouth. He had swallowed it!

'It's cold fire!' one peasant in the ring cried out.

'All right,' Black Oak said. 'You come here and hold the cold fire in your hand.'

The peasant put out his hand, touched the 'cold fire', and cried out with pain. The crowd laughed.

Black Oak was watching the Church clock. Four o'clock already! The clown came forward again, wanting to start the collection. 'Not yet,' said Black Oak.

He saw the circus folk exchanging puzzled looks. What had happened to Black Oak? Why was there no collection? The peasants would soon be driving back to their village homes, and there would be no money. Even Maria was surprised. But she had the consolation of knowing that it was not because of a woman. Black Oak had a purpose for what he was doing.

Now it was Black Oak's turn to perform. He would have to hold the crowd two more hours. Perhaps three. He must! Even if his circus folk mutinied and went off and left him here alone. He would show them one of his feats of strength, something he used to do when he was younger, in the full power of his strength.

'Give me the iron bar, Antek! Look at this iron bar, ladies and gentlemen! Feel it! I'll bend it into any shape you say. A woman's head? A bird? A heart? A rose?'

A babel of words. 'All right! I'll do a rose.'

He raised his knee. Placed the bar on it and in five minutes he held up a rose.

Then he produced an iron chain. 'Try it!' he cried. 'I'll tear it to bits. I'll bite it with my teeth. Watch!'

He wound the chain round his hands, and tugged.

'Anyone here who wants to try it? Any strong man here who wants to show us what he can do?'

Mariusia went over to him and whispered urgently: 'What are you doing, Black? Stop now!'

But Black wouldn't stop. 'I promised to show you something you have never seen before. Bring me two horses. Two strong horses. One of you will hold them by the reins. You'll use the whip to make them go, one in this direction and the other in the opposite direction. I'll stand holding the reins, in the middle and you'll see, the horses won't move.'

Juzef Granda came close up to Black Oak, with a long face. He was terribly worried. Voitek was cursing bitterly to himself. A few peasants went off and fetched the horses.

They arrived with four horses. Four strong, powerful stallions! With flowing manes and restless legs.

'I'll take the four!' Black Oak called out. And there he stood, two horses on one side, two on the other. And he in the middle. His circus folk grumbling to themselves stole away, one by one. To the tavern. Only Maria remained. But she stood there some distance away, watching.

Black Oak stood firm. He knew that he was not only holding back the horses, but the pogrom.

Then it happened. The two horses on his right took one step forward, and by just that much dragged him with them. But he had not slackened his grip on the horses on his left. He held them back. But something in his chest had snapped.

It was already getting dark when the peasants went back to their carts. The market place was empty, was quiet. The cart with the circus folk had gone. Even Maria had gone. Black Oak sat in the market place on the steps of a house, smiling to himself as he saw the lights going on in the Jewish houses in Bodsanova.

'Another drunk from the Fair,' somebody passing by muttered in Yiddish.

Black Oak looked at his hands, torn by the rope by which he had held on to the horses. There was blood on them. Presently a trickle of blood began to run from his mouth. A dog running along stopped at his side. He was no longer angry with anyone. Not with Maria, not with the other circus folk, not with the crowd of peasants. He felt wonderfully relaxed. The last light he saw in this world came from the windows of the quiet Jewish houses in Bodsanova.

ESSAYS

EPHRAIM AUERBACH

Thinking With Ivre-Teitch*

Thinking with Ivre-Teitch has a special meaning. It is thinking differently, even expressing the thought differently. It isn't the Yiddish language alone that is the big thing here, but the whole manner of bringing out the thought. And definitely with Ivre-Teitch, not in Ivre-Teitch, for it is in fact like Chumash with Rashi, or Gemara with Tosefoth. Ivre-Teitch ceases to be a language; it becomes a commentary, or a whole chain of commentaries.

Again, Ivre-Teitch is not a language, but a folk culture, a folk mentality. Ivre-Teitch is Halacha and Agadah, Mossur and the wisdom of life, story and fable, lyric and drama—a complete Jewish world in Ivre-Teitch.

When Ivre-Teitch began to take root in our life, the scholarly world of that time looked down disdainfully on the language created by the folk, for women and the common herd, for whom Ivre-Teitch was to be a road by which they could get to Judaism and Jewishness. But in time Ivre-Teitch became something valuable in itself, not just additional, supplementary, a growth on the trunk of the ancient Jewish tree. Out of the grand old tree a small sapling grew, feeding on the same old roots, but gradually growing and occupying its own area, with its own shade, its own branches, shaping differently than the father-tree.

Ivre-Teitch grew out of the great Jewish tree; from the very beginning, as soon as it sprouted it sent out a smell of ancientness. But into this ancientness it bloomed its own youth and freshness; it drew up the sap of Jewish ancientness and itself grew young. It became not only the language of the people; it also became its thought, its mood, its way of life.

The Patriarchs and the Matriarchs are different in Ivre-Teitch from those in the Pentateuch; they are even different from those in the Agadas. The imagination of the people and their mood and way of feeling has grown into them.

When we learned in chedar 'Veani' (Genesis 48.7), it became a song, Jacob's mournful lyric song, remembering in his old age how he had left our Mother Rachel in her grave on the road to Ephrath. In the Bible, when Jacob calls his sons together, to tell each what will befall him, what he sees in his vision, his voice sounds hard and metallic. He is stern, terse, concise. But the same Jacob in Ivre-Teitch is romantic, tragic, regretful. The interpretation of the 'Veani' passage in Ivre-Teitch is the folk comment on Jacob, whom it pictures as reliving his love for Rachel much more deeply than in the Bible narrative.

* Ivre-Teitch, the original name of Yiddish—Hebrew—German.   119

The Ivre-Teitch Joseph in his quarrel with his brothers is also different from what he is in the Pentateuch, and even in the Agadah. Ivre-Teitch gave Joseph more dream than the Bible gave him. In Ivre-Teitch he became the symbol of affection, piety and tragedy. How many tears the Ivre-Teitch Jews have shed over Joseph lying in the pit, and afterwards when his brothers sold him to the Ishmaelites. And the Joseph who would not reveal himself to his brothers, and went into his chamber to weep—he is the Biblical Joseph, but with Ivre-Teitch, which means with the added interpretation of the folk soul.

Since I hold that Ivre-Teitch is not just language, but a view of life and a folk-mood, I can also see how the Galuth with Ivre-Teitch has its special flavour. The Ivre-Teitch view of the Galuth is warm and affectionate, according to the interpretation made by the folk, in keeping with the folk-psychology, which finds the Galuth dear and familiar, tragically destined, like life itself.

Didn't the Ivre-Teitch Jew want to be redeemed from the Galuth? Yes, he wanted redemption no less than the Hebrew-speaking Jew, but meanwhile, till the Redemption comes, the Galuth is like the nest to a bird, though it plans to fly in winter to a warmer land. Of course, the Ivre-Teitch Jew hoped and waited for the Messiah, but as Messiah himself is a Galuth Jew, the Ivre-Teitch Jew took him into his company, took him into his Galuth home, and joined him in the rite of mourning for the Galuth.

The Ivre-Teitch Jew mourned for the Galuth with a warm heart. He created a Messiah in his own image, a Messiah who is at home with the Galuth Jews, walks about among them, speaks their language, shares their sufferings and rejoices at their happiness. The Ivre-Teitch Jew did not think of the Galuth as an idea—the concept idea did not exist for him at all. But he did build up the Galuth like an idea, he interpreted it ideologically. His mourning because of the Galuth is healthy, for he knows that if he sinks into despair he will have no strength to wait for the Messiah.

Therefore the Ivre-Teitch songs about the Galuth are not laments. Sometimes they even have a shade of irony, as in that song, 'What will we do when Messiah comes?' That song contains the entire Agadah—Behemoth and the Laviathan, and the Wine of Paradise—but right at the beginning, when it opens with the announcement of the Great Feast, we detect at once a faint irony. Didn't the Ivre-Teitch Jew believe with all his heart and soul in the Agadath of the coming of the Messiah? God forbid! He never ceased for a moment to believe, but he carried over the warm snugness of the Galuth to the Redemption. The Messianic Feast became an intimate jollification, like one of the Sabbath feastings in his own home.

The Ivre-Teitch Jew made his own comment even on the Almighty Himself. He almost forgot the God of Vengeance; he kept the God of Judgment for his prayers—in Ivre-Teitch there was only the God of Mercy. No other language, I think, has such familiar closeness to God, such intimate association with Him. When the Ivre-Teitch Jew says—'Don't punish me, God, for my words', it is as though he were talking to another Jew who is his own father and is standing beside him.

The Ivre-Teitch Jew has been cut off from the earth. In the days of Passover we recall his greatness before the Destruction came upon him. The Rising in the Ghetto is full of holy sparks of the Ivre-Teitch Jew. He is the Ivre-Teitch interpretation which the Jew gave to the Destruction.

Jewishness and Yiddish

'If God grant that the earth will be full of understanding and everybody will speak the same language, Ashkenazic, then only (the form) Brisk will be written.'

So wrote Rabbi Meir Katz, the father of the Shak, in one of his responses. We infer from his words that by 'language Ashkenazic' he means Yiddish, since Brisk is the Yiddish name for the town Brest-Litovsk. Secondly it shows that he took it for granted that the way Jews speak is Yiddish—a simple truth which we have ceased to understand in recent times. You feel in Reb Meir's words a warm attitude to Yiddish. That is how the Jewish people put it, through the mouth of its representative, the Rabbi. Times change. Who is to-day the Jewish people, and who can represent it?

There are great masses of people born Jews who live their whole life with the minimum of Jewishness, on the soul-soil of an alien way of life. We would on the face of it expect them also to abandon Yiddish, the language of that part of the Jewish people that remained faithful to the Jewish past, and we would further suppose that there would probably be such among the faithful who would wage war for their ideals, who would stand up for Yiddish.

But we don't always find the facts agree with what one's commonsense seems to say. The religious Jews say little nowadays about Yiddish, while there is a whole section among the freethinkers to whom Yiddish is an ideal, their whole ideal, in fact. How is it possible? Have we sunk so low that we can look on calmly while all that is ours is taken away from us, and we don't even see that ours is taken away from us?

Ours—for who created Yiddish? Did it grow out of modern theories? Out of the European Maskilic conception of a people—land and language, and nothing more? No, the Jewish people of old, which was the people of Judaism and the Jewish way of life, created Yiddish. Not compulsory separation in the Ghetto, as the assimilationist Maskilim wish to have it, nor just the national separation, as the nationalist assimilationists want it.

We see at the first glance that the first argument is quite untenable. For to begin with, the influence of the German Ghetto had ceased long before, and Jews had been living freely for a long time in Poland when Yiddish really flourished. Secondly, Yiddish grew out of necessity. Jews were thrust out from the 'general cultural life'. The assimilationist Maskilim are greatly mistaken when they think that the 'general culture' of those times was like the present, which keeps getting more irreligious, where people who have no relation with any religious belief can live together in some sort of indistinguishable hash.

But the 'general culture' of that time was Christian, and Jews again all lived in the way God had commanded. So how can it be imagined that they had previously both lived in one environment, and that the Jews had then been expelled from it? They could not be expelled, because they had their own great, ancient culture.

Nor can the argument of the nationalist Maskilim, national separation, be valid. What do they mean by national separation? Do they mean the factor that derives from race, from blood? It exists, no doubt. But we have no way at all of detecting its influence, and there is no people of any language in whom we find signs of a recognisable influence of race. It shows that this influence at most can be only small.

If again national separation means the historic sum-total of differences found in this or the other people, then this too is no criterion. So the question remains—where do we get this complex entity from that bears the name culture, what gives it its specific colouring?

This brings us out on the road at last. The separateness comes from the Jewish culture, and Jewish culture always grows on the soil of Jewish belief, of the Jewish faith. It was our own culture that constructed the Yiddish language out of old German.

Yiddish is no exception to the rule. The religion is with other peoples too the creator of their cultures and of new languages. And Yiddish is no exception to the rule in regard to the Jewish people itself. This same creative process was repeated several times in different periods and different places. We have the evidence of several Jewish languages and dialects to show what tremendous creative power there is in Jewishness in this special field of culture. In character and achievement there is no difference between Yiddish and Aramaic, the language of the Gemarrah, Jewish-Arabic, Judeo-Spanish (Spaniol) and the rest. But there is a great difference in fact, both quantatively and qualitatively. Yiddish embraces the largest part of the Jewish people, both in our times and in relation to our whole past, and Yiddish is the most distinctive Jewish language. The others were in practice much less differentiated from their non-Jewish parallel languages, and not one of them had worked out such a distinct form of its own. In other words, Yiddish is in this point the only language that lives only on the Jewish tongue. For even the holy language, Hebrew, was spoken by other peoples as well.

Where the influence of the faith ends, there also ends the culture-creating process, and the deep differences between peoples disappear, as we see it among

Jews and among the other peoples. One glance at Europe provides ample material of such facts. But our Leftists have gone blind where spirit is concerned, and they don't see it, and that army of freethinkers which has turned Yiddish into a banner is using the creation of the faith against itself, in the belief that the force which created it is now old and decrepit, and the child can manage by itself. The 'Yiddishist' war against the faith, which is mostly waged also against Hebrew, sometimes blinds one of our own too, so that he sees only the danger of Yiddishism, and sometimes doesn't even understand the role of Yiddish, especially if he has been unconsciously infected with Leftist views. He is too short-sighted to see that there is no difference between Yiddishism on one side and Hebraism on the other, that they are both the same irreligious nationalism in different dress. He doesn't see that the whole conflict Yiddish-Hebrew, folk language-national language, is only a conflict between true brothers, that Hebrew is not the holy tongue, though to the Bolsheviks the Torah and Tchernichovsky, forgive me for coupling the two, are both the same enemy.

But the people knows that under the smattering of Hebrew words lies apostasy, assimilation, non-Jewish life—and the people disregarded the slogan 'Hebrew or Russian' and simply held on to its mother-tongue.

Even in Western Europe you can meet already to-day people of the second immigrant generation who can speak Yiddish. This too is characteristic—that we see reports from time to time from Israel about a meeting in a Synagogue, where someone wanted to speak in Hebrew, and the assembly of religious Jews protested vigorously, insisting on Yiddish. They were not fooled, it seems —they sensed the profane under the sanctity. The people also realise that the ostensibly practical argument is hollow, that it won't do to be for ever teaching millions of people to speak Hebrew, because a Polish and a Moroccan Jew sometimes meet. Where it is necessary they understand each other, without any theories, and without that sort of Hebrew which is just as mechanical and soulless as Esperanto. But this is not understood so well by individuals at the top, who dismiss Yiddish contemptuously.

This contempt stems from two roots of the Haskallah, whose influence is much more powerful among us than appears at first sight. The attitude to Yiddish shows it clearly. The Maskilic hostility has slowly eaten its way into us. The two roots are stuck in nationalism and in the earlier assimilationist views of certain West European orthodoxy. The Maskil, whether nationalist or assimilationist-orthodox, lives in a world which is not in essence Jewish, or only half-Jewish, and has therefore among other things also lost its language, or is losing it. One lot of nationalists think and speak all the time of the importance of the national form, and they don't see that before their eyes they have complete and ready, alive, the very thing about which they keep weaving elaborate theories. Their influence is also felt among us, not so much in words as in consequences.

The Maskilised orthodox again (and this is perhaps a diminishing category) fails to understand that God's command to be different from the nations is greatly facilitated if we are also different in language. Not only does he miss seeing the great value of Yiddish for the maintenance of the people as a whole and of its soul, but he also can't understand the importance of the form in the whole structure of Jewishness, from which we derive the second fundamental value of Yiddish. So that being under these Maskilic influences he stands with blind eyes and repeats all the silly absurdities: Yiddish is really not our own language, it isn't a nice language, it's a mixed language, it is a corrupt German, no other people in the world speaks it (!) and other such bright clever things, which both Jewishly and scholarly are nonsense.

There are many examples of the extent to which Maskilic psychology has spread its influence over us. I want to mention only one instance which has to do with the language itself. The old Haskallah created an ugly, Germanised corrupt language, and modern Haskallah has not of course improved it to make it more Jewish, though it has departed from the openly Germanised path. The religious Jews have in recent times hardly bothered to guard their old language, and have sometimes admitted the new influence even in the Yiddish translation of the Bible text. And now, when Yiddish has come into wider use they have simply taken over the language of the freethinkers, which has assimilation in its soul, their words, their forms, their syntax. We hadn't the strength to construct something of our own. They introduced a Germanised orthography, which looked philologically stupid—and we followed them in this, and are holding on to it tighter than they are, for they have already replaced it with some brand-new spellings—and it's even a good thing for us to be dancing in their footsteps, because the old Germanised orthography is still less Jewish. Who among us thought that our own old orthography was not so bad, and that we could easily build on this base a scientific and national orthography? No, it didn't occur to us. 'Language ... orthography ... not important!' We neglect our own affairs; we don't consider that Jews must conduct themselves finely in everything, and in so important a matter as language as well. The language of a people should be something well-shaped, and it isn't all the same whether its writers kill the language, or they take pains to bring out the order and the beauty which lie in the language itself.

Nor should it be said that this needs philological preparation, and the subject is too dull. First of all, not everybody need deal with it, and secondly it is the same everywhere: details are not dull, if you know why the work is being done—and the purpose is to form, to refine, to beautify the instrument of our worship and our service, and so better it. We must serve God with beauty.

Now we come to the third value. The value of separation and the value of form which I mentioned before bear a relation to the people as a whole. Demanding aesthetic treatment of Yiddish because it is a means of service, we approach the territory of the individual. And here we see that the importance of Yiddish is just as great. A language that is spoken has a direct impact, and does not need the middle-road of the mind. Rabbi Nachman of Bratzlav knew what he was doing when he left instructions in his will that his stories must not be published otherwise than with the Yiddish original. That is how we must also understand the fact that Chassidism strengthened the position of Yiddish. When Chassidim wanted to pour out their soul they found the way in the language which was on their tongue. That is how the holy Levi Yitzchok came to sing in Yiddish. It is interesting in this regard to note the difference between Jewish changes and Maskilic reforms. The strengthening of Yiddish did not diminish by a hair the importance of the holy tongue—while the West European Maskil's way of thought went like this: The holy tongue is hardly understood now, or perhaps no longer understood at all. Therefore it must be discarded, and we must say our prayers in the language which the people speak. This is not a problem of language, but of psychology. The prayers in German did not oust the holy tongue, but Yiddish was dying among these people, so Maskilic psychology thought up such things. Where Jewishness flourished the people used the religious values of both languages, as the women's Techinoth testify.

But Yiddish entered the religious life not only in the field of emotion, but also of the mind. Here we have the fourth great value of Yiddish, the intellectual and the pedagogic. This means, Yiddish was used for intellectual purposes, for literature, chiefly translations, paraphrasings, commentaries. For the fact could not be ignored that there are parts of the people for whom the road of the holy tongue is too hard or even impossible, and it was realised that they must not just be left out in the wilderness. A whole people can't all be scholars—and they must have God's word in the speech of those who achieved something with their publications. It is important to remember that this part of the people was a large one because it included a whole half of the people— the women and girls, besides many men. This also strengthened the emotional factor. Translations were made of the Bible and some of the other literature. The large number of these translations, paraphrasings and commentaries show how well the matter was understood. There is no need to quote examples from the leaders of the people, such as the approbations of the Bible translations by

Blitz and Witzenhausen, (which incidentally have only the translations, without commentary). There were also original works.

I think that the value of the older Yiddish literature is not appreciated as much as it should be. Who knows where we might have been to-day if Rabbi Isaac ben Reb Jacob had not written his Tze'enu U'renu. I mean, it is quite unnecessary for any little youngster to-day to shrug his shoulders and sniff—'Womanish stuff!' He doesn't realise that without the Tze'enu U'renu he might not be studying his Gemarrah now.

The most important intellectual victory of Yiddish is the fact that we learn everything in Yiddish. The small boy in Chedar and the Gaon are linked together in life and learning through the language. We mustn't think that only what is printed is a fact which counts. No, because the spoken Yiddish is the garb of the intellectual life, its importance is beyond calculation, even if what is said in Yiddish is afterwards written down and printed in the holy tongue and Halacha language.

The division of service between the sacred tongue and Yiddish still exists to-day. Here too we could have an extension of the role of Yiddish. We can easily picture a great scholar writing a new commentary in Yiddish, and from what we have seen till now, it will not oust Rashi, God forbid, and the sacred tongue will not lose its greatness, sanctity and practical value. In this field the position will probably remain like that. But in other fields the rôle of Yiddish is growing, and it will have to occupy a great place in our literature. There are masses of people who must be given both fine literature and scientific knowledge on the basis of Jewishness, not popularisation nor trash, but classic works. (I don't of course mean that classics can be created by programmes).

In the modern period the people were not given anything, and this often led them to turn to the irreligious literature in Yiddish. The end of it is irreligiousness or at least a strong Maskilic influence. True, the modern literature is cutting itself off from the Jewish tree and cannot endure, but meanwhile it is doing damage among us, and we have no gain from it, nor from the modern Hebrew literature—they are only European literatures in supposed Jewish language.

It will be something quite different if we have a Jewish literature in Yiddish, which will spread from end to end, on every side, and in all fields of Jewish life and Jewish ways. Then we shall be privileged to read poems and songs by truly great poets, not as to-day where the poetry we have is written by irreligious people, and if we get any poetry of ours it is bad versification. And it is rarely lyrical—mostly so-called epic, on historical themes. Is it only chance that we have no poets to-day who write songs of God's ways? Are we still justified in calling ourselves the people of faith? Apparently religious

Jews think it is beneath them to write poetry. King David didn't think so. There is only one thing to keep us from despair—there still are folksongs, and we still have a folk who sing the holy Rabbi Levi Yitzchok's songs.

God gave us such a precious possession, our own language, and if we continue in the same way as now we shall fritter away His gift. One of the reasons for which the people of Israel was redeemed from Egypt, says the Gemarrah, was the language—'Because they did not change their language.' Let us hope that we shall one day, in the coming years, be entitled to claim the same privilege for ourselves.

AARON ZEITLIN

Isaac Katznelson

In our generation every Jew, even if he hasn't himself been in any of the ghettoes and extermination camps, should consider himself not as one who lives, just that, but as one who has remained alive, which is more and different. One who has remained alive after a shipwreck still feels the tragedy of the shipwreck. That is how every Jew should feel the disaster of the six million. If it is fobbed off with official remembrance days it is forgetting by remembering. Theatralised grief is a desecration.

There was a great fuss made about Anne Frank's Diary. What are twenty such Diaries against one page in the records of Isaac Katznelson, written in the concentration camp Vitel? Every Jew who wants to remember must read again and again Isaac Katznelson's journal that he kept in Vitel. He must keep returning to such works of the Churban as Katznelson's 'Song of the Slaughtered Jewish People'. That is more, immeasurably more than he can get from the best memorial speeches. Reading Katznelson is to suffer, to be destroyed with the Jewish millions, to be burned and to rise from the ashes and demand a reckoning.

In writing that work the martyr Isaac Katznelson became himself a survivor, one of those who have remained alive. He will always rise from the ashes to demand a reckoning from those above and those below.

Till the Churban, Isaac Katznelson was a graceful, musical poet with a Heinesque manner and a bent for feuilletonism. Even his ponderous poems—and they were not rare—gave the impression of something light, because while the poet wept, his rhyme frolicked. In his Hebrew poems Katznelson often surprised one with his playful inventive rhymes, smooth and gay. His facile swinging rhymes prevented us from taking his song and his grief seriously.

He came from a good comfortable home, gently nurtured, surrounded with parental affection, a wonder-child, an infant prodigy dancing into our literature. Afterwards he was a teacher, in constant contact with children; he wrote songs for children, children's plays, all sorts of things like that. He never grew out of being a wonder-child, not even in those works where he tried as a mature artist to express himself to his world. Katznelson who wrote Hebrew and Yiddish poems, many of them weighty and original, though unintegrated, who wrote a robust prose, and fine one-act plays, and all sorts of things, big and small in various literary genres, strained every nerve to achieve a crowning work. But he could not get away from his playful rhymes.

Also Katznelson was not the kind of man who was out for success. He didn't try to get ahead of anyone. He kept aloof from the market place, where they sell a hundredweight of immortality for an ounce of talent. He didn't want to make a career. So he got no place at the top, where the literary peers sit.

The Churban shook Katznelson. The tragic experience moved him so intensely that it lifted him up to greatness. Yet had it come as suddenly as that there wouldn't have been any transition from the pre-Churban Katznelson to the Katznelson of 'The Song of the Slaughtered Jewish People'. The fact is that the flaming love of Israel that burns in the Churban poems was already evident in his fine dramatic sketch showing how Jewish gentleness bleeds when it hits against the rough alien world of the Czarist barracks. The wonderful love of the Jewish child which moves us so much in 'The Song of the Slaughtered Jewish People' was always characteristic of Katznelson who, a lovely child himself, identified himself in his work with the world of Jewish children. We may say that in the later Katznelson the lovely child merged with the tragic mature Jew who immortalised the cry of his slaughtered People. 'Jewish children', he writes in his Vitel scroll, 'Jewish children in Lithuania, Volhynia, Poland . . . children—meek as the Godly man Moses, poor and suffering like Job, beautiful as Joseph in the strange land Egypt, in the Egyptian bondage.' A People's children reveal the kind of people it is. The prematurely aged Jewish child in the years of the extermination appears to him the embodiment of grandfather Israel. The Jewish child is great and ethical to the point of holiness. In his small, starved body that the enemy doomed to destruction lives the soul of a great doomed People that is being slaughtered because it always gave birth to Prophets and Messiahs.

In the sixth chapter of his Lament for the slaughtered People Katznelson describes with burning pathos the orphans of the Warsaw Jewish Children's Home, and when he calls them 'Holy Messiahs, sanctified by suffering' it does not sound sentimental. You feel the love that bleeds when it looks at the child and sees in him the living symbol of the suffering People. There follows his outcry—at the beginning of the same chapter—'Oh, livelihood-seeking and God-seeking Jew.' The love for the Jewish child is at the same time love for his father who, seeking to make his living, sought also the Father in Heaven and found his death at Gentile hands.

In the doomed and dying Jew of the Churban Katznelson saw the highest, supreme and ripest expression of Jewish existence. The Jew of the Churban was to him greater, more Jewish than the Jews of all the previous generations. We see that in his Vitel journal, which deserves special attention. The sentences here are raw wounds; the syntax is bad, the sentences are not always completed, but it fits the frightful tragicalness of what is said, or rather shrieked, just as 'The Song of the Slaughtered Jewish People' is not written according to any rules; the technical helplessness is part of its strength. The sentences in the Vitel journal are heaped together feverishly, one on top of the other, and you fever with them. Katznelson's vision of a People that is being slaughtered because it is different and higher is transmitted to the reader with suggestive force. It is a defiant idealisation which derives from pain and compassion, for the same Katznelson with scorn expels from the Jewish generality the rabble, the dregs, the Jewish ghetto police, whom he hated for helping the Germans to exterminate the Jewish child. He hates all who are like them.

'The Song of the Slaughtered Jewish People' was written by Katznelson, like his journal, in the French concentration camp Vitel, from which he was then returned to Poland, to his death in Hitler's gas chambers. Vitel was a temporary prolongation. As though the poet's life had been extended only to let him write this poem. Sealed in three bottles and buried, it lay in the ground waiting to be resurrected. Katznelson was gassed, with his people. But he still lives—and he will live as long as there will live in the hearts of the generations that world tragedy which because of the poverty of human language we call the Churban.

H. LEIVICK

Jerusalem and Yiddish Literature

There never was such a need for the Jew as an individual to search his soul and to see where he stands in the world as now. Now, after that indescribable disaster of the Hitler period. After all the poetry and the prose works written about that disaster it has not yet been pictured or comprehended. Now after the establishment of the State of Israel, which is still forced to be armed, military, instead of being peaceful and Messianic, as we all ardently desire. Jews are building a State because they are both persecuted and just, and want to do justice. Now when we accept it as a historic and at times a mystic fact that it is against the six million Jews destroyed in Eastern Europe that we have the rise to-day of over six million Jews in America. It is something we must reckon with. Now, in face of all the circumstances, it is tremendously important for every individual Jew to search his soul and render an account to himself.

There isn't in the world to-day anyone who has like the individual Jew simultaneously stepped over the threshold of national redemption and yet has the feeling that the world around him is a gaping abyss luring him on to fling himself down and be lost in it. Yes, simultaneously redeemed and lost, confused, both a riddle to the world and a still greater riddle to himself. And this does not exclude the individual in Israel. For never has the Jew so felt the secret of his existence—both the wonder and the restlessness of his existence. And indeed, here on the soil of Jerusalem, on this earth where our foot touches this forever sanctified ground. The secret and the tragedy of our existence in the world. The secret and the tragedy of our contradictions, which need straightening out; the secret of our wonderful but blood-drenched millenia hovers over the face of the earth; the secret of our wanderings through so many exiles and dispersions; the secret of our struggles, our martyrdoms, our revolts, our Messianic uprisings and collapses; the secret of our frightening seclusions and God-visions; the secret of our wonder-men in darkest poverty; of our lowly water-carrier hidden saints, by whose merit the world exists; of our Gaonim, our great Rabbis and scholars, those of us who sit on the ground and mourn because of our Exile, who have raised this mourning to holiness; the secret of those of us who go to the barricades and to the gallows; the secret of our Shlomo Molkos and Hirsh Lekerts; of our Baal Shems and our Brenners; the secret of our Trumpeldors and Anilewiczes; our Vilnas and our history-transforming Ein Harods.

Here, on the soil of Jerusalem I say, as I have said it over and over again, that the Golus, the Exile, is bad, is ugly, and we must be redeemed from it. But the Jew in Golus was wonderful, glorious, and it is a pride to be descended from this glory. Poverty is dark, dismal, black, but the poor man is purity itself. Prison is darkness and gloom, but the prisoner, if he is guiltless is sublime. The Inquisition is criminal, murderous, blasphemy, but the Jew in the cells of the Inquisition was holy.

Why do I say this? To emphasise our unique worth through thousands of years, which must never in any situation be minimised or, God forbid, denied by ourselves.

What I am aiming at is to bring out the idea, my profoundest belief, that the basis of the life of every Jew, both in the State of Israel and outside is not negative but positive, not denial but affirmation. The foundation and the secret of our existence is always an intimate linking on and continuity. It must never be conceived in terms of a sharp commencement, a Genesis. Only once was the word Genesis used—when God created the world. Since then everything is in the process of flow, of lines that extend and bear within them the great desire to complete themselves in circles. The circle, as I see it, is the supreme achievement touched by the wings of God. I would like to hope that our Jewish history is now undergoing the process of completing itself within its circle, where every dot, every stroke is an essential ring in the circle, in this chain, where the smallest detail must not be profaned, must not drop out, for if you cast out the slightest stroke the whole circle breaks up.

I say this as a warning against the danger of the idea that would conceive the rise of the State of Israel as a Genesis, broken off from our whole yesterday, with all its characteristics, liberated completely from all yesterday's influences. A Genesis, a something sprung up out of itself, like a leap over the generations of two thousand years. And here I would like to take up the view that Ben Gurion expressed in his correspondence with Professor Nathan Rotenstreich. With many of his judgments about our history and about Messianism I am in complete agreement. But I hold his idea of making a leap, jumping over two thousand years of Golus straight back into the three thousand years ago, what he calls the Bible atmosphere, I consider that dangerous. Not because I don't value the Bible, but on the contrary, because I hold that the true bond between our people, between the individual Jew and the Bible was made not in the days when the Bible was in process of creation, but precisely in the two thousand years of Golus, of Exile. It was in the Exile that our people moulded its grand image. The Prophets entered into the hearts of our people only in the generations of Exile. The same with the Psalms. The same with the whole Torah.

In general, when we say People of the Bible, what does it mean in concrete terms? We must see the individual Jew in this. I hold that the Golus figure Sarah Bath Tuvim is a more Biblical figure than Bath Sheba, for whom King David committed plain murder of an innocent man.

Yes, Bath Tuvim is a nobler figure than Bath Sheba. And the young Jewish generation, both in Israel and everywhere should know more about Bath Tuvim than about Bath Sheba. I hold that the stories of a Jew who is a martyr figure are more Biblical than the story of the concubine in Gibeah. I hold that the story of the young shoemaker's apprentice Hirsh Lekert who fired a bullet into the head of the Governor-General of Vilna for having Jewish workers flogged on the First of May, and went to the gallows for it is no less Biblical than the story of the young shepherd boy David who slung a stone at the head of the Philistine giant Goliath. Yes, that is something Jewish children should learn about, not making the leap over this and similar wonderful great Jewish events. They should see the living simple Jewish man with his full heroism. Not as the conception of some new thing, the rise of a new Genesis. It must all be brought within the process of continuity, back to the lap of its lawful mother, the past, to grow naturally into the future.

Every prolonged exploitation of the idea that is called New Beginning in relation to our Jewish national revolution must lead to both a national and a cultural tragedy, to decline.

We had a cruel, brutal lesson not only with German Fascism, with Hitlerism, which set itself up with the idea of a German New Beginning. We had the same cruel, brutal lesson with Bolshevism, in all its forms, from Lenin to Stalin and to its present representatives. We have seen how this mad idea of a supposed New Beginning worked, to change into the complete contrary of what had been hoped at first. The dreadful tragedy of that part of our people living in the Soviet Union began and developed there so fatally not only because of the hideous Stalinist dialectic alone, but because the Jewish Communist leaders and writers who became complete masters over Jewish culture and Jewish intellectual life in the Soviet Union and the other countries under Soviet Russia's influence had—even more so than the Russian leaders and writers—fallen into a terrible Genesis trauma—the idea that Jewish history started from 1917, and that everything which existed before was nothing but mustiness and mildew. The Yiddish writers in the Soviet Union didn't like it when we warned them of the danger of conceiving Jewish life as having begun with 1917. To-day they can't even admit their mistake, for they are all lying dead, slain by the slayer whom they deified. But even if this had not happened, and they had not been destroyed by the Stalin idol, they would have succumbed of themselves if they had clung to their mania of seeing the history of our people only in the light of their own New Beginning.

I am dwelling on this point because it is necessary to emphasise again and again that it is a calamity for the world to adopt the theory that a man can create a yes out of a no, that in order to bring redemption, or to turn oneself into the image of a World Redeemer one may or one should walk arm in arm with Satan; that in order to bring love one may and should first get drunk with hate.

All this has a bearing on how we to-day value the tie between Israel and the Golus. How we value the concrete individual Jew in the State of Israel and the concrete individual Jew in Golus. What are they one to the other?

I use the word Golus, not the camouflage term Diaspora. Though I do not figure as a Zionist I hold that a Jew who for one reason or another is not in Israel, in the Land from which his people was driven out and to which it must return, that Jew lives in Golus, in Exile. Even America, as I believe, is on the banner of Jewish History Golus. I say it about myself. I am in Golus. Though I love America, both for herself, and because on her earth millions of our people have found freedom. But it is clear to me that as long as a Jew carries in an active form within himself the destiny of present-day Jewish history and his bond with the great unbroken Jewish past, then no matter where he is he longs and yearns for the return to the Land of Israel. A Jew who consciously dis- cards this longing, consciously abandons it, denies and forfeits, loses the main essential of his national biography, which basically is also his own personal biography. He has thrown away one of the most obvious features of his Jewish image.

I go further. And I say it with the knowledge of my own life experience, that a Jew in America who really feels that he is no longer in Golus, loses the essential point of being a Jew. But I also say that a Jew in Israel who declares that every Jew outside Israel has no longer any fundamental relationship with himself, or is at best something inferior, such a Jew in Israel saying such a thing—such a Jew too has lost the essential of being a Jew.

A Jew in Israel should be and is nationally a happier man, spiritually more at peace with himself, at home. And that should be and is the chief reason for envying him, and being drawn towards him. That is the everlasting emotion which draws us towards the Land of Israel, and is always a living factor in us. It does not mean however that it gives the present-day Israeli Jew the right to the arrogant assumption that he is not only at rest in his own home, but that he is also morally better, more ethical than his brother-Jew in Golus. We must never forget that the longing for the Land of Israel was always linked with the desire for justice and righteousness, for the ethical perfection of the individual Jew. For true Messianism. For the celestial Jerusalem.

But this desire, this longing always went together in partnership with the idea of the Perfect Man, the Adam Elyon, over the entire wander-world. In the world of suffering and purified grief. This Messianic longing was never arrogant, egocentric, contemptuous with regard to any Jew living in some forsaken spot. Whoever introduces in the relationship of Jew and Jew the approach of superior and inferior, of one sort of Jew who is better and another sort of Jew who is worse, undermines the foundations of our people. At best he is creating a kind of 'co-existence' between the Israeli Jew and the Golus Jew.

I say this because the argument and the rating of superior Jews and inferior Jews still goes on in part of the Israeli Press and Literature. Sometimes openly, sometimes hidden. It has a definite bearing on our whole national-culture problem, our education problem, our literature problem, our language problem. We have here the tragedy reflected in our life between Yiddish and Hebrew and culture in Israel and culture outside Israel.

I confess I am tired of our culture and language tragedies. I am too proud to go about to-day demanding respect from Jews for Yiddish. I do my thing, as I am called upon to do it. I know too that whoever we may be we are all of us not the ultimate judges to make the final decisions. Not we—the party involved—are the full and absolute lords over our history, even if we are at certain moments its masters and builders. There is a higher Power above us.

I must say it fills me with fear and grief that large sections of Jews in America are flinging out Yiddish and Hebrew from their spiritual life—the two languages that both gave us great national values, a great national literature, full of our own kind of people, with our own songs and art-forms and symbols. They are transferring completely to English, to an Anglo-Jewish literature, which must be without roots, without deep folk symbolism. And with few exceptions it must therefore be essentially empty. It can't be otherwise. Without Yiddish and without Hebrew it is impossible to-day to create in any other language any national Jewish culture worthy of the name.

I am also distressed when I hear people talk of Hebraising America at the cost of an ousted Yiddish—which means in effect completely Anglicising Jewish life in America. Before one Jewish house in America is Hebraised hundreds, thousands of Jewish houses will be Anglicised. There is a similar process at work in Israel in relation to the Yiddish language and to everything created by Jews in Golus. It affects not only the world of the writer, the poet, the novelist. It affects the world of every single individual Jew.

I know there have lately been big changes in certain circles in Hebrew literature in Israel in favour of Yiddish and in favour of our whole culture created in Golus, in favour of our entire Jewish existence, our Jewish life in

Golus. I am of course delighted with these changes. But then I read that a Hebrew writer in Israel has said in a public speech that with Yiddish the Golus Jew, the Ghetto Jew went to the gas chamber; and with Hebrew the Israeli Jew went to the Battle of Sinai. I know it was only one individual who uttered this nonsense. But I attach great importance to what is said by an individual, especially when he is speaking in public. I must add that I have heard from several others muttered undertones which are not far removed from this terrible nonsense, which goes together with a tendency to ignore, to go out of their way to avoid even mentioning the great Yiddish literature, which has played and is still playing a wonderful rôle to-day in the life of our people. It is only one remove from the speaker who can talk with contempt of the Jew who went with Yiddish to the gas chamber, thinking that in this way he was elevating the Israeli Jew who went to Sinai. He is mistaken. The affront to the Jew who went to the gas chamber is an affront also to the Jew who went to Sinai. For it is a lie to say that with Yiddish the Golus Jew went only to the gas chamber. With Yiddish the Golus Jew went also to the barricades and fought in the battles of the revolution. With Yiddish the Jew in the Warsaw Ghetto fought almost unarmed in the Rising against the powerful German army. The Baal Shem spoke Yiddish, this great Golus Jew who lit the fire of Chassidism. Rabbi Nachman Bratzlaver told his marvellous stories in Yiddish. Rabbi Levi Yitzchok Berditchever spoke in Yiddish direct to God. The Bratzlaver Chassidim in the Warsaw Ghetto Rising cried out in Yiddish, 'Jews, don't despair! Never despair!' We have in Yiddish created a great literature. And even if it should be true that the Golus Jew went with Yiddish only to the gas chamber, I can only say this: Bow down before this Yiddish! Bow down before this Golus Jew! Bow down and kiss the ground on which this Golus Jew trod on his holy way to the gas chamber!

Our Yiddish poetry has elevated these Jews who went to the gas chambers, rightly so, with great love—these bright, radiant Jews. This term, radiant Jews applied to the Jews who went to the gas chambers belongs to a wonderful contemporary Yiddish poet in America, Jacob Glatstein. And in Yiddish too a wonderful Yiddish poet in Israel, Abraham Sutzkever has sung with radiant words the march to Sinai.

ABRAHAM GOLOMB

Rambam or Maimonides*

I have been reading a fine piece of work about Rambam by a good Jewish scholar, a Jew with all his heart, who also knows the sources in their original. But he holds that 'the Yiddish language is already a lost cause in America', and that we must teach Jewishness to Jews in 'their' language. I read his work, which is really written with a great deal of knowledge, but I didn't find the Jewish Rambam there. What emerged was a work about the philosopher Maimonides. But there is a gulf between the Rambam and Maimonides. Very different associations are evoked in Jews by the name Rambam. The Rambam played an altogether other rôle in the history of the Jewish people. There are two different sets of culture involved in Rambam and in Maimonides, though they are the same one person.

For us the Rambam or Rashi or the Ari, or the Chai Adam and the like, whoever it is of our great men, is not a person with a biography, but a collective culture in Jewish life, a sum total, an aggregate of thoughts, ideas, formulations of Jewish Torahs. We call a man according to the works he has created, not the works according to the man. We say among Jews that someone is a grandson of the Tosafot Yom Tov, and we study the Chai Adam, not Rabbi Abraham Danziger. Not the works according to the man, but the man according to the works.

The name is no more, it seems, than a name, yet it is much more than a name. For eight hundred years Jews have associated very different problems and different solutions with the name Rambam. And all these problems never had anything to do with Maimonides. The Jewish people even created legends about Rambam. They have no relationship with Maimonides. Maimonides is one of many renowned philosophers. One of many. He belongs to the whole world. Maimonides is universal. But we had Rambam. Rambam belonged only to us. He suffered our sufferings, fought our fight, worried about Jewish worries, agonised over the tragic present of his people and trembled for its future—a Jew like all Jews, who at the same time with truly legendary powers bore up the heaven of Jewish eternity. In all this Maimonides played no part. A Jewish Jew, an ardent Jew undertook to tell the estranged, alienated sons of the Jewish people about the Jewish Rambam, and he wandered away to the non-Jewish Maimonides, forgot all about Rambam.

* Rambam, the initials of Rabbi Moses ben Maimon, known as Maimonides, born in 1135 in Cordova, died in 1204 in Cairo. Talmudist, philosopher and physician, one of the greatest men of Jewish religious thought, 'The Second Moses'.

138

True, the Rambam himself also sinned considerably with alien tongues. He wrote many of his works in Arabic. He sinned, and he was punished for his sin. This is how. Eternity is only for the Rambam. Only the books he wrote for Jews in a language for Jews or translated immediately into Hebrew for Jews.

But what was connected with Maimonides, what he left in Arabic, at that time the rich language of civilisation and culture for the great outside world, that has remained in museums and archives for a few specialised scholars. Rambam is eternal with the eternity of the Jewish people. Maimonides is eternal with the eternity of world philosophy. In the eternity of his people, in the Jewish eternity, the immortality of Jewishness, in that Maimonides has no part.

That is how this scholar lost Rambam and was left only with the non-Jewish Maimonides. Can a Jewish work in a non-Jewish language achieve immortality among Jews? Among the living Jewish people? It has never happened till now. The great *Wissenschaft des Judentums* in Germany is dead. Over a hundred and twenty years of creative Jewish work in Russian, the result of great faith and even greater pride in the 'language of Turgeniev' were lost, with all their works, and even the names of their creators. The English-speaking Jewish people too is gradually moving away from the Jewish work created in English.

What drove the Rambam to think and write, to go on working above and beyond all human strength? What took him to philosophy? Philosophy is the daughter of a quiet peaceful life. It is the possession of people whom God Himself released from the task of having to work. They had slaves to work for them. So they could sit and fill their time with art and with lofty thoughts, with disputations with the Muses. Such was not the lot of the Jewish Rambam. A son of the hunted and persecuted Jewish people, the Rambam himself had to flee to save his life. A son of a people longer lived than all its contemporary nations, that has never yet lived securely, a people whose symbol is the fiery furnace of its first ancestor, a people with a bent towards destruction, yet given the longest life, a son of a people forever wandering from land to land, so that the Wandering Jew became a legend among the nations, so the Jewish Rambam wandered, and in his wanderings worked and created. When he was able to stay quietly in one spot and pursue his medical profession (he became the physician to the Sultan Saladin in Cairo) he worked all the hours of the day and night, seeing patients even when he was in bed, exhausted by his labours. As the most eminent Jew of his age he was consulted by Jews in trouble everywhere, suffering from discrimination and persecution. As the recognised authority on Rabbinic law a stream of correspondence flowed to him asking for his views about disputed points of belief and practice.

In his time, the twelfth century, the ancient Jewish people had already created many Torahs. Two whole epochs had ended. And the Rambam knew, as the sages before him knew, that the Torah of the first epoch—the Tanach, the Bible—could no longer serve as an elixir of life. It belonged to an earlier period, was too far away, too remote from the real life of the day, too universal, not close enough to the folk. So the Jewish Rambam devoted himself to reducing and systematising the grand 'sea of the Talmud', and with his 'Strong Hand' he succeeded in creating his 'Second Talmud' (Mishna Torah and Yad). In his Foreword to this gigantic encyclopedia of the Talmudic Halacha he says that in these hard and bitter days there is no time and no opportunity for studying the entire Talmud—the Torah of the second epoch. Here his book would help. His book, which it is hard to believe could have been the work of one single man. One man—and the whole Torah!

What is philosophy? And what is Torah?

Philosophy—beautiful, profound, clear ideas about man and the world, the product of a few select exceptionally gifted individuals who stand higher, much higher than the entire people, the folk. That is philosophy.

And Torah? It is the distinctive life of the folk, for ourselves alone, otherness, different, peculiarly our own, spiritually and culturally independent, sovereign, though without territorial boundaries—that, formulated in principles and laws, in codexes for the near future—that is Torah. It was that which the Jewish Rambam created. And in all this Maimonides had no hand. Thus Rambam ensured the continued existence of his people, its immortality. And therefore he himself earned his private portion of immortality, his share in the eternity of the Jewish people.

Rambam, loaded with all the rich treasures of his people, is himself a pillar equal with Moses, equal with the Prophets, equal with Rabbi Akibah—a pillar of Jewish immortality. Yet he carries with him also a legend that for a time he had to wear a Moslem mask. But Rambam kept comforting and giving courage to the persecuted suffering Jews in Yemen and elsewhere, though he was himself being devoured by doubts about the continued existence of his people. (His Letter to the Jews of the South of France). He encouraged and comforted—with what? With faith and with the Halacha. With both together—in his Jewish creative work. With the creative work of Rambam. Not of Maimonides. That stayed in the Archives.

The Jewish people became a people and remained a people not with material possessions, but with its distinctive and for itself practices and way of life.

Not with property, but with proclivity, not with its possessions but with its qualities. In a foreign world, and yet for itself. Once this for our-selfness called itself Torah. Another time Halacha. And still later laws and ordinances. To-day it is falsely called religion.

This for our-selfness, otherness in our way of life was always confronted by various perils. The Prophets fought against the impulse to ape, to imitate. In those days it was called 'serving other gods', following in foreign ways. To-day we call it assimilation. Later came the danger of adopting alien theories, alien ideas. Not only forms of living, but also ideas.

In our own Land the first Prophets believed that the existence of our people was bound up with the existence of the Fatherland. Only after the Exile in Babylon one saw the complete, thorough assimilation of those who had remained in the Land. And those who had returned from Babylon, who had withstood the assimilationist pressure of the rich dominant cultures of the powerful nations, were gradually disillusioned about their belief in the holding power of the Land, of all material attributes for the existence of the people. Then those who were the bearers of Jewish immortality put up a fight for our own distinctive separate way of life. When belief in the worldly power of the State did not avail, they built a Jewishness independent of the Land, of the State, of Dynasties, of Kings who waged war against each other, and through civil war hastened the Destruction. Halacha (Way of Life) over everything! And the fight was also against the petrification of Jewishness, which wanted to keep and to guard only the ancient writings, but not the new folkish culture that had grown up. The war against the Saducees. In the Diaspora, which had already become powerful, the war for Jewish eternity took different forms. In Alexandria the Jews were nationalistically minded, religiously minded, but linguistically and culturally they assimilated. And that brought about their decline. The same happened with the Jews in the other Roman Provinces.

It was different in Babylon, where the Jews lived separately, retained their Jewish speech and their Jewish way of life.

Maybe objectively in regard to culture they were inferior to the Jews of the Roman Empire, but in their way of life they were more themselves. Linguistically they were not assimilated. And they were more active in forming and guarding their own separate distinctiveness, their for themselfness. This was how the Talmud was created—the greatest creation of the Jewish people, which laid the true foundation for Jewish immortality. There was one other important principle that the Talmud-creators observed. They did not seek the giants, the great creative geniuses who stand heaven-high above the ordinary folk; on the contrary, they tried to gather up and preserve all that the ordinary folk possessed. Even the Torahs of the great and the exalted were taken over as they were reflected in the folk mentality and the folk tradition. They had an unformulated generalisation: from the folk back to the folk, after sifting it, after working on it. Therefore what was not yet formulated, what was not yet written down, not defined, was more important than the old which was written and sanctified in the Torah of ancient times. To-day we would formulate it in this way: The culture of the other day is more important for the life of our people than the culture of days long ago, though this is holier and more accepted. At that time they formulated it differently, in what has to-day become distorted and misunderstood. They said the Torah on the tongue of the people is more important than the Torah in writing. Not the rich and elegant Greek language of philosophers and poets, nor the grand philosophy of the Greeks and their Jewish disciples like Philo and others; not these promoted Jewish existence, but the ordinary separate folk way of life of Babylon —this, thanks to the Talmud created Jewish immortality, even if some foolishnesses and confused legends sometimes occur there.

The Greek philosophy in its Arab form came to dominate the intellectual world. And three dangers at once faced Jewishness: from the Karaites, who wanted a Jewishness fixed in the ancient long ago, without the folkish still unfixed Talmudic element; from the renascent Greek philosophy; and from the continual threat of physical extermination. First Saadia Gaon demolished the Karaites; then Yehuda Halevi and after him the Rambam decisively routed the philosophy. And here Rambam was helped by the philosopher Maimonides. If the Rambam had himself to flee from enemies, he gave comfort and strength to all who were in physical danger. He rendered the philosophy harmless. He taught the perplexed, whom Greek philosophy had confused and bewildered and made them doubt Jewishness. With superhuman spiritual power he simultaneously challenged all the enemies of Jewishness. It is true as Professor Tchernowitz (Rav Zair) said, that the Rabbinic Jews overcame the Karaites only thanks to Rambam's achievements.

Maimonides was only a small part of the great Rambam. And in the same way the Rambam's medical writings too were only a part of that great teacher Rambam, the leader and the guide of the perplexed.

We must not interchange the two ideas expressed in the words Salvation and the World to Come. Salvation in the Christian religions means saving the soul from the fires of Gehenna. The World to Come means rewarding the soul with Paradise, Garden of Eden, in return for its services in this world. There is a gulf between the two conceptions, their development and their place in the life of the nations.

At first the Prophets beginning with Moses had only one thing in mind:

If the Jews live good lives things will go well with the people as a whole in the land which God has given them. Hard to find in the writings of the First Temple period anything that suggests reward and punishment for the individual. The words Garden of Eden and Gehenna (Gehenom) denoted actual geographical spots on this earth. They had nothing to do with the World to Come. The fortune or the misfortune of the individual played practically no part in the teachings of the Prophets. It was only on the eve of the Destruction that Jeremiah brought up the good of the individual. But still no other world.

What had happened? The worldly State was going to be destroyed. Jeremiah foresaw that clearly. Who would then watch over and secure the existence of the nation? Who would see to it that the people would not assimilate? And here Jeremiah came forward with his assurance that 'Each man shall die for his own iniquity'. Over the course of centuries this rôle of the individual in safeguarding the Jewishness of the community as a whole became a complete system of reward and punishment in the next world. The Garden of Eden and Gehenna were no longer geographical spots on this earth, but they were in the next world. And together with it grew up the theory of a Guardian Providence, with the belief in Resurrection, which is not hinted at anywhere in the Books of Moses. So the belief in individual reward and punishment arose as a means towards the larger aim—the continued existence of the nation. But the larger aim still remained the final goal and the purpose of Jewishness.

It was quite different with the Christians. They took over the belief in Paradise and Gehenna from the Jews as already completed. But for what purpose? What can the individual gain by keeping the commandments and not sinning? There were of course no national aims. The Christian religion has no relation to the national life. So the good or ill of the individual, what happens to his soul in the next world was left to be the final purpose of being good and devout. Salvation, saving the soul from the fires of Gehenna is the sole purpose of a good and religious life. So Salvation and the World to Come remained two different ideas with very different aims. And they must not be confused. The mistake is in using foreign languages.

It is not true to say that the Pharisees made a private personal share in the World to Come the essential of Jewishness. The fact is that the Pharisees looked for the Le-osud Lovo, the Hereafter, as the time of the coming of the Messiah for Jews and for the whole world. The Le-osud Lovo however can come only when Jews as a body, as a whole people will have earned it, when they will observe Jewishness. The private reward and punishment was only in the sense that every individual must take upon himself the yoke of the commandments and the sins, and why every individual should serve the interests of the entire community.

The trouble is with the foreign language, with taking a Christian interpretation as an original Jewish conception. Those who used Germanic words translated the Jewish ideas. Foreign words make Jewish ideas un-Jewish.

All who start writing about Jewishness in foreign languages, as the Jewish scholar with whom I began did, soon go on to the idea of God. As though Jewishness had to do only with God. For Christians Jewishness is indeed no more than a religion. But Jews must see it as something much bigger than religion. It took Jews a long time before they liberated themselves from all anthropomorphic conceptions about God. There are such anthropomorphisms in the older Books of the Bible. Afterwards when in place of the folkish tales and songs we got the individual writings of the Prophets and thinkers coming into the Bible, the primitive anthropomorphic conceptions were dropped. And the Talmudic sages thought even less anthropomorphically. The Rambam fought against all anthropomorphisms, against all that was material in relation to God. And the sources of his antimaterialism must be found in the Talmud, not in Aristotle. In Rambam, not in Maimonides.

Jews like to boast about great Jews, about world figures who may have had a Jewish grandfather. I don't know what there is so noteworthy about somebody having had a Jewish grandfather. What is characteristic in all this boasting is that it is mostly about people who are estranged from Jewishness. I have rarely heard such boasting about Rabbi Akibah, or about Rabbi Jochanan ben Zakkai, or Rashi, or Rabbi Israel Salanter, or the Chofetz Chaim, men who really were a summation of the Jewish spirit. But of course these are not known as the others are to the outside world.

The whole thing seems wrong—as though the Jewish people exists only because it presents the world with great men, that we live by virtue of the giants. You have to have tons of uranium to produce one gram of radium.

That is not a Jewish approach. It is the approach of those who take pride in Maimonides and forget the Rambam. The Jewish approach is to consider a man great according to how far he summates the spirit of the people. He reveals what is hidden, latent in the people. The Talmud loves to express profound ideas in the form of a legend. The Pentateuch tells us that when the Jews made a golden calf God's wrath waxed hot, and He said to Moses that He would destroy the entire Jewish people and would make of Moses a great nation. The Talmud says that Moses answered God: 'Better that Moses should die and a thousand like him, but no harm should come to the Jewish nation.' That is a deep truth. The soil is more than the fruit which grows on it.

Sanctuaries in Ruin

I don't mean to speak of the sufferings of the living Jews in the Ghettos and camps. I want to write about the ruins, about the dumb silence that cried aloud to me from the ruins.

I wandered through the empty streets of the Vilna Ghetto. Day after day I vanished in the labyrinth of connecting courtyards. I got entangled in them; I was caught as if in ancient catacombs, in caves full of prehistoric graves. The sense of bereavement fascinated me, the emptiness took away my speech. The seven narrow little streets hung on me like seven stone chains, but I didn't want to release myself from the chains; I wanted them to cut deeper still into my body, into my flesh. I felt the dark coagulated mass creeping into my soul from under the closed gates and doors. I felt the broken windows staring through my eyes. That's right, I told myself. I want to become a ruin.

It wasn't the first time. I had several times been wandering around, and lost in thought had come to the gate of the Ghetto—one step more and I would be on the other side. It is evening. It grows dark among the ruins sooner than anywhere else. The night begins here at a mound of junk, like a beggar without a home. From here the darkness creeps out down into the town, where people walk about, talk and laugh. Vilna is gradually beginning to live again. I hear in the distance a lot of heavy measured footfalls. These are soldiers marching. A military band starts to play. The soldiers sing. I say to myself: These who are marching and singing are the victors. But the Ghetto did not live to see the victory. I turn back hastily into the little streets. I am the watchman who must not go away. I hear the dumb silence asking me: 'Watchman, what of the night? Watchman, when will the night end?' And I, the spirit of the ruins, answer: 'Here the day has died, and it is desolate like the night. The week has here seven whole Sabbaths, but the Sabbath is here forever accursed, the Sabbath that Moses cursed in the cursings on Mount Ebal.'

What are you seeking here? What do you still expect? Ask the mysterious silence. I search. I mutter to myself. I expect the moon to rise and spin from its cold rays a spider web in my brain. I want to see the silver beard of an old Jew leaning out of a window. Perhaps a Jewish girl in a long white moonlight chemise will come fluttering down a collapsing staircase. She will with her long flowing black hair jump up out of her hiding place, will fall on me, weeping, and huddle against me. Perhaps someone has remained alive in his hiding place and won't believe that the Liberation has come. Let this man, gone mad with terror, come out and laugh with a wild laughter. He will laugh. And I will shudder. I want to be shattered. But the moon is afraid. The moon avoids the Ghetto. The images of the night spun from my dreams do not appear to me.

I go home, and gliding behind me comes the Ghetto, with all its broken windows, like blind people groping their way along the walls. Behind me is a procession of blank walls and black sooty chimneys. Hunched roofs and limping rooms follow me like cripples, but they don't stamp on the ground like soldiers with heavy boots. They rise and soar, and no one but I sees them. Around me electric lamps blazing, people streaming past on all sides, and I stand among them like a great rock lifting myself out of the water. I think: Who is calling me back? Have I left something behind in the Ghetto?

I go back. The little streets are dark. A lamp at the exit from the Ghetto sheds a red beam of light as if it had drawn a blood-stained knife against me. I hear something rustle at my feet. Crumpled leaves from Hebrew prayerbooks, scattered pages from sacred tomes. The wind dragged them out of the attics and cellars. Two years since the Ghetto was slaughtered, and these pages still wander around. It seems to me as if the dead came back at night to study their books and scrolls. The section they have studied, the pages they have read they tear out, and give them to the wind to give to me, who have come back from my wandering—so that I should see what has happened to the People of the Book. I pick up the pages. I stuff them into my pockets. I shall straighten them out in my room, smoothe them. I may recognise the finger that folded and crumpled them. I shall perhaps hear the voice of the scholar who broke into the dispute of Abaye with Rabbath in the Gemarrah. Perhaps the tears that drenched the Techinas will live again for me; perhaps my own boyhood face will shine out as so many years past, and I will be able to go on dreaming over a book of wonder tales.

Do you remember, I say to myself, do you remember this story that you read when you were young? A pious Jew got lost on a Friday night in a forest. The sun was setting, and the Jew wept with grief that he would not be able to keep the Sabbath. Then he saw between the trees the lights of a palace. An old man came towards him and beckoned without a word to the lost man to follow him. He led him to a fragrant stream to bathe, to purify himself for the Sabbath. He gave him precious garments to put on for the Sabbath. The guest wanted to question him, to ask something, but the guardian of the palace motioned to him to be silent. He took him into the first chamber, that sparkled with silver and gold and precious stones. He conducted him to a second chamber, where menorahs and chandeliers shone with the brightness of the seven lights of the six days of Creation. Dazzled the guest went from chamber to chamber, each more richly and wonderfully furnished than the one before. In the seventh, the last chamber, seven old men with white beards came towards him, and they looked like a forest with snow-covered oak trees. They greeted him, and said that now he had come there was a minyan. He couldn't understand—there were seven old men. With him there were eight. With the old man who had met him in the forest, nine. He saw no tenth. But he felt that the tenth was everywhere, like the radiant Shechina, and he was filled with awe. But the ordinary fear that makes a man's limbs tremble was not in his heart. He saw an old man with a kingly crown go and stand at the reading desk, and he sang the Sabbath evening service with such sweetness as though he were the Psalmist. After the service the guest was told to wash his hands, and he ate meat which had the taste of the Great Ox, and he drank wine which had the taste of the Heavenly Wine. So he spent the whole Sabbath with the old men, praying and singing table hymns, and studying holy lore. And if he attempted to say one word of ordinary talk they motioned to him to be silent. When the Sabbath ended he was given such fragrant herbs to smell that they had the scent of the Tree of Life. Then the same first old man took him to the forest and murmured in his ear that he had been in the Garden of Eden, that the old men were Abraham, Isaac and Jacob, Moses and Aaron, David and Solomon. And he, the servant of the Sanctuary, was Eliezer, Abraham's servant. And the tenth who made the minyan was the Holy One, Blessed be He Himself. The palace vanished and instead of the seven chambers in the palace he found himself in—the seven bereaved little streets of the Vilna ghetto. And the Patriarchs are the shades of the slaughtered. And the prayers he had heard were those in the torn pages at his feet.

That was how I spent my nights and days in 'The Big Ghetto' as it was called. I knew I still had to endure the agony of absorbing into myself 'The Little Ghetto'. The two were divided by the 'German Street' and by a guard of living Germans. 'The Little Ghetto' consisted of the Synagogue courtyard and several adjoining little streets. The Jews who had lived there were massacred in 1941. The whole area had been empty for four years.

I went there the first day of Rosh Hashona. The autumn sun in the midst of a clear blue sky spread pure gold. Around the Synagogue courtyard all was happily peaceful and empty as if all the Jews were assembled in the different little sanctuaries there, waiting with bated breath for the sound of the shofar. On the wall there was a poster from before the war: 'Buy Tozereth Haaretz!' (Buy Palestine Goods) signed 'Women's Federation'. Where the shops were, as if to infuriate the shopkeepers, a slogan with red letters: 'Long Live the Jewish Workers' Party'. The slogan of the Jewish Socialist Bund on the eve of the Jewish Community elections in 1939. Next to it a screaming Revisionist slogan: 'With Blood and Battle for Freedom in Palestine!' On the iron gate a signboard: 'Baths in the Synagogue Courtyard'. I shudder—the first time that terrible shuddering I wanted. I shut my eyes. Is it perhaps all a bad dream? I feel the sunbeams on my face, but I am cold. The sunshine silence steals into my bones like a frost. I open my eyes and see a whole row of broken windows in the Strashun Library. From the building opposite a huge shadow falls on the wall with the posters like a black cloth hung over a mirror in a house of the dead.

I crawl over great heaps of rubble into the Synagogue Square. I want to go up to the Vilna Gaon's little *klaus*. The stairs have been torn away as if the ladder of Jacob's dream had been knocked over. I look up to the black space of the *klaus*. Over the entrance the sign is still there: 'The Beth Hamedrash of the Gaon Reb Elijah, his Memory for a Blessing'. The sign hangs over the entrance like a bird that has returned to its nest and finds its tree chopped down. Frightened by the evening dark in the forest the bird utters no sound but stays hanging on its exhausted wings in the air.

I shudder. I slip and fall. I look around with such fear as if the dynamite the Germans had placed under a Jewish house several years back had only just exploded. I knew Vilna was in ruins. I knew no one was left. But that the Beth Hamedrash of the Gaon could crash, that I had not imagined possible. From childhood Vilna was for me interwoven with the legend of the Gaon, as fire is with light. So I looked at the devastated building where the Gaon had sat and studied as though it was only now that I realised that Vilna was destroyed.

'The seed of Israel will not perish.' I thought I heard a voice, I thought someone was trying to help me to my feet. But it was hard to rise from the heap of lumber. So I lay there and recalled my last hour in Vilna before I fled. The streets were swamped with people. The young strode along at such a pace as if they were trying to eat up the miles. Hardly touched the ground. A Jew with a pack was taking leave of his wife. Children held on to his pack, crying. A man ran by with a baby in his arms. Behind him a starved-looking young woman running, and unable to catch up with him. Behind her an old woman, running, yet all the time falling farther behind. Wringing her hands, and crying: 'Daughter mine, dear daughter, where are you running to? The Vilna Gaon blessed Vilna that it will never be destroyed!'

I rise with difficulty, and drag myself on further. Here is the gravediggers' little Synagogue—now itself a grave. God wants His houses of worship to soar in the sky like clouds, so that we should not be able to get to them. I look up. That was where the bimah stood. I remember how, still a young boy, I sat one Ticha b'Av in my stockinged feet on the bimah on a low stool, reading Lamentations aloud to the assembled worshippers in this Synagogue. No bimah left now. No more this little boy who had lamented, 'God is righteous; For I have rebelled against His word'. On the eastern wall, high up where the Ark of the Law stood, one word, beaten in copper, has remained: 'Onochi' (I).

I want to cry out, but my breath is stone. I feel my feet are being taken away from me. A paralysis creeps nearer to my heart. There is deathly silence all round me, and over the ruins one flaming word, the first word of the First Commandment of the Ten Commandments—'I'. 'I am the Lord thy God.' Or it is perhaps the passage in Isaiah: 'I am He who comforts you'. Or perhaps: 'I am He who is guilty'?

I shudder at the thought. The 'Onochi' seems to me moving. It will soon fly down like an eagle and peck out my eyes for the blasphemy. I stand open-mouthed, as in my boyhood in this Synagogue on Yom Kippur when the whole congregation fell Korim, prostrate on the ground before God. I look at the heaps of earth from the ruins of the Vilna Synagogue Square, and they are to me like the bowed backs of grey-haired old Jews kneeling during the recital of the service of the High Priest. I turn away, and see the 'Old Synagogue'. Ancient Fane, it is of you that the Prophet laments: 'God has cast off His altar. He has abhorred His sanctuary. He has given up into the hand of the enemy the walls of the palaces'. Your front wall is torn down, like your silken curtain that hung before the Ark. The heathen and the uncircumcised see how your tottering pillars try to hold up your vaulted ceiling, and the adversaries laugh. Ancient Fane, are you waiting for a Samson to shake your pillars and hurl them down to bury the blasphemers, the plunderers? They are climbing up your windows to take away the wooden frames. They are breaking down the oaken doors of your walled-in bookcases. Your carved lions and deer they tear out, set fire to them and cook their pots of unclean food on them. What the German bird of prey left our neighbours the Edomites, the Poles and Lithuanians have taken away. Your ruins look to me like towering marble rocks with a gleaming crown of gold and snow. To my eyes you are Mount Nebo where Moses died. You look like Mount Moriah on which the Temple stood. Your crumbled walls bar my way, so that I cannot pass to the other side. But there is more Synagogue Square there, more tortured holy soil. It is impossible to get there; therefore I want to get there. To plant my foot there. Where none can reach, all the deep mysteries lie open.

I climb over heaps of stones and iron girders hanging in space. I crawl through holes and crevices. I am smothered with plaster and dust. I emerge into the second half of the Synagogue Square. I am surrounded with wild prickly weeds. Plants spring out of the walls, twist and twine themselves around the empty buildings, obscuring the names of the little synagogues—

<header>Chaim Grade</header>

'Chevra Poalim', 'Tifferath Bachurim', 'Kaidonover Shtibl', so that they should not be shamed by their nakedness. The Vilna Beth Midrashim did not experience the miracle that came to the gates of the Temple in Jerusalem, which sank into the ground. But the inscriptions on the buildings refuse to be hidden by the vegetation; the letters burn and fall like sparks on my face. We were built, these small synagogues tell me, in the year 5,622, in 5,632, in 5,693, in 5,509. 'Here is a grave', cry these dumb synagogues, 'here lie buried the prayers of Jews for centuries.'

Here is the Old-New Synagogue. To keep it from falling it was propped up with an outside wall; the worshippers inside held it up with their prayers. The Synagogue was built by the great philanthropist Yehuda Sapora Vedeina, who bequeathed a fortune to the Synagogue on condition that his son-in-law, Reb Samuel, would become the Vilna Rav. The wardens of the Synagogue agreed—but after the father-in-law died they found themselves in conflict with the son-in-law. And they so humiliated the Rabbi that he fled from the town. When he died the community repented what they had done to him, and out of respect for him abolished the title Ab Beth Din. They put a stone beside the Holy Ark in the Town Synagogue, so that no one should sit in the place of the last Vilna Rav. Now all Vilna is a gravestone for the last Jew. In the place of the Jews Gentiles sit now like crows in the ruins.

It seems to me that the vegetation has grown higher in the time that I have stood here in the midst of it. The plants enfold and entangle me, to stop me from getting out again. I tear myself free and try to climb back. But bricks from the ancient Synagogue fall on me, as though God had heard the prayer of the ruin—if no Samson comes the Almighty Himself will break down His House, that the robbers should no longer defile and plunder it. It frightens me. Must I remain a captive here, imprisoned between falling walls? Near the ground I see the windows of the back of the Vilna Town Synagogue. I'll drop in through them, I tell myself. I will run through the Synagogue and go down the front steps and so get out.

I walk through the Synagogue with bowed head. I want to see no more. I have filled myself enough with the ashes of the ruins. The brass handrails of the front staircase shine as they did in the old festive days when the people used to crowd and jostle to hear the cantor and his choir. I look up to the vestibule, and see the charity collecting boxes still intact, collecting boxes for the sick, for the Home for the Aged, for poor students, for Reb Meir Baal Ha'Nes. The emptiness of the Synagogue blows at my back like the Arctic Ocean. I stand frozen. I can't move away. I turn slowly and see—the Synagogue has grown, like a corpse whose nails and hair still grow. Without the rows of seats one behind the other the Synagogue looks twice as big, more

<footer>150</footer>

spacious. The four huge pillars round the Balemar and the colonnade of veined marble on the bimah look like fountains flowing together in semi-arcs. The gratings of the women's synagogue burn in the sunset like bars of gold. In the place of the sunset clock that used to hang in the west there is now a flaming real sunset like a polished mirror. Its rays cut through the length of the Synagogue, till the whole bunch of rays falls into the black depth of the torn-out Holy Ark. And in the black depth of the eastern wall there is a shimmer and a sparkle as though a great diamond were hanging in the empty space of the broken sanctuary. The diamond floats out of its hiding place and comes nearer to me, as though it wanted to suck me in. It shines with all the fires of the stolen crowns of the Scrolls of the Law. It is radiant with all the radiance of the torn mantles of the Scrolls, embroidered with silver and purple thread, and studded with gems. I step back from the brightness of the Shechina floating towards me—and immediately the diamond is extinguished. Over the Omud where David's harp and the holy creatures hung I see an orphaned text: 'And you shall put my Name upon the children of Israel, and I will bless them'. I stare up to the steps of the Holy Ark, where I would have looked for the Cohanim. How can the Cohanim come and bless us with the priestly blessing if their bodies have been burned? Should I perhaps go and waken the Golem of clay that the Vilna Gaon made? The Golem lies in the attic of the Synagogue, buried under a heap of torn pages from sacred tomes. How can I get to the attic when the wooden stair leading to it has fallen down? And why should I wake the legend of the clay Golem from its century-old sleep? Whom will he save now if he could not save them before?

It grows dark. I start to go and stop, frozen. I hear a strange sound. I feel eerie. I make an effort and look round. There is something dripping from the ceiling, slowly and monotonously, like in a cave in the mountains. There has been no rain in Vilna for months. Is this rain water that has collected under the roof during the whole past year or two years? There is a coagulated silence all round; ice-cold drops fall on the stone floor, one by one, one by one, and their echo is full of sadness and sorrow. They fall on my head and reverberate in my skull. A chill runs through my bones. I shudder at each drop, as though a needle had been stuck through my brain, as though a slithery snake were gliding over my spine. It is the tears of Vilna Jews that are dripping down. They have gathered in the roof of the old Vilna Synagogue, and they are telling me what happened:

'You have returned from far distances, with a hidden question in your heart. You fled northward and lived among an alien people skilled in the arts of war. They went to war with the Germans, their enemy who attacked them from the west. The wild power of the victors amazed you. And you demand from us, Power! You ask, Why did you not resist? You saved your life. Now you want us, the dead, to save your supposed honour, so that you can boast to the world that you are the last of the slaughtered heroes. You want us to answer the strong and powerful people who live by the sword, to say why we did not take revenge. Don't you know we were deceived? Those villains sent traitors to us to persuade us that by working we would save ourselves from death. Nobody came back from the grave. The woods round Ponar have hidden from the birds the secret of the mass graves. The overseers of our own nation, so that they might live one day longer than we, comforted us after each cruel attack, saying it was the last. We had little children, and wives and aged parents. We were tortured and tormented to make us lose our human dignity. We were stripped naked, to make us break down under the shame. We ran to the pit under a hail of blows and laughter. We ran. For do you know what it means to lie in a field surrounded with hangmen and see others led to their death, with you left till later? What a release it is to die just one moment sooner. And you demand from us heroism, that we should with our dead hands hold up your dignity among the nations of the world who do not prostrate themselves before suffering, only before strength and power.

'And you, strong-heart, what did you do while we were dying? And your brothers in the far-off places in the free world, what did they do? Did they go on their knees and plead with the nations to save us? Why did you not lie down in the streets so that the world should not pass by while we were slaughtered with silence? Why did you not rend your garments every day, every hour, every minute? You showed no Jewish self-sacrifice for us, but from us you demand the might and the strength of Esau! Who says we are guilty because we were weak has no compassion in his heart.Who says we sinned, blasphemes. It is Rosh Hashona to-day. Pray for us. Our lives were broken. Our pages torn out.'

That was what the drops said as they fell from the ceiling and wept into me, drop by drop, word by word. Till it was dark and a wind began to howl from all sides in the great empty stone Synagogue. But I did not go away. I stood nailed to the spot, as if I had after long searching found the hiding place of the spirits who were tormenting me.

'Leave me alone! Leave me alone!' I muttered. 'How many more yellowing folios do you want me to swallow? How often must I tear my fingers against rusty nails? How much more ash do you want me to put on my lips and drink into my lungs? How many times do you want me to curse the world when I see a Jewish small town that has remained whole? The graveyard is intact, the shops are intact, but the shopkeepers who stand at the doors are Gentiles. How many texts do you want to cut themselves into my mind and lie in the folds and creases of my face? I lift my head and look for them, the words, the letters that were left hanging on the ceilings of the synagogues, the single limbs of a torn body; but in the ghetto prison I had to bend down to the ground to read what a small Jewish boy had scratched on the wall: 'Yossele is preparing to go to Ponar'. 'Leave me alone! Leave me alone!'

But the ruins would not leave me alone. On Yom Kippur, on Kol Nidrei night I went to the Great Synagogue, the only one left whole in Vilna. Once Maskilim and enlightened rich folk used to worship there. The bimah stood by the Holy Ark as in a Reform Temple, and the wardens wore short tallithim like scarves. Now the entire remnant that has remained gathers there—the partisans from the forests, those who crept out of their hiding places, those who returned from Russia. They all twined themselves together into one bitter cry as the flames of the Yorzeit candles lighted for the dead fused into one. I did not say the Kol Nidrei. I stood among the congregation dumb and strange. Before my eyes stood the ruined Synagogue Square at night.

On Yom Kippur day, just before noon, when the entire congregation was for a moment silent, before it burst out into the wail of the Yizkor, I ran out of the Great Synagogue like one fleeing from a flood. Now, I said, is the right time to go to the Beth Hamedrash of Reb Saul Katznelenbogen in the Yatkaver Street. There I had played as a child among the seats where the learned sat. There every path was blocked with shelves of books. There worshipped the most pious and devout. In Reb Saul's Beth Hamedrash so much Torah was studied day and night that the benches were treif, unclean with the melted tallow from the candles. But their hearts were kosher, clean. So a great preacher had once said.

I pushed with wild force against the barred door. It groaned and creaked like a wooden gibbet when the body is taken down. In the dead ghetto the silence roared, as if the ruins were outraged because I was desecrating Yom Kippur. I went on pushing with fury till the rotting boards gave way. I went, in, into the Beth Hamedrash. A ruin, like all the sanctuaries. In the northwest corner a plaque had remained on the wall, whose wording I remembered from my boyhood: 'The woman Libbe, daughter of Reb Ezriel Hellin, left three thousand roubles for keeping up the studying in the Beth Hamedrash'. I walked across the little synagogue and saw a second plaque on the wall: 'This stone is a memorial for Reb Joseph Shragai Trakinitzky, who in this Beth Hamedrash pitched his tent for Torah and prayer for nearly fifty years. He was warden here for forty years. Reb Joseph Shragai died Yom Kippur in the town Seattle, in America, where he was passing on his way to Palestine'. 'Indeed', I addressed the plaque, 'it is as the Gemarrah says: "The feet of a man are surety for him. They lead him where the Angel of Death waits for him." '

I looked to the bimah where on Sabbaths and festivals the Warden Reb Shragai stood allotting the Aliyas. I thought of another Jew who had stood on that bimah, the shammas Reb Dov Ber Galein. Reb Dov was shammas and shocket. A terrible zealot. His thick black beard and big black eyes blazed with anger because of the worldly Jews. He made his sons rabbis, and held himself in high esteem for that. He was even prouder that the Chofetz Chaim stayed in his house. When I stopped studying in the Beth Hamedrash and he saw me in the street he turned his head away. On Yom Kippur he stood on the bimah and sold the honour of opening the Ark to the highest bidder.

I look at the bimah, and a cry bursts from my throat, a strangled cry as if someone were throttling me. Twenty thousand Jews were there to open the Holy Ark. But the gate of Heaven did not open. Forty thousand Jews to open the Holy Ark. But the Gates of Mercy remained closed. Seventy thousand Jews perished. Jewish communities vied with each other—who would offer more victims? Yet none of them succeeded in getting the Gates of Mercy to open. Reb Ber, bring down your hand on the reading desk: 'Enough victims! Turn your black burning beard and your black burning eyes towards me and burn me up for my reproach and my scorn, Reb Ber!'

The Beth Hamedrash is empty. Silence hovers over it. I go slowly down the steps. Where shall I go? What shall I do? All the Jews have been slain, but their Yom Kippur sits in me, weeps in me, yet I cannot pray, neither for them nor for myself. Why did I run away from the remnant of the survivors? Why don't I go to rejoice with the last few Jews who were saved?

Another small synagogue—the minyan in the Shavel Street, where poor artisans worshipped and hard-worked shopkeepers used to drop in to say Kaddish. When I was a young student I came to this Beth Hamedrash seldom. I sat among the great scholars in Reb Saul's klaus and dreamed of becoming one of them. I crawl up to Yogiche's klaus, and stop in amazement. Out of the grubbed-up ground a whole field of yellow roses has grown. The flowers reach above my head. Radiant golden light, as though a thousand suns were circling round each other. They sway with a yearning happiness as though the souls of those poor Jews who worshipped there had been reincarnated in the yellow roses. They shake their heads towards the empty Ark of the Law, as if the open sanctuary were full of Scrolls of the Law.

I wept silently. I closed my eyes and felt I was being woven into the sweet silence. I felt my face wet with tears. My pain began to thaw like ice. I made no sound, but smiled to myself and wiped the sweat from my brow. With tottering steps I came down the stairs, not to waken the prayerful silence of the glowing yellow roses at the hour of Nielah.

SHOLEM ASCH

Triumphal March

At last, at last, at last. After all those years of pain and grief and anger the tormented population of the martyr town Warsaw crept out of their graves and out of their holes to welcome their liberators. The Red Army with the Polish Liberation Army and the heroes of the partisan movement, of all parties and all trends, marched into Warsaw in a triumphal march, from the Mokotov side, from the Vistula, along the broad tree-lined Uyazdovska Avenue through Krakovskie Przedmiescie into the heart of Warsaw.

All the church bells were ringing. What was their tune? Chopin's Funeral March. In memory of all the dead. The military bands too played it, the Funeral March, for on the day of liberation Warsaw could not forget—the liberation armies marched into Warsaw with bowed heads, to the strains of Chopin's Funeral March.

There is no city where Chopin's Funeral March is so fitting as in Warsaw, in that part of Warsaw through which the liberation armies march. The Warsaw streets sing to it, accompanied by the ringing of the church bells, the sound of the trumpets and the beat of the drums.

Drawn by the music and the marching a part of Warsaw's population appeared in the streets that had not been seen for a long time in the Warsaw streets. They have come to welcome the liberation armies. They are natives of Warsaw, people who had lived here, were brought up here for centuries—the Jews, a native, inalienable part of Warsaw life. The Jews came—not only from the Nalevkis, not only from Krochmalna, Tvarda, Grzybov, Novolipa, Lesna, from all the Jewish streets. They came soaring out of the air. One saw them, yet did not see them. They were here, filling the Warsaw streets. They go to meet the marching armies, streaming towards them, out of all the side streets; they come from Praga, from the Jerusalemska Avenue, through the adjoining streets, from Marszalkovska, from the Old Market and the Franciszkana—to meet the marching armies.

It seemed that the church bells were ringing for them, the military bands playing for them. They move to the beat of the Funeral March. First come 170 virgins, young girls between ten and eighteen, the youngest first, the older following with their teachers. All dressed in white, with veils over their faces, and lighted tapers in their hands. Their feet do not seem to touch the ground as they come nearer, till they rise up and vanish in the heights.

After them, alone, comes Dr. Korczak. He has grown taller and thinner.

His face shines with celestial joy. In each arm he holds a child, two small Jewish children with earlocks and silk skull caps and fringes showing from under the spencers that their mothers had put on them for the occasion.

And the Warsaw population does not jeer, does not sneer at these Jewish faces, at their earlocks, at their fringes. The Warsaw population fall to their knees on the pavement when Dr. Korczak, the saint, passes with the two Jewish children in his arms, followed by a long procession of orphan children from his Home. Then more children, row after row, children from the Medem Sanatorium, with their teachers, all perished in the gas ovens, where they were burned. Look at their faces. Pale. But their cheeks are red. I will tell you a secret—they are consumptive. That is why their eye-balls blaze like stars in the sky. Some wear skull caps and earlocks, and the fringes show from under their spencers. But most of them are modern, wearing the peaked Jewish caps. Look at their hands, so thin, so thin. They carry banners, red banners with slogans of the good times coming; what a wonderful world it will be when Messiah comes—I mean the social revolution. They are singing, with husky voices, from their sunken tubercular chests; they are singing the Shevuah, the oath they swore when they were driven to their death in the gas chambers.

Their parents have come, out of their graves, from the Franciszkana, where the poorest of the poor lived, fathers and mothers, Warsaw Chassidim, Warsaw load-carriers, mothers with sheitels, happy to see their children, as when they used to wait for them at the Otwock Railway Station, coming back home from their holiday.

Behind them come armies of children, children from good homes, with good shoes and coats, the girls with pig-tails, children in silk gaberdines, and children ragged and barefoot, or wearing their parents' shoes, torn shoes, shoes too big for them. But all the children have wings. And they fly from all directions, to welcome the liberation armies. Then suddenly they rise in the air and are gone, like the Moishelech and Shloimelech in Bialik's poem.

Next come a group of the most venerated Rabbis of Poland, headed by the Warsaw Dayanim. Who wasn't there? Torah like the waters of the sea, the Gaons of the generation, scholars whose names resound far and wide, the heads of world famous Polish Yeshivas, great Chassidic Rebbes with their followers, talking Torah, praying, studying, some wear Tallith and Tephilin and hold prayer books and works of Hebrew learning in their hands; all with shining eyes, full of ecstasy and devotion, just as they went to their death. You can see in their faces their yearning to join themselves to God's Shechina. Some walk with their heads in heaven, their eyes closed, their hands uplifted, lost in God's Oneness. The Shechina shines from their faces. Their eyes are filled with the light of God which they saw at the moment of their death.

And marvellous! The Warsaw population does not scoff and mock, no one twists his coat tail into a pig's ear in derision, no one cries: 'Dirty Jews! Go to Palestine!' No one calls: 'Beilis!' But all, young and old, fall to their knees, bow their heads, lift their arms to heaven. Some burst into tears, cross themselves, stretch out their hands to the Rabbis: 'Forgive us, holy Rabbis, for the indignities and the shame to which we subjected you, for the wrongs we committed against you. We did not know how to value you'.

After the Rabbis Hebrew writers, artists, journalists on the big Yiddish papers, Professors in the Institute of Jewish Studies attached to the Tlomacka Street Synagogue, the teachers of the Hebrew High Schools, the teachers of the Yiddish Schools, the whole Jewish intelligentsia of Warsaw.

Who wasn't there? At their head Hillel Zeitlin, the spiritual leader of religious Polish Jewry, the man who was all spirit, whose religious influence on our youth was powerful. Even his outward form was that of a Prophet. His red-grey hair, his noble features, his red beard, and his dreamy eyes always staring far away into hidden worlds. A sacred fire burned in him. That was how they saw him last, going to his death. He is talking to his colleagues. They listen to him eagerly, as he expounds a Midrash, full of deep meaning, a passage from the Zohar, fitting for this present day.

Immediately after him comes Professor Balaban, scholar and historian. His monumental works on Lemberg and Cracow, his 'Frank and the Frankists', his hundreds of essays on Jewish history have made him the great historian of Polish Jewry. He is talking to Dr. Schipper: 'Tell me, Dr. Schipper, why must you busy yourself with politics? You are a scholar. Your work is research into Jewish economic and cultural life. Leave politics to Deputy Gruenbaum. Let him lead the Jewish Parliamentary Club. Please, Dr. Schipper!'

Professor Stein, that modest unassuming scholar, walks quietly behind him, keeping carefully out of everybody's way, trying not to attract attention. Greek scholars who know half as much as he does have a world reputation. His Hebrew monograph on the Greek Jew Philo is a monumental work.

There are the younger men, my own colleagues, writers, poets, brothers of the pen. Oh, my dear colleagues, my brothers, if I had been with you I would have found myself together with you. But I am with you. I am here with you to meet the marching liberation armies.

My colleagues, my brothers, Hitler is dead. We are dancing on Hitler's grave, as Itzik Feffer sings. We may do it, brothers! Feffer is one of us. Come, let us all hold hands. We are all colleagues. We all belong to the same shelf of books. One will take us in, one will throw us out—they have all died with you, and we all live with you in Jewish literature, in the Jewish spirit.

Next comes the Warsaw Jewish population, the people. Look at them! The elite, the aristocracy, the big merchants of the Nalevkis, of Gesia, the worshippers in the Tlomacka Synagogue, with their high hats, the Jews of the Mosaic faith, who preach in Polish on Yom Kippur, the Zionists of the Nozik Synagogue, merchants, bankers, currency brokers, shipping agents, metal merchants. Look at them—half to God, half to man. They keep the 'Hazefirah' going, they buy the Shekel, but they send their own sons to Polish High Schools, because of their career, and their daughters to Polish finishing schools. But I must not criticise now. That is all past. Now we are all going to welcome the liberating armies, which are settling accounts with Hitler.

We all sit at the same table. Come here, assimilationist Jews, Zionist Jews, all sorts of Jews. Make room! The Bund is coming, the old and the young, the shoemakers, the shoe-upper machinists, with walking sticks, with rubberised collars, weavers with sunken breasts. Clerks and book-keepers, who on 200 zloty a month keep a sick mother and a mother-in-law, yet manage to contribute to the Party, and to the Jewish Community. Hungry by day, cold by night, living with hope, with the faith of the idea which the Party gives. Please don't quarrel with your brothers of the Poale Zion, I beg you. Look, here they come, Poale Zionists of all trends, from the Hashomer Hazair to Zerubabel's left, to those who are under Gruenbaum's and Schipper's influence. Don't quarrel! To-day we all march together. Look! You have all sprouted wings. We could no longer stay on earth, so we are all together in heaven. At least, in the same gas oven, all burned to death together. Hitler threw us all into the gas oven. Jewish history has lifted us all up to heaven.

Here come the ordinary folk, the common people. Who isn't here? The streets are black with them. A sea of heads and hands. Look at the heads— Chassidic shtreimels, velvet hats, small peaked caps, all sorts of hats, and the modernists bare-headed. The vegetarians are here, the nature-lovers. Look, look, all Warsaw is here! Chassidim, just like at the Vienna Station when the Gerer Rebbe was leaving to take the cure at a spa. Hats and bare heads, like at a Bundist demonstration on the First of May. Here are the load-carriers from Krochmalna and from Grzybov, with coils of rope slung round their waist and over their backs, their teeth missing, knocked out in street fights, with oaths and swear words on their lips: 'I'll break that Hitler's bones, I will! I'll rip his bloody guts out!'

And quiet, soft-spoken, pious Jews. A Sochachev Chassid, with a smile on his lips over his long flowing beard, stands swaying to and fro, as if in prayer in his Rebbe's court. They are all here. Here are the women. Look at them! Bonnets and coifs and sheitels. Hats with feathers, and many with their own hair. Paris models and berets. Women of the Sabbath Observance League, who go from door to door collecting for Sabbath loaves for the poor, and women of the aristocracy, of the societies for helping the poor and the sick and the old. Some have babies in their arms, the poor have them at their breasts, and some still have them in their wombs. They are all here, they have all come, filling the streets, which are densely packed with them. No room to drop a pin.

Last of all, a column in good marching order, as if on parade, rank on rank—no uniforms, half-naked, their bodies full of wounds. Stand still, hold your breath, bow your heads before these hero-martyrs. General Klepfish at their head, a hole in his heart torn open by a German bullet, which he shows proudly, like a medal. He has a revolver in his hand. He heads the march. Two adjutants on his right and left, Shlomo of the Hashomer Hazair and Itzik the Bolshevik. I knew them both. Like Klepfish, the Bundist, they were neither of them proletarians. They came of good families. One day I shall tell you their family tree. Now I must tell you of the march they are leading. In front goes the flag that flew to the last minute, the blue and white, riddled with bullet holes, torn in shreds, spattered with blood. Now it is carried high, with pride and honour. No enemy's hand defiled it. It flew till the last breath of its defenders, and then was consumed in the flames. When the Germans reached it, Yekel, the shoe-upper machinist, a member of the Young Bund, lying mortally wounded, pressed it to his breast, stained it with his blood, and jumped with it into the flames. He brought the flag with him on high, untouched by a German hand. Now he bears it aloft, Yekel, the shoe-upper machinist, his breast torn open by a German bullet.

On either side, escorting the flag he carries, Nechome, the Chalutza, and Borenstein the Communist. Nechome the Chalutza kept encouraging the others—Am Yisroel Chai! When the ammunition ran out, and her comrades lay dying in pools of blood, her Am Yisroel Chai was the last cry they heard.

Borenstein the Communist, whose Party name was Vicher, which means stormwind, a thin, pale, shrivelled young man, went like a storm through the German ranks. He stole like a shadow through the gates, smuggling revolvers and bullets into the Ghetto. The Germans caught him in the end, and made a sieve of his body. Now he has bound up all his wounds, and goes limping along with a smile of victory, with the banner. All his wounds inflicted by the Germans have been patched up, only his leg which was twisted in a Polish concentration camp, where they put him as a 'Jew-Bolshevik', has stayed as it was.

So, united, Zionist, Bundist, Communist round the Jewish flag of the Battle of the Warsaw Ghetto they now come marching down the pages of

Jewish history, after their death. A warning for the present, consolation for the future.

The martyr-heroes march together in closed ranks, united as they were when they fought together, in the streets, in the bunkers, in the cellars, on the roofs, Zionist, Bundist, Communist, religious Jew, Chassid and assimilationist, all together, each marked with the seal of Kidush Hashem by God's angels. Each wears the distinction of German knife and bullet wounds, all dripping blood as they go. It is the same blood from them all, Bundist, Zionist, Communist, religious Jew—all Jewish blood. The same devil shed it all. The same enemy, the same vengeance, the same triumph, the same liberation and redemption. The past is one, and the future is one. Am Yisroel Chai!

Then by herself, alone, comes a Jewish mother, tall, wrapped in the folds of a black mantle, carrying a dead child in her arms; she weeps quietly to herself, like a dove. Like Mother Rachel she complains to God. She has only one complaint: 'Abraham was only tried. From me you took the full sacrifice'. That is all she has to say.

This was the end of the march of the dead. Then came the march of the living.

Suddenly everything vanished. Like a dream. Gone were the crowds, the sea of faces had disappeared as though they had never been there. The whole Jewish population of Warsaw had flown up into the air, and left the earth free. The air was silent. Only the bells went on ringing to the tune of Chopin's Funeral March, echoing the tramp of the entering liberation armies.

Out of a side street came a small group of people with torn clothes, barefoot, with dishevelled hair. Mothers looking like madwomen, with flaming eyes and sick children in their arms, or leading them by the hand. Fathers, wild-eyed, with flying hair and beards, rifles slung over their shoulders, the wounded flesh showing through their rags, their naked feet torn and bleeding. The eyes of the children wide with terror, looking round all the time, terrified, as if pursued.

This group of people came rushing towards the advancing liberation armies. Suddenly everything was silent. The music stopped, the church bells no longer rang. The General leading the liberation armies shouted an order, and his armies withdrew, making room for the oncoming group with their tattered clothes and bleeding bodies, and each whispered to the other: 'These are all that are left of the Jews of Warsaw'.

The General dismounted from his white horse. 'I bend my head', he said, 'to the Jewish martyrs of Poland. You are Hitler's greatest victims, yet you are also the greatest heroes of the Hitler war. You, with your endurance, won the war against Hitler.'

The Generals of the other liberation armies and of the Polish armies all came forward, bowed to the handful of surviving Jews, and said: 'Warsaw will live. Warsaw will live, with you. There will be no Warsaw without Jews'.

Suddenly a voice rose, the voice of the half-million Jews of Warsaw, the voice of the three million Jews of Poland. The voice came from invisible heights, falling down to earth, the voice of the whole Jewish population that had lived in Poland, all the Rabbis, all the writers, the social workers, the thieves, the fighters, the vulgar common folk, the Chassidim, the Communists, the Bundists, the Zionists, all the women and children who perished for Kidush Hashem, by all Hitler's terrible ways of slaughter. The voice cried: 'Jews of Poland, your blood is Jewish history for a thousand years. In your heart beats the pulse of generations, of scholars, Rabbis, writers, leaders. Jewish destiny depends on you. You are the remnant of us all. You must live! You will live! In you we all shall live!'

Then came an echo, the voice of hundreds of thousands, of millions of Polish people whom Hitler tortured to death, and they cried to the Jews: 'Jews of Poland! We died for a free Poland. Without you, without the Polish Jews, there is no Poland. Live, live on!'

MELECH RAVITCH

Why Not Canonise a Second Book of Books?

The question is posed here clearly—why shouldn't we put together and
canonise a second Jewish Book of Books, such as our old Bible is? Yehoash's
Yiddish translation of the Bible, and the exactness of his translation gave the
Bible a new lease of life among modern Yiddish readers. Many Jews who had
studied the whole Bible, like myself, in their youth, but had in the course of
years forgotten most of their Hebrew, had practically stopped looking into
the Bible. Reading the Bible in a European translation is something cold and
distant and alien if one has studied the original text; and as reading it in Hebrew
is difficult we had completely abandoned this practice of reading the Bible
from time to time, turning its pages—the oftener the better. Then Yehoash
came, and now we no longer need to read the Bible in a foreign language.
Yehoash saved the Bible for thousands upon thousands, millions of Jews.

I don't want to go into the question of Yiddish and Hebrew. Of course,
it's a good thing if a Jew knows Hebrew and remembers it all his days. But
what if he doesn't? What was permitted to most Jews in the Land of Israel
itself for centuries may surely be allowed to-day to the Jews in all the lands
of the Dispersion.

The greatness of the Bible is first and foremost that it is not an apologetic
book. It scolds and reprimands and admonishes and denounces; and if it lifts
the idea to the heavens it hurls down with double force to the earth those who
should have been the bearers of the idea, and they were not.

But the canonised Bible is over two thousand years old, and a great deal
has happened since then. It would be a good thing for us if we had a second
Jewish Bible now, or a second great part of the Bible.

A Bible is not an anthology, nor a history, nor a collection of documents.
It is all of these together. The most important thing in a Bible is the bold,
courageous, manly, human idea—the flowing line, not the precise dot. And the
line is, that man *is* good, and that absolute justice does exist, and that it will
one day prevail; and that the Jews work for it and suffer for it, and though
they often suffer more for it—for absolute justice—they don't stop working
for it, work more for it, in fact. But all this must not be said, must not be
brought out apologetically.

Yes, and they must not sign the Book as its compilers, though they will
very much want to—because the big difference between the great Jews of old

and the little Jews of to-day is that once they were a people of the Book, and to-day we are a people of books.

What a second Jewish Bible should comprise, should take in? First, there is the name. It could again be called as it is to-day in Hebrew T'Nach (Torah, Naviim, Chsuvim—Law, Prophets, Scriptures) for we shall need to take in new Torahs, new Naviim, new Chsuvim.

New Torahs—the new doctrines about God Himself, the doctrines of Maimonides, and Spinoza, and even Bergson. And the new social doctrines, of which those of Karl Marx are surely a constituent part. And (after Sholem Asch's courageous stand we may say it openly now) the definitely Jewish prophetic speech, interwoven with parables, of Jesus, the man of Galilee. And just as in our old Bible we have the centuries all intermixed, so they should be intermixed in the new Bible.

Of course, the new Bible should begin where the old stopped, at the period following Ezra the Scribe. But when it reaches the time of Jesus, the man of Galilee, it must leap boldly across to our own time, and include part of Sholem Asch's book about the first Reformer of Jewish Law, who for a thousand and one different reasons became a reformer not among Jews but a missionary of the Jewish God to the Gentiles. Why should we take a fragment from Sholem Asch's book? Because never—since the time of Paul—has a Jewish hand which remained absolutely Jewish, taken such a stand on this whole matter as have the hands and heart of Sholem Asch.

The new Bible must have lyrics, the endless longing of the Jew for the land of the old Bible. Rabbi Yehuda Halevi. And there should be a chronicle of the pogroms. A chronicle of fifteen centuries. The Bible itself has whole chunks of archaic statistics. So this part of the new Bible should have a masterpiece of new statistics, bare figures—naked as skeletons—that will send a shudder down the spine of the world. And lyrics, from the oldest up to Frug and Bialik.

I mentioned Spinoza—his speculative conception of God should receive a place in the new Bible. But there should go with it the text of the decree of excommunication with which he was excluded from the Jewish community, and other such excommunications. Because a Bible is not a work of apologetics —it follows a line, it has an idea, as strong and powerful as the sun.

There should be a special Book of Hate for the blasphemers, the apostates and all kinds of antisemitic doctrinaires—with no apologetics, with no defence advocacy. If there is an idea it will shine through and shame the lot. The way of the old Bible was naked and ruthless truth; it should be the same with the new.

The existence of the Jewish people till to-day—and this is clear from the Bible itself—was possible only thanks to the dogmas contained in the Ten Commandments, to which the Jewish people clung like steel to a magnet.

163

There were no interests that compelled them to do this, only an inert force, like that which draws the steel to the magnet—a higher power, anchored in the primal mystery of nature.

The existence of the Jewish people till to-day shows that besides the inert power of the Ten Commandments there has been another inert power at work, but it was never since the first Ten Commandments put into concrete form as dogmas. The task of the new Bible should be to search out these dogmas and put them into concrete words.

So we speak here—besides the new Bible—also of new dogmas, of new commandments? Yes. All this, all this together would ensure the further existence of the Jewish people for another two thousand years, and—what is more important—it would be a sharp step forward by the world as a whole towards its Redemption.

There is a gulf between the Judaism of to-day and of the time when the Bible was put together, or rather when the finest parts of the Bible were composed. It would not be enough to say there is a link missing in the chain between that Judaism and the Judaism of to-day. Not only a link in the chain—the whole chain is missing. For a Bible is not a link—it is a whole chain. But only in the literary sense. In the higher spiritual sense it is a bridge—a bridge between a permanent past and a permanent future.

We Jews—who are Jews and not pseudo-Jews, we Jews who are, or at least want to be genuine Jews and not a surrogate, we Jews who don't put on Tephilin and don't go to Synagogue, and need no symbols, because we have taken the essential into our hearts and minds and have thoroughly digested it, we Jews who know that there is constant change and transformation in Judaism, we who know that conservative in Judaism is like fire in water—we Sabbath and Festival Jews without Sabbaths and Festivals—we really feel the lack of a continuation of the Bible like a long hunger. Our hands are stretched out all the time for a second Bible, and woe to us when our hands strike only against emptiness. And if the generality of our people has not till now given expression to this thought which is as clear to us as twice times two, it is no proof that we have not felt it clearly and plainly, like twice times two, even if only subconsciously.

All Jewish spiritual disasters come from the lack of this bridge between the Judaism of old and the Judaism of to-day.

Symbol of all that is already in the Pentateuch. Moses and Aaron. The Judaism of Moses is contained in the Pentateuch. The Judaism of Aaron plays a secondary role there, often antipathetic. The Judaism of Moses was never interrupted till to-day, but it was overlaid in the wilderness of 2,500 years under the sand of the Judaism of Aaron. A second Bible would be both a new stream out of the sand and a bridge over the abyss of millenia.

Who should put the second Bible together? I don't know. I don't even dare to want to know. It would be best if someone suddenly appeared—a little-known man with a considerable knowledge, and he would put together a Book of about a thousand pages which would take in that undefinable material which a Bible should take in. Jews on all sides and of all movements would hurl themselves on this Book—some with fury, some with clever arguments, some with piety, some with seriousness; and there would be one among them who would do it better. And another better still. Afterwards the three might get together and make the Book what it is to be in its final and best form. Then the Book would be here. Of course, the process of birth would take years.

The Book would not be complete. A Bible must not be complete; it must not be perfect. It would contain nonsense, 969 times nonsense, like the years of Methuselah. And it must contain the supreme wisdoms. It may contain wearying monotonous recitals, like the lists of hundreds of names, unnecessary and boring, and it must contain the utmost dramatic tension. A Bible must not be perfect—like an ancient tree it must burst with autumn and decay on one side and blossom with spring on the other.

Therefore the writing and the putting together of the Bible must not be organised. I don't know who should put it together. No one may call the man, and appoint him. He must do it on his own. He must be a man without a name, or at least a man whose name is of little concern to him, as little as it concerned the compiler of the Psalms or the writers of the single groups of Psalms or the separate individual Psalms contained in the Psalter.

I don't know and no one has asked me who should compile the new Bible. How can anyone know?—even the man who will do it doesn't know it yet.

It is not Yiddish chauvinism that makes me say that large parts of the second continued Bible should be in Yiddish. It should of course take in big sections in Hebrew. As the first Bible took in Aramaic elements. It could also include small parts in Ladino and perhaps, too, in Judeo-Arabic and in other living Judeo languages, like the Judeo-Tat of the Caucasian Mountain Jews.

A Bible must not occupy more than about a thousand pages of a normal book. It could, if it is preferred, be divided into ten volumes, to look like an encyclopedia, and to take half a shelf in a bookcase—each volume conveniently sized to slip into the pocket. A Bible should be able to accompany a man everywhere, in any situation, as an integral part of himself. Or at least, like an article of his clothing. A book that one could take easily with one into prison

—not only when one goes to prison for an ideal, but even for ordinary crimes. And one should be able to take it along when one wants to rest from the world, and from books, when one wants to be alone.

That is why the Book should not be any bigger—so that one can always have it with one, whenever it is needed. To read at any time, without any tricks, without magnifying glasses, just simply and plainly with your own eyes.

When the first Bible was canonised they hadn't our present technical means and accomplishments. Above all, two important elementary things have happened since then—printing on the one hand, and the almost general ability to read on the other.

Can everything be got into about a thousand pages? Of course, it can—if it was possible to include in the first Bible over three thousand years of history, and actually billions of years. Yet everything is there—nothing is missing. So we shall certainly get everything into about a thousand pages.

The argument that one Bible is enough for us—for the Jewish people—is untenable. It can't be taken seriously. Even less the argument that we have managed for nearly two thousand years without a second Bible and therefore we have no need of one now. To begin with, it is very probable that the second half of the first Bible as we have it to-day is already in fact a second Bible. For the Pentateuch alone, the Pentateuch in itself alone is already a kind of Bible, a Book which contains all the Bible elements. And if the other parts of the Bible following the Pentateuch had been, God forbid, not canonised, or if they had been completely lost, the Pentateuch would have been the whole Bible. Actually, the new Bible would be a third, not a second Bible.

The reason we didn't go further in this matter of the Bible may be that the first Bible had been canonised, a little too much canonised. Now the times are freer in the religious sense, and that is symptomatic, more open to ideas about a second Bible which do keep coming up. In olden days people would have been stoned for even having such thoughts. Perhaps the idea came up at some time, perhaps it was even carried out, but the Book was 'lost'. One could believe anything of the officially pious. But for a miracle who knows if we would have had the first Bible, because of the pious clique whose object is to stand like a solid wall between God and man. The truly pious, those not in the clique, stand like an open door between God and man.

The world mutely demands a second Bible from us. It will get it; and it will be the Book of endless understanding, and therefore it will also be the Book which will be endlessly understood by the world.

Not because of our race—for there is no race—race-characteristics disappear in the first generation. Not because of our proud lineage, because there is nothing in pride of lineage. On the contrary, it is often a warning to be on guard against it, because the finer your descent the more danger there is of a reaction from it in the opposite direction. Not because of our destiny. For destiny is something we have not yet been able to look into, and it proves nothing. But because of our dispersion all over the world we have been the best agents for the first Bible, and we shall be even better agents for the second.

Now is the time for putting together the second Bible. It may be that there have been times such as these before. It may be. If so, it is high time now, the last time to put the second Bible together.

The times are disturbed, the people are torn and sundered outwardly and inwardly—is that an argument against putting together a new Bible? On the contrary, these are arguments for rather than against. Were the times when the first Bible was compiled quieter, more united and whole? Were the technical means then more suitable than they are now? No, now is the time to produce such a work for the world, for the Jewish world, for the whole world. It is the time of times.

By my soul, has our end been written anywhere in the stars, is the scapegoat of mankind now about to be cast down into the pit for the last time, never again to rise? Then it would surely be necessary to leave at least the Book behind us—to leave it for the world, for humanity. Is this the time when the phoenix, the fire and the light of mankind burns for the last time, and when it now rises it will no longer need to burn? Then surely it is good to have such a Book as a reminder of the long past, almost an eternity, a warning for the coming eternity. However this may be—the time is now, high time, perhaps the last opportunity.

Postscript: This essay which Joseph Leftwich, my friend for many years, has compiled from several of my essays was written in the years 1937-43. It therefore contains thoughts with which the author is to-day only partly in agreement. For that reason I ask my readers for indulgence and forgiveness.

SHLOMO BICKEL

The Argument Around Shylock

It's easy for those who have and feel no relationship with Shylock. For three centuries now they have shuddered watching Shylock stubbornly and pitilessly demand his pound of flesh. And for just so long they have been morally recompensed for their fear and trembling by Portia's sharp and subtle interpretation of the law, by which she saves the noble Antonio and turns the tables triumphantly on the cruel Jew. They have been able to leave the theatre not only happy and rejoicing over Antonio's lucky escape, but armed also with another literary symbol, a synonym for avariciousness and vengefulness—the Jew Shylock.

It's we Jewish Shakespeare readers and theatregoers who find it hard. We can't make up our minds what to do with Shylock. We feel the moral grandeur of the Shylock figure, but we are afraid of completely accepting it. We admire his challenging aggressiveness, but we shrink from its logical consequences. We are repelled by the subterfuge with which Portia obtains her verdict, but we applaud her, so that we should not be ourselves accused of Shylockism. We find Shylock's unrootedness, his Galuth feeling close and familiar, but we haven't his broad shoulders to carry it about openly with us.

So we are prepared to deny Shylock. Yet we know that he is putting forward in our name such a justified and fundamental historic grievance and complaint that it must not be left unsaid. We can't enter into judgment with Shylock. We try to refine him and civilise him with moralistic interpretations and conceptions—and by doing so we make him smaller and paler and colourless—and ourselves as well.

This specifically Jewish psychological problem with regard to Shylock was raised with me a few years ago by a Jewish teacher in a high school not far from New York. He had come across an article of mine on the subject which had just appeared, and he wanted my advice about a practical problem of his own in pedagogics.

The school curriculum required him as the English master to do two Shakespeare plays each year with the students of the upper classes. Being a Jew he always chose 'The Merchant of Venice' as one of the two plays, and every time it turned out to be more or less a failure. The non-Jewish part of the class shuddered of course at Shylock's stubborn and vengeful cruelty, and then rejoiced at the way Portia confused and overthrew him; and they applauded her. While the Jewish students, or most of them, were stirred by Shylock's great monologue and, like their teacher, put all the stress on Shylock's questions. You could see the Jewish student spiritually uplifted when he declaimed aloud to the class: 'If you prick us do we not bleed? If you poison us do we not die? and if you wrong us shall we not revenge?'

But the pound of flesh, and—nearest his heart? Such malevolent, relentless vengefulness! The Jewish students applauded wise Portia just as the non-Jewish students did.

Year after year it was the same, over and over again. Till finally the teacher decided to choose a different play for his classes. 'The Merchant of Venice' was not suitable—neither for him nor for his students.

But when he came to ask my advice—it was in the summer of 1943, when we already knew something about the chapters Treblinka and Maidanek in the long story of Shylock's sufferings and martyrdom at the hands of Antonio—he felt this was the time when it was his duty to do Shylock with both his Jewish and his non-Jewish students. Now it was possible by the flames of the gas ovens to read in Shylock's words and actions not only a pack of rhetorical questions about the victim's sufferings, but also the grim facts of the diabolical butcheries committed against him. Now the story of the pound of flesh had gained a new meaning in respect of vengeance and humanity. Now a Jew might dare to proclaim the truth openly.

Four years passed—with all the events of those Judgment Day four years—and I met my high school teacher again. At a first night of the New York Hebrew Theatre group 'Pargod'. And the play was Shylock.

The producer, Peter Frey, using Shakespeare's text in the Hebrew translation made by the poet Simon Halkin, tried to do something with it that would meet Jewish susceptibilities and bring the play into line with Jewish ideas in our day. The three acts of Frey's adaptation, which he called 'Shylock 1947', showed us not only Shylock on the stage, but Jewish actors in 1947 struggling to bring out a dignified Jewish conception of the Shylock figure.

In the first act—supposed to be ten days before the production of the play —Heinrich Zwick, as the producer, a Jewish refugee from Germany, tries to explain to the cast that Shylock must on the stage cut a ridiculous figure, a buffoon, to make people laugh at him, and so destroying the myth of Shylock as a representative Jewish figure.

A Jew making fun of Shylock? Most of the cast object that Zwick's conception is undignified, is an affront to Jewish feeling. Most of the fuss is made by one of the younger actors, Judah, who takes over the production on entirely different lines.

Judah's conception of Shylock, as it finds expression in Act II, turns out to be what we are accustomed to call apologetic. Judah transports Shylock to a ghetto in eighteenth-century Germany, so that in this atmosphere of intolerance and moral and spiritual persecution he can as far as possible justify Shylock's vengefulness.

Are we to justify vengefulness? Jews—says the Jewish refugee from Germany—never demanded vengeance. For vengeance, he explains, means destruction and self-destruction. With these words Heinrich Zwick regains the upper hand in producing the play. In Act III we have the trial scene as it is in Shakespeare's text in his Act IV. Only it is played in modern dress.

Shylock, a clean-shaven Jew of the twentieth-century, demands his pound of flesh. Portia is a social worker of the same period who finds the legal loophole by which she saves Antonio from the Jew's vengeance. Both sides are aware that they are in a modern court of law, so there are no histrionics. There is no attempt to justify Shylock's vindictive vengefulness, nor is there much applause for Portia either. But when the court asks Shylock if he is content with the sentence, to become a Christian and to record a gift of all he dies possessed to his Christian son-in-law Lorenzo and his daughter Jessica, and Shylock answers, 'I am content', the producer in this version shows Shylock a prouder Jew than Shakespeare's Jew in Venice. Shylock strides up to the footlights and cries into the body of the theatre: 'No! We will not accept the sentence! We must change the ending of the play!'

Now how does the producer, after hurling that defiant challenge at his audience, change the ending of the play? How? He leaves everything as it is —Shylock cruel and vengeful, Portia successful and wise, and Antonio delivered and free.

Only what? Turn Christian? Go to the font? No! Shylock will not do that! Shylock remains a Jew! How does the Yiddish folk song go?—'What we are, we are, but Jews we are!' And Jews we remain!

As we left the hall the teacher came up to me and asked me: 'Can you tell me why this Jewish company with a competent producer had to struggle through three acts to give us this banality?'

Instead of dealing with his justified complaint, for which I had no real answer, I asked him how he had got on with his own Shylock problem at his school. He seemed to have been expecting my question.

'After my talk with you four years ago', he said, 'I sat down and thought it all over very carefully, and I 'discovered America'. Shakespeare is a giant, and what he wrote is like something in the Bible. Just as we mustn't change and try to improve things in the Bible, but repeat it, as the Rebbe taught us to repeat the stories in Genesis. The teacher must be clear in his own mind about what he is repeating, and if he is clear about it his students will be even more so. I think I can say that all my students, Jews and non-Jews, are quite clear now in their own minds about Shylock's moral greatness.

'Why does Shylock insist on his pound of flesh? Because he is a cruel monster? Because he is vengeful? It's nonsense to judge Shakespeare and a Shakespeare hero in this shallow fashion. Shylock knows that suffering is perhaps the only way to rouse the senses of the 'Good Antonios', so that they should see and should feel the sufferings of their victims. It is only when 'Good Antonio', and light-hearted Bassanio and 'Gentle Portia' will feel the stab of the knife and the sting of pain, the grief of humiliation and the pang of impotence that they may perhaps come to realise the most simple and most primitive fact, which is that their victims too are human, that 'if you prick us, we bleed'.

'Out of that realisation, born of our own sufferings, there may perhaps grow up that common humanitarianism that will stop dividing people and nations into torturers and victims. Thus Shylock's vengefulness carries within it the noble vision of a new humanity. Shylock's cruelty is essentially his noble passion for humanity, and in the court scene it is almost victorious. Any moment now, it seems, and the torturers will be driven into the narrow corner of history from which there is no way out, and they will have to assume the burden of suffering.

'I must confess', he went on, 'that this is not my own personal discovery. After the revelations about Oswiecim and Treblinka it was in the air, so to speak, in America and in England. Everybody, headed by President Roosevelt and Winston Churchill adopted Shylock's demand for the pound of flesh, not only to punish, but by their suffering to convert the German 'Antonio-people' to humanity, to human solidarity.

'That is as far as I got in 1945. Now I go much further—and that 'further' too is already in Shakespeare's play. This Shakespeare was a giant, and a prophet. He foresaw everything. When they were already on the road to humanity, they brought in the code of law with its legal quibbling and hair-splitting, and the New Testament, with its moist pages of mercy-teaching, and —the hangman became the victim, and they branded the victim as a cruel monster.'

That was a few months ago, on one of those terribly sultry nights we get in New York in midsummer, with a Hebrew amateur theatre group struggling with Shylock on the small stage of a New York uptown hall. Now it was autumn, and with our freakish New York weather it was as hot as in midsummer, and Maurice Schwartz's fine, well-equipped Yiddish Art Theatre was playing Shylock on New York's East Side.

In the Hebrew production Peter Frey had rewritten Shylock to refine and explain his Jewish vengefulness by transplanting him to an eighteenth-century ghetto in Germany, where the atmosphere of hate and persecution would supply the psychological and moral justification for Shylock's stubborn demand for vengeance. In Maurice Schwartz's Yiddish Art Theatre too the whole emphasis seemed to lie in trying to justify Shylock's vengefulness.

It was a new play called 'Shylock and His Daughter', and the author, Ari Ibn-Zahav, and the producer, Maurice Schwartz, did not go to the trouble of transporting Shylock from Venice to Germany. There was no need. For the Venice ghetto in the days of the Inquisition, of Popes Paul III and Paul IV gave a Jew no less justfication for hatred and vengefulness than did the life in a German ghetto in the eighteenth-century. But to make Shylock's demand for his pound of flesh ring more true, the author, Ari Ibn-Zahav, chose both in his original novel and in his dramatisation to stress not so much the Jewish group sufferings in the Venice ghetto as Shylock's personal sufferings at the hands of Antonio and Lorenzo. In his version Antonio not only borrowed three thousand ducats from Shylock, but borrowed them expressly for the purpose of seducing Shylock's servants and conspiring in Jessica's flight. Lorenzo is presented not only as a Christian who loves a Jewish girl and persuades her to turn Christian, but as a kind of Aryan commissar placed in Shylock's bank to destroy him. The inference is that anyone, even a Christian noble, would in these circumstances be as vengeful as Shylock.

Does that make the Jewish Shylock figure nobler, morally greater? On the contrary, Shylock's vengefulness loses much of its ethical passion when behind it stands only the whimpering of a hurt Jewish father, as Ari Ibn-Zahav has it, not the historic cry of an outraged people, as we have it in Shakespeare.

In Ibn-Zahav's dramatisation Shylock is only one real individual Jew whom a Christian has injured, mortally injured, firing him with determination to be revenged. In Shakespeare's 'Merchant of Venice' Shylock is a Jew—a symbol, speaking in the name of a whole people, and even the pound of flesh ceases to be real and becomes the symbol of that people's sufferings at the hands of Antonio, of whole nations of Antonios, who can feel only through their own pain that 'if you prick us, we bleed'.

It is said that the great Shylock monologue has paled and weakened to-day against the flames of the Treblinka gas ovens in which Antonio burned Shylock. It is true. The words Shakespeare put in Shylock's mouth in that monologue are insignificant against the reality of Maidanek. We want deeper, stronger words for our grief and woe.

Has Ibn-Zahav brought us these new words? No! He has only injected into Shylock's great national grief and protest some small personal grievances, and he imagines that these will give Shylock the strength and power to cry out from the depths, to find the true word—and that the world, and we Jews ourselves will at last understand and justify his vengefulness.

Adding Shylock's personal troubles, as Ibn-Zahav does, seems in the light of Maidanek only to diminish the dignity and the moral significance of the age-old national lament that Shakespeare's monologue sounds.

Therefore I can well understand why the Jews of Venice headed by their Rabbi, in Ibn-Zahav's own play, couldn't make head or tail of Shylock's exaggerated unrelenting vengefulness. For is he indeed the first Jew whose daughter was seduced by a Christian? What? The Christian seduced his daughter with her father's own money, money that he had himself borrowed from him? What of it? Is that a reason for such savage vengefulness that might bring down disaster upon the entire Jewish community?

In Ibn-Zahav's play Shylock has grown small and weak and narrow-minded. The law court has not made any difference to Shylock, as it does in Shakespeare. No, the Venice court of justice was very fair. It awarded Shylock his pound of flesh as provided in the bond. Only Shylock comes out small and untragic, because he can't have his revenge, because fundamentally he has nothing for which to take revenge. As in the old days of the Yiddish theatre we hear at the end of the play the happy-sad news that Jessica has returned home—but no longer alive.

I can well understand the Venetian Jews who put their ban on this diminished Shylock. For a Jew who will because of his personal troubles imperil the whole Jewish community deserves the ban.

Not Shakespeare's Shylock. Shakespeare's Shylock deserves no ban.

ITZIK MANGER

The Poetry of Our Holy Days

My friend Joseph Leftwich said: 'Write something for the Rosh Hashonah issue of the "South African Jewish Times" '.

'About what?'

'About Rosh Hashonah. About the Holy Days. Jewish Holy days.'

My friend knows that I am no theologian to write about the Jewish Holy Days. But I am a poet, and I know something about the poetry of the Jewish High Holy Days. One God in Heaven knows that there was and there still is a great deal of poetry in our Machzor. That there was and perhaps still is a great deal of poetry in the Jews who still say their prayers. In all the places where Jews pray on the Jewish High Holy Days. But the landscapes which were an organic part of the Holy Day atmosphere in my childhood years have vanished for ever.

When I stood a year ago beside the mounds of ashes in Maidanek, I saw that they were the ashes of our Sabbaths and our Holy Days. What does it mean to be burnt to ashes; what do they mean, the ashes of our Sabbaths and our Holy Days?

The wise and witty Abbé Galiani in a letter to Madame Epinay brushed aside Voltaire's onslaught against the Holy Days. 'Voltaire thinks the Holy Days were made for God. He is wrong. Man needs them. They have their roots in man's innermost nature.'

Paraphrasing Galiani I would say that the Jewish Holy Days, both those of joy and those of sorrow, and of the innermost searchings of the heart have grown out of the deepest needs of the Jewish human being. He gave them colour, he breathed into them his song, his faith, his woe.

I ask myself—in all your wanderings, where did you feel the Jewish Holy Days? In Paris, in London? No! It does not mean that there are no devout Jews in London and Paris and elsewhere who keep the Sabbaths and the Holy Days. God forbid! But the Sabbath-Holy Day radiance on everything around us, that I felt in Poland and Lithuania. Read a chapter of Mendele Mocher Seforim, and you will feel what I mean.

A Jewish cart crawls through Gentile roads and fields. It is Selichot time. Listen how the mood of the old bookseller transforms the entire landscape through his mood into a Jewish Holy Day-eve landscape.

Read a chapter of Asch, and you will feel the Sabbath-Holy Day radiation of the Jewish mood upon the landscape. A Jewish chedar-lad watched the play of clouds. What did he see? A Bible landscape with camels. Jews going to Jerusalem. The dark had caught them on their way. So they were spending the night on the road, and to-morrow they would, with God's help, continue their wandering.

Sholom Aleichem's little Jewish boy steals into a Gentile garden and makes havoc of the cabbages. He is fighting a battle against the enemies of Israel, putting them to rout.

There is Peretz's wonderful story 'Between Two Mountains', of groups of Chassidim walking in the fields. And the whole landscape became alive and sang. One grand harmony.

Jews have Biblicised the Polish-Lithuanian landscape and therefore it became homelike, intimately Jewish. The Sabbath candles shed their rays through the Jewish windows and made the Gentile outside world Sabbathlike. The Yom Kippur candles wept through the Synagogue windows, and the surrounding countryside became Yom Kippur-like.

It took thousands of years, this process of making the week, the Sabbath and the Holy Day at home with, intimate with the foreign landscape. After the Biblical classic this was a tremendous achievement, a Golus-classic.

The Sossover Rebbe, Moishe Leib, in his peasant fur. The Berditchever Rebbe who argues with God, half in Yiddish, half in Ukrainian. The Polish Rebbe who declares his love to God in Polish, 'Moy Kochany', 'My Beloved'.

It is style, integral Jewish style. You could not escape from the Sabbath. Because the Sabbath caught you on the road and you had to keep the Sabbath en route. You could not escape from the Holy Day, because the Holy Day caught you on the road and you had to keep the Holy Day en route. And if you did not want to keep the Sabbath and the Holy Day, because you were freethinking, you felt an outsider. Outside, excluded from something which embraced most Jews. I hadn't this feeling in Paris, and not in London. But I have it in the towns and villages of Poland and Lithuania.

Unforgettably lovely in our memories are the Saturday nights when our mothers murmured in the twilit rooms, 'God of Abraham'. The nostalgia for the departing Sabbath engraved itself deep in our temperament, not to be forgotten. Every Jewish home was then a glorious Rembrandt painting, composed of light and shade, with our mothers in the centre.

Yiddish literature has echoes of that mood. Both in poetry and in prose. Yiddish literature has fixed for generations a mood, a sentiment which though it has disappeared from reality will long, long echo this Sabbath-Holy Dayness for coming generations. If you want to know the Jews and the Jewish women and the Jewish children both in their work-a-day week and in the Sabbath-Holy Dayness turn the pages of Yiddish literature, and you will meet them as if alive, you will see them revelling on Simchat Torah, forgiving each other on Yom Kippur eve, sending gifts on Purim, frying Latkes and playing with Dreidlach on Chanukah, gathering greens for Shevuot, mourning and grieving on Tisha B'Av. You will see how Jewish children have turned every hillock outside the town into a 'Mount Sinai'. You will hear how Jewish saints on foreign roads were wafted across. You will encounter, in reality and in dream, the daily dust and the legend of a people. The Sabbaths and the Holy Days did not come like shamefaced beggars somewhere in an alien foreignness, but to their own home, homely, at home.

This lovely and classic Jewish style and way of life became, as I said, possible through the Jew acclimatising himself, growing to be at home in the Slav landscape. The Baal Shem revealed himself in the Carpathian Mountains. Reb Nachman Bratzlav improvised his marvellous tales during his walks across the Ukrainian fields.

Jews and Canaan-landscape were an organic whole. Result: Style, Hebraic style and the Bible. Jews and the Slav-landscape became an organic unity. Result: Style, and its radiation in Yiddish worldly and religious literature.

Both styles, the Hebrew and the Yiddish, did not die a natural death, the death that comes with over-ripeness. The Hebrew style was brutally cut down by the Roman sword. The Yiddish was sadistically murdered by the German sword.

We are still too near the destruction of our Yiddish-European style to be able to give a clear account of the terrible catastrophe. But deep in the hearts of each of us who was by chance saved or escaped in all the corners of the earth, vibrate the echoes of this Jewish style of life. Let us acquaint our children with it, let us teach them the lesson 'Continuation', for indeed this style was terribly lovely, authentically Jewish, and if the word classic still has any sense and meaning, it was in our day 'classic-Jewish'.

ZALMAN SHAZAR

Shigayon Chagall

I

Inexplicable are often the strange introductory passages with which the ancient editor of the Psalms described the different chapters of the Book. We have for instance among them one superscription which is used in the Psalms only once, and is hardly capable of explanation: Shigayon L'David.

It is difficult to give the true meaning of this rare word Shigayon, but it is not hard to get at the intention of the word. Shigayon appears to derive from the phrase Shuga B'Dimyonoth, that is, taken up with dreams, and Shuga B'Ahavah, taken up with love, swept away to distant, dreamy, nostalgic, wonderful dream worlds. If you like, there is even the semblance of Shegiah and Shigagah, which mean error and mistake, that is, a revolt against the accepted legality, and almost a twin of the word Sheguon, which means ecstasy, exaltation, and denotes in the Bible the man of spirit who lives outside the accepted laws of Higiun (logic). Yet if you like, it is very close indeed to the word Higiun itself; only a single letter divides the two twin-words. And if you venture to shift only one dot on the shin, from right to left, the word becomes bound up with tremendous greatness, and it means the supreme, the highest.

Why can't I free my mind of this ancient, unusable, unique yet significant superscription ever since I was surrounded with the songs on canvas of our great artist Marc Chagall?

An old-time editor, with a love of language and a sense for the word-play on names, if he were looking for a superscription for Chagall's picture-visions, which are pure transports into fantasy and love, and break all the accepted rules of our reality, coming to rest where the roads part between exalted enthusiasm and wise logic, and are tremendously great in their beauty and their sublime poetic content—he would not be able to resist setting over them all the vague yet meaningful word-play and unique superscription: Shigayon Chagall.

II

Since the miracle that came to us on the threshold of our newest generations, and we experienced in our revival upsurge the great flowering of our liberation expression in art, since our national genius opened wide the doors of the world, few among us have been so fortunate in winning the minds and hearts of the finest judges and lovers of art in the outside world as our Marc Chagall.

His exhibitions are held in all the capitals of the world, and an entire literature has grown up around his pictures. The world is amazed and astonished, captivated, struck with wonder. Distant worlds have accepted him as close to them. He has succeeded in being both honoured and condemned. He has been both highly praised and banned. Yet in times of honour and in times of obloquy he remained rooted fast in the hearts of the artistic world, as few among us have.

And like few among our choice spirits whom the world has drawn into its magic circle, Marc Chagall has stood out as a Jew, who is deeply rooted in Jewish memory and derives his sustenance from the sources of ancient Jewish fantasy and the familiar figures of the Jewish shtetl, which only recently was still flowing with life and has now been cut off and is no more. Liozne, the shtetl to which he used to go as a youngster to see his grandfather whom he loved belongs now to the past. Vitebsk, the town of his young days, is in all his pictures in flames and dying. 'The song is ended, only the echo rings out.' And no foe can take away the echo from him, for it is anchored deep in his poet's heart.

When the art spirit rests on him, and he soars up into the heights, armed with his colour-signs, he spreads the wings of his Jewish antiquity and lately almost forgotten fantasy, and from his faithful heart rise on the world stage the people and the little streets of his youth, who have cut themselves into his memory—and no enemy fire can consume them and no forgetfulness has power over them.

One often thinks—the old human art of creating Aggadoth, stories and fables, has here taken on new life, as in its first spring, and it is the Jewish child dreaming on the canvases of this modern Aggadist.

It seems to me that a grandchild of the ancient Rabbi Bar Bar Hanna has arisen here—his power of imagination, his endless exaggerations, his tall tales. Then one looks further and sees: he is at the same time a flesh and blood brother of Sholem Aleichem's Mottel Peise the Chazan's. These are his hometown figures, his shtetl pictures. Chagall welds them both into one body with the enchantment of his colours that capture the eye with their interplay, and he alone knows the hidden secret of their combination. He has indicated to us the mystery of enjoying them.

III

But not too much 'interpreting', and not getting alarmed if something does not look 'understandable'. Aggadoth are never taken by the force of our reason. Certainly not pictorial Aggadoth. Here the enjoyment is that of feeling. The figures speak to us in the speech of colour, and memory has wings, and they are flooded with light. The figures that the painter sees with the eye of his poetic memory are full of childlike cleanness, exalted beauty.

Therefore no insisting on trying to understand everything by plain meaning. Of course a picture also has its plain meaning, but besides that it has suggestion and exposition and mystery; and if you try to close all the doors except that of plain meaning you will not find the plain meaning either. Aggadah is a sister of mythos, and is often subject to the requirements of a dream rather than of true everyday reality, and one doesn't ask questions of a visionary mythos.

But Chagall is a modern visionary, and the suffering of his generation is his pain; and the hope of his generation is his bright light. Like a true brother of Mottel Peise the Chazan's, his pictures derive from his father's house. Both when they are inanimate objects and when they are living creatures they all breathe ancient compassion, are saturated with a child's love, full of beauty, and they have the power to warm the heart all through life. Look at them: the wise cow, the calf's eye, the fiddle and the book, the clock and the ladder, the shofar and the chuppa poles, and the Sefer Torah. They are a child's letters carved for eternity. And when the poetic spirit possesses him he adorns them with his strongest colours, natural colours and passion-colours, bringing them closer and moving them off to a distance and setting them in a row, as the poet arranges his rhymes and rhythms, and 'writes' his canvas pictures with them.

He is like the tree in the Psalm, that is 'planted by streams of water'. The trunk bathes in childhood memories and the crown shines with the vision of the generation, and the whole flutters with its multi-coloured spring blossoms.

IV

'The language of visions' was Bialik's designation for 'the language of all languages.' He sang it in his poem 'Habrocha':

'There is a quiet language here, the language of mystery. No voice, no sound, only all colours. And it has magic and splendid pictures, and abundant images. In this language God reveals Himself to His chosen.'

That is the language in which the mermaid confided her secret to Bialik. In this language he told us afresh the mythos of 'Megilloth Esh'. With this language he brought out his father's image from the deep pit of his faithful memory. In the same way Chagall can't get away from the image of his father, the sad, silent man. That is how he draws from his memory image after image, dream after dream—'in the quiet divine language', without voice, without sound, all in colour.

For what the word is in its many forms to the poet, colour is in its many stages to the poet-painter. And our heart looks and cannot be sated, is wonder-struck, excited, exalted and grateful.

V

So we shall do no searching for a moral, nor for a story. The visionary-artist is absorbed with his love. Each speck of colour is to him a cry from the depths of his heart. And his childlike naivete is exalted, against all the errors of everyday logic.

Remember, his Liozne is no more. His Jewish Vitebsk has gone up in flames. It is only in his imagination, in his fantasy that they rise up for him. His fantasy is full of yearning. From afar he sees how the fire burned, and his hand—like every human hand—was too short and could not save them from forgetfulness. Here they breathe again and dream before our eyes in his songs on canvas.

And when Vitebsk, burned down, rises from his nostalgic memory to artistic life, its symbols rise in its place. Its soul arises, because the simple ob-jects are now immersed in symbol, and they all obtain a different colour and a different order. Not according to their chronological order, but according to the intensity of their impression on the painter's memory, they now ascend on the ladder of his creative imagination. Only open your heart to it, and you will convince yourself—the same ladder stands with him and with you, and its top reaches to the highest heights.

VI

Look at the red skinned calf that hangs crucified over the whole town. Like the true crucified, like the father of all the crucified of the world, since the prevailing of wickedness of a living creature over a living creature. See how the redness of its blood cries out, see the cruel cut of its split body, see the purity of its face—Is there another such crucified among all the crucified?

Were we not all shocked in our childhood seeing the local shochet killing our loved calf? Isn't Feierberg's 'The Calf' truly Jewish for all time? Is there a truer sense of pity for the lot of the powerless? And a stronger outburst of wrath against the cruelty of the heartless? Is not Chagall like Feierberg?

Chagall may not know what our poetess Rochel sang to us about the cow in the stall:

'My life is sistered with hers,
With a thousand secret threads.'

Here we are interwoven in the ball of these threads. We breathe the mystery that the painter-poet has unrolled for us with his simple genius and childlike dreaminess. Look closely and see the climax, the culmination of human wickedness peering out from an idyll which is all pure sublimity.

Here you have an uncle of his, a butcher, going on a journey with his favourite goat on the cart, taking it to the slaughterer. The goat shines in the memory of the painter, adorned with the most legendary colours. And in this shine as of a dream, there is in all this everyday world no such multi-coloured goat; and the little golden sheep that lies like a crown on his aunt's head—look at its eyes. Isn't it a human face? And the aunt herself, does she not look like a variation of the legendary 'faithful shepherd' who with immense compassion rescues a weak little sheep that had strayed from the flock? And the friendly mare that pulls the cart, isn't she as good as gold with her wonderful roseate appearance? She has about her the sanctity of a mother-to-be—for the child's eye of the clairvoyant poet sees clearly and shows us the unborn foal in the mare's belly. And all this pious and idyllic procession, full of beauty and cleanness and simple-mindedness is taking a goat to the slaughter.

And the permanent wedding, with the chuppa poles and the musicians, and the astonishing love of the two, the everlasting union of the passionate violet with the absolute pure white by the light of the Paris Eiffel Tower, as the bodily nakedness beckons from somewhere in the distance to the moon, and the pure little calf, like a symbol of pity and compassion, looks closely, deep and understandingly, and from high up blesses the fiddle and the ancient book, and the eye of the goat, all three interwoven in one, as they were from his early youth lovingly interwoven in his memory, and the dear chanticleer carries them as if on eagle's wings high, very high over the roofs of everyday reality, to the distant clear heavens...

Or the profound loneliness of the petrified Jew with the pitch-black eyes, wrapped in the absolute white, clear shroud, the death-kittel, holding the red, rescued Torah Scroll, and accompanied by the friendly wise cow and the silenced fiddle lying on the ground—is there anywhere a finer commentary on the brutally-tragic passage in Lamentations: 'Let him sit alone and keep silence'?

And all these dear familiar objects that have now become symbols and unite almost all the pictures in one great poetic vision—they don't leave the poet-painter even when he lifts himself to his greatest heights in his Biblical paintings. Here he permits himself to show as he sees—with no barriers between yesterday and to-day, between outside and within, in the chain of generations. And as he sees, so he shows, and as he shows, so we see. Mysterious and plain, exalted and naive, agonised and festive and full of grandeur.

VII

And all these qualities have blossomed more ripely in the new artistic gifts that he has given the world and us in the eighth decade of his blessed life. In the twelve windows of the Hadassah Synagogue in Jerusalem the exaggeration has given way to the childlike picturing of the Biblical texts, and the explanations he heard from the Melamed in his chedar years. All twelve are winged with the intoxication of the natural colours of the Land of Israel and the old-Yiddish mythological flora and fauna that adorn the legends about the ancient Jewish tribes. Prophetic and Midrashic metaphors have here come alive. And a sea of faith and nostalgia is poured out on each Tribal window.

And from the singing radiant ceiling of the Paris Opera House which seeks to unroll in rich colour before the eyes of the enraptured beholder the mysterious Cosmos of artistic creation, of his genius in all its most masterly revelations and diverse motives, he does not cease to enchant us with the familiar sounds of his inherited treasures of beauty.

And as with the ceiling of the Paris Opera House, so also with the murals of the Lincoln Centre in New York. Everywhere, in all his greatest world-visions his faithful companion is always his deeply rooted festiveness and his ecstatic enthusiasm.

VIII

Seven great and long generations back, in that same shtetl Liozne and in that same Jewish Vitebsk, the Father of Chassidism in Lithuania, the Baal Ha-Tanya, thought out and sang the unforgettable melody that is known as the Tune of the Old Rabbi. This melody which rises to the very heights and penetrates down to the last depths—Chagall can still sing it to-day as he heard it in his childhood and youth in the homes of his parents and relatives. Who knows if it is not the Tune that his grandfather played on his fiddle, sitting in Vitebsk on the roof, while the corpse lay on the ground with death-candles round it, the widow weeping and wailing, the strange watchman with the broom in his hand sweeping the street, and the neighbour in black carrying a ladder which is to reach to the very top of the fiddling grandfather. Now Liozne is no more, and Jewish Vitebsk has gone, and all Jewish creative work in the whole of Lithuania is silenced and broken off. Here their broken-off melody rises again, coming from the rich and faithful painter-poet and joining before our eyes the splendour of world-art.

MOSHE DLUZNOVSKY

The Old Tree in Vence

We liken trees to people. If a man has a good figure we say—straight as a tree. When a man ages well we say he is like an old oak. When a man falls and breathes his last he fell like an oak tree.

I want to speak now of a tree in the small town of Vence, in France, near the famed Riviera resort Nice. It lies among mountains and valleys, in the midst of rocks and flowers; a real beauty spot. A mass of green and silver and gold, red and blue, snow and sunshine, rain and storm.

There is in Vence a tree that covers almost half the town. It must be thousands of years old—stands there perhaps since the first six days of Creation.

Half the population spend their time under the tree, from early morning till late at night. The other half hold back, unwilling to mix with the common folk. The branches of the three—long arms, prongs, fingers—spread benediction and repose over the heads of the inhabitants. Its hands reach out with tender leaves, with golden green in summer, with naked, ruffled branches in winter —which is really autumn there—reach out far and wide.

Children play under the branches and the foliage, crawl into the hollow belly of the tree, playing hide and seek. Old folk sit under its shade, enjoying the fresh cool. In the blue evenings the inhabitants of the town sit there, telling stories that never were on land or sea, all sorts of gossip about their neighbours who happen just then not to be with them under the tree, and about all the things that happened in the town to-day, yesterday, a year ago, many, many years ago.

There is a stone well under the tree, full of deep clear water. The women of the town do their washing there in the early morning, and their chatter and laughter gets caught and entangled in the branches. And to the well, to drink, come people, natives and strangers, asses and dogs, cattle, birds, horses. There are seats under the tree, and in the evenings comedians come to amuse the people with comic performances and mocking satires. A barrel organ plays Viennese waltzes, tangos, all kinds of dance music. Jugglers and acrobats come from far away, and here under the tree they spread fun among the people, and laughter under the branches of the tree.

Vence is world-famous. The name is known everywhere. Some time before the Second World War the great French painter Matisse worked there, painted wonderful frescoes inside the Church, and thousands of people came on pilgrimage to Vence to see them. Some time after the Second World War the great Jewish painter Chagall came to live in Vence, and put the town on the map of the world.

Chagall painted a number of his masterpieces in Vence. Thousands of people came on pilgrimage to Vence to visit him and see his work. In Vence, Chagall conceived the twelve stained-glass windows which are now in the Hadassah Hebrew University Memorial Centra Synagogue in Jerusalem, and his ceiling in the Paris Opera House. He has painted a huge canvas that he calls 'Vence', which was exhibited in New York.

What does this canvas show? A candelabrum with lights and roses, a fish swimming under a clock on the wall, over which the crucified hangs naked, a calf smothered in flaming roses, a lot of silver, snow, and over the snow a bit of a sledge. This is how Chagall saw the little town Vence in the French Riviera, which has been his home for years. Vence was also the scene of a film made there which has the title 'Chagall'. It shows the artist in his atelier, at work, out for a walk, stopping to look at flowers. On Chagall's canvas Vence has emerged as altogether dreamed poetry, vision and silver, red and truly Chagallesque blue, which is unique in the glorious nuancing of a blue.

Marc Chagall lives in this little French town Vence. The people there love him and feel proud that he has settled there. Under the tree the inhabitants speak more gently than usual about the great artist who has carried the name of their town out into the big world, giving it prestige and distinction.

It is said that even a Sepher Torah in the Sanctuary must have luck. And Vence has had a lot of luck, enough to make any other such small town famous. Before the Second World War I was in Vence often. I lived several winters in Nice and was a frequent visitor in Vence and in another small town near Vence called St. Paul. In the Middle Ages this was a royal residence for the whole region of Provence. You get your first glimpse of the town over the top of a cliff, and it looks like a dove's nest. There is an ancient cannon at the entrance gate, a relic of its days of royalty. The walls old and crumbling, the windows grated, thousands of dim corridors, narrow streets with steps leading up and down. The surrounding landscape is bewitchingly beautiful, hills and valleys, the gold of the sun, the gold of the oranges on the trees. Painters have been coming to St. Paul for a long time to paint its beauties, and writers too, poets, and people wanting to escape from the world, to find peace. There is a hotel in the town, and its walls are covered with paintings by renowned artists who paid in this way for their board and lodging. There is a big book in the hotel, you might call it a Golden Book, a Visitor's Book. You will find famous names there—Rudyard Kipling, H. G. Wells, Bernard Shaw, Zalman Shneour.

You make your way from St. Paul to Vence. I loved to sit under the ancient tree in Vence, listening to the talk. One old Frenchman speaking Provençal told me about a thin little man with flaming eyes who spent weeks there, painting that tree. They didn't know where he came from; they don't know where he went. One day he disappeared. He had spoken to no one, and no one had dared to speak to him.

He had only painted that tree, painted the branches, the leaves, the beauty of the tree. The old man seemed to have no great liking for this strange painter who had taken the image of the tree out into the great world. One felt a kind of envy—that the old man had a grudge against that strange painter who had transferred his tree on to his canvas. One detected a fear that some day the tree would be chopped down, and that would be the end of the tree.

The town, he said, is growing rich. New shops are opening. The tree is getting in their way. It takes up too much space in the centre of the town. There could be big new buildings put up instead. It would be better that fewer strange people should come and take away the beauty of the tree.

I had known, as it happens, about a famous Jewish painter who had come to live in France and had a habit of painting that particular tree. He had for years been painting landscapes in the south of France, in the Riviera.

Then the Second World War came. I escaped from France. I often thought of that old man in Vence, and his fear that the tree would be chopped down, and his grudge against the strange painter who was taking the tree away with the paint on his canvas.

A few years ago the Museum of Modern Art in New York had a big Exhibition of the work of the great Jewish painter Chaim Soutine. There were 103 paintings on the walls of the museum. I wandered through the rooms, fascinated by the colour and the theme, by the genius and the vision of the Jew Chaim Soutine, who had come from the poor Lithuanian shtetl Smilovitch to Paris and had conquered not only Paris but the world. We saw his Old Mill in deep green and gold, sides of raw meat, slaughtered hens, plucked geese, red roofs, trees in a stormwind. Then my eye fell suddenly on the painting of the old tree in Vence, standing between two rows of houses. And there was the description—'The Tree in Vence'. Here it was, growing in all its majestic beauty, the deep green, the leaves and the branches like long fingers, like the prongs of so many forks. Only the children were missing, and the old people, and the well.

There was the old tree standing in front of me; I even heard the people laughing and chatting. And I saw the old man of Vence, like an old rooted tree himself, with his grudge against the strange painter.

Who knows, I wondered to myself, if the tree is still standing there in Vence, if it has not been chopped down to make room for more shops. Yet it was enough that a great artist had carried its image out into the world.

Chaim Soutine who had painted innumerable landscapes, great chunks of nature, had gone in fear of nature. You see in his landscapes fields, trees, branches, something terrifying, menacing, transient. It is all painted with such power and vision that you stand in front of his paintings with a mixed feeling of shock and admiration. He has given the tree in Vence immortality.

Vence has been lucky. Three great painters have in the last three decades immortalised it and its tree—the Frenchman Henri Matisse and the two Jews Marc Chagall and Chaim Soutine. Blessings on this place where they contrived as if by magic through colour and tone a tree, a man—the sparks of God's Creation.

PLAYS

SHOLEM ASCH

A String Of Pearls

PROLOGUE

Rome. The Arch of Titus. In the background Rome at sunset. Messiah in the garb of an old beggarman sits by the passage through the Arch. It is not noticeable that he is chained to the Arch. A shofar near him on the ground, and a jug of water. A few people, men and women, pass. Some notice him. A few throw him bits of food. Most don't see him. Messiah rises from his place, and his chains show.

Messiah (looking round): You have opened my heart to feel the sorrows of the world. But you have not given me the power to heal them. So there are endless sorrows in my heart. Every wrong, every evil makes stronger my chains, and I have no strength to break them. People and beasts look for me, run around with unrest in their hearts and fear in their eyes, asking one another: where is he, our saviour, our Redeemer? Why doesn't he come? And when our eyes close at night and we sleep, it is with the hope that he will come and wake us. So generations sleep and wait, in the everlasting night on the other side. And I see the dreamsmile on the face of the night, asking—Where is he? So I hear all the sorrows of the world. And I have no power to help. Lord God, when will the time come? In each generation great spirits arise. And they file at my chains with the Divine Word. In every generation fresh blood flows into my old bones. And I become rejuvenated, renewed. Perhaps this is the generation that is worthy to release me from my chains.

(He strains his ears, listening. From the distance comes martial music, drums and flutes and cymbals).

What do I hear? Who comes? Now! At this time!

(Enter Titus, a warrior, with sword and shield. Wants to go through the Arch. But Messiah bars his way).

Messiah: Where are you going, Titus? The time is past when you incited men against men, and sent them with weapons and hate to fight each other. Great spirits have risen in each generation, and told people how I stay here bound with chains against this wall. One day they will take away your ancient weapons, and remove the helmet from your head. They will stroke your cheeks as though you were a child, and will say to you: 'Stop playing the fool!' They will put you into a museum, together with other idols of the ancient past.

Titus: Still dreaming, old dreamer? Since I brought you here from Jerusalem, and fastened you to this Arch raised in my honour, you go on dreaming all the time and fail to see how Time has passed you by, how you have grown old, with your dream. Your bones are old and hard and stiff. In each generation you have sent out great spirits, yet nothing has changed. Your great spirits came to me. They do homage to me. All their wisdom is for me, to increase my power. On land, on sea, in the air new inventions are made to serve me, to advance the art of war. The poets sing odes in my honour. If I order it brothers will fight brothers, fathers their sons, offering themselves as sacrifices to me.

Messiah: You may well boast, Titus! You have spread hatred and enmity among people. But now your time has come! Your power is ended. Your coming here has helped me.

(He tears at his chains, which make a loud ringing, clanking noise).

Titus: Cast away your dream, old dreamer! Come and serve me! I am Power!

Messiah: Your power is only for a while. But Truth is for ever. Your time is past. Enmity and war is for a while. Peace and love are for ever. Soon the people will turn from you with loathing and abhorrence.

Titus: I'll show you how people abhor and loathe me. (Exit).

(A sound of cheering and loud clapping is heard. With martial music).

Titus (returning, crowned with wreaths and garlands): Man is a glorious creature when the noble savage is roused in him. When he smells blood. When his eyes glare, and his nostrils quiver, and his hands stretch out to strike. Maidens love the young warrior. When he returns from the battle-field they dance towards him, straight into his blood. Put away your dreaming, old fool. Take my laurel wreath. Wear it! (He places the wreath on Messiah's head). Follow me! I am Power!

(Cries from without: 'Come to us, great King!').

Titus: Stop dreaming, old fool! Follow me! (Exit amid acclaim and jubilation).

Messiah (as the noise dies away, frightened): And I thought my time had come. How long, O Lord, how long! How long must I wait? Everything has already been said. Everything has been done. Yet man is no better. Is Titus right? I have sat here and dreamed, and grown old with my dream, and nothing has changed. Lord God, give me a sign! Show me that I am wrong. That things have changed, that the time is nearer. That people are waiting for me. That evil will end. That there is somewhere a border-line, and on the other side there is justice and hope. Show me the border-line, Lord God! Let me see its light from afar, that I may have patience to sit here and wait, knowing that the time will come.

(A woman in black approaches, walking slowly like a Queen).

Messiah: Who is this, that walks like a Sabbath Queen, clad in sorrow? (The woman comes close up, and seats herself beside Messiah). Who are you, woman, bearing your sorrow in silence like God, and deep down in you like a human being?

The Mother: I am the mother of the child. And if I am immortal, human suffering is my suffering. None can feel the sorrow of a child more than its mother.

Messiah: (Bowing low) : I bow before your pain and sorrow, Mother!

Mother: Why do your chains sound so restless, Messiah? I heard them from afar, and came.

Messiah: Free me from them, and give me back my power. You can do it with your sorrow.

Mother: You know that God has ordained that the children should come to release you. We must both wait for them to come. The children are not yet ripe for it.

Messiah: I have grown impatient waiting for them. I sit here, chained, captive to Titus' Arch of Triumph. I have sent out messengers to tell the children that it all depends now on them.

Mother: The spirits no longer understand the people. If you were in their place, you would doubt as they do.

Messiah: Send me to them.

Mother: Can you do this? Can you endure it? To see the suffering and not have the power to help?

Messiah: I will become one of them. I will let the divine in me die. Let the human in me live. Let the human sorrow pass through my heart, so that I will feel it, and understand them, and know how to wait for them.

Mother: Give me the shofar. But do not seek in your heart to release them. Release only their sorrows. I take from you the power. Be one of them. Go to them.

(She removes his chains).

Messiah: I am free! I have not the shofar with me. Sorrow is the power of the Mother. Suffering gives strength. Titus, I call you out to battle! You with your power! I with my sorrow! (Exit).

EPILOGUE

The open highway, lined with poplars. Fields everywhere. Night. Occasionally a drum beats, and trumpets from the military camp. Jews keep arriving, at first singly, with burning torches to light their way. Then whole groups arrive.

191

Sholem Asch

Several Jews (directing the newcomers): Over here! Careful how you go! Careful! Careful with the children! The road is treacherous.

A Jew: The children mustn't cry. If they are heard, it will endanger us all.

Women: God in Heaven, help us!

(A cart comes along the road, with Reb Melech, hardly able to walk, following it, one hand on his son, Shlomo's shoulder, the other on that of his wife Malkele. Behind them their daughter Rebecca, dressed in black, her head bowed. Near her David and a group of Jews, one of them carrying a Scroll of the Law wrapped in a Tallith).

David: Stop! Stop for a moment, friends! Reb Melech can't go any further. (Some of the people come forward, anxiously asking, what has happened?).

Reb Melech (faintly): Don't stop! Go on! This road is dangerous!

David: Bring the cart over here! Reb Melech can't walk any further. He must get into the cart.

A Jew: Tell the women to get down from the cart. To make room for Reb Melech. Let the dead and the children stay.

Reb Melech: No, no! The women are ill and frail. I can still walk, thank God! (Tries to walk and falls).

A Jew: Let's stop here for a while. Till Reb Melech feels better.

First Jew: Why is God punishing us?

Second Jew: God is just and His Judgment is just.

A Voice: Who knows if there is anyone who sees our sufferings and hears our woe. Who knows if there is a hand to count our sufferings. Who knows?

First Woman: You mustn't talk like that! There must be a purpose to our sufferings! Else why, God forbid? What for?

Another Woman: Who knows?

First Woman: You mustn't say such things! This kind of talk can drive one mad.

A Man: This kind of talk is blasphemy! It makes God angry! Are we not suffering enough?

A Young Man: We should do what Job did. It is better to die than to live in shame.

Reb Melech (Making an effort): Complain to God, little petty Jews, complain to God that He created you Jews. (Lifts his arms to Heaven): I thank You and praise You, Lord God, for the sufferings we endure because we walk in Your ways. You have bestowed this great gift on us that we should bear the sorrow of the world, because the world has not yet reached perfection. The nations shoot their arrows at us, angry because you lead them with Your strong arm in the right direction. The nearer they come to the goal the more their eyes will shine and they will feel ashamed because of the sufferings they have inflicted on us. Complain, little petty Jews, weekaday Jews! You have forgotten what it is all about. God will by force compel you to be Jews! Remember, you are not alone. You are but a link in the chain. Come, let us join hands, and go dancing towards God, dancing and singing to Him, praising Him because He has created us Jews. Now at the height of our sufferings and our sorrows let us sing and dance. Because we know what it means to be Jews.

(He takes the Scroll of the Law from the man holding it, and makes weak dance movements with it. He sings):

Help us, God, we beseech Thee.
Prosper us, God, we beseech Thee.
For He is good to us!

(Several of the older Jews join in: Help us, God, we beseech Thee. The cart begins to move, and the people follow. Reb Melech takes a few steps with them, but falls).

David: Stop! Make room for Reb Melech in the cart! He can't walk.

Reb Melech: Please go on! Don't stop for me! Leave me here. I'm an old frail man, sated with years. Leave me here!

Malkele, and the crowd of Jews: You mustn't talk like that! Let us lift you up into the cart.

Reb Melech: Leave me here! I put an oath on you! Leave me here! You go on! Save yourselves! Save the children! Save the young people. Don't lose time arguing with me. The soldiers may get here and then you won't be able to escape! (He falls).

Malkele (screaming): Don't leave us! Stay with us! Reb Melech is dying! Bring water! Bring a lantern, over here!

(Jews come running up with water and a lighted lantern).

Reb Melech: I told you to go. I told you to go. I put you under an oath to leave me here! Save yourselves! Leave the old and the sick behind. Our Father in Heaven knows everything, sees everything. He will lead you in the right road.

(The people move off, dejectedly, reluctantly, shamefacedly. Only Reb Melech, his wife Malkele, their daughter Rebecca, their son Shlomo and Rebecca's betrothed David remain).

Reb Melech: I told you to go, Rebecca! And you Shlomo! And you, David! You are young people. Go! Save yourselves!

David: Please don't drive us away!

Reb Melech: You have no right to stay with me. You must go away, and live.

193

Your lives do not belong to you, but to God. Go, David! And Rebecca and Shlomo! Please go!

Malkele: Why do you drive them away, Melech? They want to stay. Let them stay.

Reb Melech: They mustn't stay! I am dying, Malkele! My Father in Heaven is calling me. Don't cry, Malkele! God is a merciful Father. I shall not fear to stand before His Judgment Seat. Or—perhaps they are right.

Malkele: What do you mean, Melech?

Reb Melech: I mean, perhaps those others are right. Perhaps we have deceived ourselves. Perhaps there is nothing where I am going—only black night. And I shall have no one to tell about our sufferings.

Malkele: What talk is this, Melech, God forbid!

Reb Melech: Who can know? What human being can tell? Have we waited in vain, Malkele? Is there nothing on the other side, only night? Is everything permitted, may anything be done? Is there nobody who measures and weighs our sufferings, our tears?

Malkele: What are you saying, Melech! Think of God!

Melech: I search, and I find only night. Black night.

Rebecca: The dark is dimming your eyes, father. Let me give you light. Look at my pearls (she puts on the pearls and they shine in the night).

Reb Melech (happily): I see the Sabbath candles. I see your mother blessing the Sabbath candles. I hear singing. It is the Holy Sabbath. There is silence all over the world. The Sabbath is coming with holy tread. Malkele, put on your Sabbath dress. The Sabbath is coming. The candles are lighted.

Malkele: What you see is the light from Rebecca's pearls.

Reb Melech: Good pearls, beautiful pearls. Cover me up, Malkele. I'm cold. I want to sleep.

Malkele (putting a coat over him): Your father is asleep. May God strengthen him in his sleep. Perhaps God will work a miracle and he will be better when he wakens.

(Rebecca and Malkele sit on the ground, side by side, near Reb Melech. After a time they too sleep. A strange light like the dawn breaks. Becomes brighter, very bright).

Reb Melech (sits up and cries out): Malkele, Malkele! Call the children! I want to see them before I die!

Malkele: How can I call the children together? Who knows where our sons are, on what battlefields they bleed.

Reb Melech: Call them from the battlefield. Call them! Let them stop their bloodshed! Let them come to me here. There is something I want to tell them before I die!

Rebecca: Go to the edge of the field, mother. Stand there and call Chaim and Moshe! Call them! Father wants them to come here.

Malkele (stands at the edge of the field, calling): Chaim ben Melech, your father calls you! He wants to bid you farewell before he leaves this world. (Pause. Chaim, the eldest son comes from the field; a bearded Jew in the uniform of a Russian soldier, with one lame leg, looks round astonished, wondering).

Chaim: Who calls me? (sees Malkele and Reb Melech). Who are you?

Malkele (cries out with joy): Chaim, my son!

Chaim (recognising his mother): What are you doing here, mother, on the battlefield, in the midst of the war? Where is my father?

Malkele (pointing to Reb Melech): There is your father. (Chaim walks over to Reb Melech).

Malkele (seeing he is lame): You have been wounded, Chaim?

Reb Melech: Is this my son Chaim? Yes! I recognise you. My son Chaim!

Chaim (kissing his father): How do you come to be here?

Malkele: They chased us out of our town, together with all the other Jews.

Chaim: Who did?

Malkele: Soldiers in uniform like you.

Chaim (sees Rebecca): Who is this?

Malkele: Your sister Rebecca.

Chaim: No! It can't be Rebecca! This is an old woman!

Malkele: That is what they made of her.

Reb Melech: Where is your brother Moshe, Chaim?

Chaim: I don't know. He was living in Vienna. He must be in the Austrian army, our enemy.

Reb Melech: Where is the enemy?

Chaim (pointing): On that other side of the field.

Reb Melech: Go and call Moshe, Malkele.

Malkele (stands at the other edge of the field, and calls): Moshe ben Melech! Your father calls you! Come here!

Chaim: What are you doing, mother? That's the enemy over there. (Moshe comes walking towards them, an elderly Jew in Austrian uniform, his head bandaged).

Moshe: Who is calling me? Mother!

Chaim (Runs at Moshe with his rifle): Our enemy!

Malkele (Rushes between them): Don't! He is your brother!
(Chaim and Moshe drop their rifles and stand looking bewildered).

Reb Melech: Why is there blood on your clothes, my sons?

Chaim and Moshe: We have come from the battlefield, father. We have been fighting, killing the enemy.

Reb Melech: Fighting? Killing? Didn't I teach you that the Torah says 'Thou shalt not kill!'

Chaim and Moshe: The Fatherland called us and said we must kill!

Reb Melech: What new Moloch is this Fatherland, my sons? Why do you worship this idol? Have I not taught you that there is only one God, and there is no other God beside Him, the Ruler of the Universe?

Chaim and Moshe (staring at each other): And I shot at you!

Malkele: How is it possible, God in Heaven! These are both my sons! I gave birth to them both. I suckled them both! And they fight in opposing armies against each other! Wound each other! Might kill each other!

Moshe: Why are you here, father, so near the fighting line! And who is this?

Chaim: Our sister Rebecca.

Moshe: Rebecca! Who has done this to you, Rebecca!

Reb Melech: You have done it! All of you!

Chaim and Moshe: We?

Reb Melech: Yes! You went out with sword and gun to kill people on the other side. Somebody's brother, somebody's father. A sister. A mother. A human creature!

Chaim and Moshe: We were made to, father. It was compulsory. We were forced.

Reb Melech: Forced to be murderers! To kill your brothers! To offer human sacrifice to your idol, your Moloch, the Fatherland! That is why God has punished us. (Lifts his hands to Heaven): I let myself for a moment fall into doubt. I began to question. But now I understand. Thank you, God, for letting me see before I close my eyes how right Your Judgments are.

Chaim and Moshe: What shall we do, father?

Reb Melech: Serve God as you have served till now your idol, the Fatherland. Go and find water and wash the blood from your hands, and pray to God to forgive you. May God have mercy on you. May He forgive!

Chaim: Forgive me, brother!

Moshe: And you, forgive me, brother!

Reb Melech: Who will forgive the shame done to your sister? Who will forgive that?

(The brothers turn to look at Rebecca, but the light from her pearls dazzles them, and they back away).

Chaim and Moshe: What is that great light shining from Rebecca?

Reb Melech: The light from the pearls that our tortured daughters wear. It is the witness to their chaste purity.

(Song approaching in the distance):

The pearls shine that our sisters wear.
They sparkle and shine, with a light holy and rare.
They were saved from the unclean; our daughter, our child.
Escaped from the evil-doer, undefiled.

Rebecca: Don't you recognise me? (She stands transformed in the form of the Mother. All back away. She steps slowly towards Reb Melech, the pearls shining at her throat): My son! You have been silent for long. You have swallowed your pain and your grief. My house is destroyed. You have been hunted across the earth, and you have kept silent. Take this shofar (hands him the shofar) blow to the right and blow to the left, and proclaim to the whole world—Salvation has come! Brother has recognised brother! Hallelujah!

Reb Melech (blowing the shofar): Salvation has come! A great Salvation has come over the whole world. Brother has recognised brother! Hallelujah! (The Commander runs up from the battlefield. Sees the two soldiers, Chaim and Moshe).

Commander: What are you doing here? Get back to the battlefield! Fight the enemy! (Suddenly becomes aware that Moshe is wearing enemy uniform. To Chaim): What are you doing, fraternising with the enemy! Treason! Shoot him down!

Chaim: He is my brother! No enemy!

Commander: Treason! (calling across to the battlefield): Soldiers! There is treason here! Come and arrest these Jews!

(A sound of singing comes from the battlefield):

Say it to the right, say it to the left,
A great Salvation has come to the world.
Brother has recognised brother!
Hallelujah!

Commander: Mutiny! You're behind this, you old Jew! (recognises Reb Melech): You're that old Jew I had trouble with before! Soldiers, arrest him! He is our enemy!

Chaim and Moshe: He is our father!

Commander: Who released you from your chains? Who gave you back your youth and strength?

Reb Melech-Messiah: The sufferings you inflicted on me, Titus, made me strong! Made me young!

Commander: Soldiers, I order you to arrest this Jew!

Reb Melech (blows the shofar. The singing from the battlefield comes nearer and nearer):

A great Salvation has come to the world!
Brother has recognised brother!
Hallelujah!

Commander (runs away, shouting): Treason! The Jew has organised a mutiny! (The singing grows louder and nearer. The stage darkens, leaving only Reb Melech dying on the highway, with Malkele and Rebecca at his side).

Rebecca: I've had a strange dream, mother. I dreamt that I had grown old, had become an old Jewish Mother.

Malkele: I too dreamed. I saw my sons in my dream, all of them together, holding hands.

Rebecca: I dreamt that father had become a young man again. Young and strong.

Reb Melech (with a last effort): Malkele, I hear the shofar being blown. Has Messiah come?

Curtain.

May 25th. 1915.

DAVID PINSKI

Small Heroes

PERSONS:
Fourteenyear old.
Thirteenyear old.
First Twelveyear old.
Second Twelveyear old.
Elevenyear old.
Tenyear old.

TIME:
The Present. Place: A ravaged village in a country at war and defeated. A big living room in a peasant cottage badly damaged by gunfire. A shell has ripped through the roof, leaving a big hole in the floor. Bullet marks in all the walls. Every window broken, the doors hanging loose on the hinges. Bits of furniture hit by the gunfire in heaps on the floor. Only a long bench and two chairs have been left whole.

The Fourteenyear old (enters, looks round angrily, stamps his foot, shakes his fist at the broken windows).

First Twelveyear old (enters and stands at the door, afraid): Worse than with us!

Fourteenyear old: Where are they, all of them?

First Twelveyear old: I don't know. I haven't seen them. (Looks up at the hole in the ceiling). Went right through! You can see the sky. That must have been the shell that killed your mother!

Fourteenyear old: Tore her to bits.

First Twelveyear old: Where was she?

Fourteenyear old: Over here. Standing against that cupboard.

First Twelveyear old: And they shot the cupboard to bits.

Fourteenyear old: Those are the bits and pieces. All over the floor.

First Twelveyear old: Smashed up the whole of your furniture. (Bangs his fist on the bench, as if testing its strength): And smashed us up too!

Fourteenyear old (angrily): I know! They hardly touched your place. Everything there is almost as it was.

First Twelveyear old: Yes, but there's a whole wall smashed down. And the chimney. And the barn, burnt right out. They killed our dog. And broke up his kennel. And my grandmother died of fright.

Fourteenyear old (looking out of the window): They're late. Playing ball, I suppose, and forgot the time.

First Twelveyear old: Nobody plays ball now. Nobody plays anything now. I'm ever so sad. I hide behind the house. I just hang around. I'm hungry. Haven't you got a bit of bread?

Fourteenyear old: Not a scrap!

First Twelveyear old: Some of them went to the enemy to try to get bread.

Fourteenyear old: Ought to be ashamed of themselves!

First Twelveyear old: But they're all hungry. Aren't you hungry?

Fourteenyear old: I wouldn't touch bread from the enemy.

First Twelveyear old: Your father wasn't killed in the war. My father got a bullet through his head. (Enter the Thirteenyear old and the Second Twelveyear old. Speaking to them): Look! Look at that! That was a shell that went right through the roof. And through the floor.

Fourteenyear old: Is this what you think is coming on time?

Thirteenyear old (bending over the hole): What a huge hole!

Second Twelveyear old: Must have been some bang when that hit!

First Twelveyear old: Tore his mother to bits, that's what it did! And smashed up the whole of the furniture. Look at those bits and pieces lying on the floor.

Thirteenyear old (stretching full length on the bench): I had to stay and look after my little sister. She keeps crying, says she's hungry. I gave her my finger to suck. She nearly bit it off.

Second Twelveyear old: My mother keeps crying, sobbing the whole time. I had to sneak out so that she shouldn't see me go.

(Enter the Elevenyear old, dragging the Tenyear old with him):

Elevenyear old: That was some job getting him here! He wouldn't move!

Tenyear old: I'm hungry!

Elevenyear old: Look at that huge hole!

Tenyear old: If it starts raining this place will be flooded!

Thirteenyear old: You're telling us! (He goes on, speaking to the Fourteenyear old, who paces up and down impatiently): You've got quite a meeting here!

Fourteenyear old: I've got a plan. I want to talk it over with you. I need your help.

Elevenyear old (settles down on the floor, with his feet in the hole): What a huge hole!

(First Twelveyear old squats beside him. Second Twelveyear old tries to do the same, and then changes his mind and sits down on a chair. The Tenyear old sprawls full length on the floor, resting his head on a heap of smashed furniture).

Fourteenyear old (heatedly): Aren't we the only men left now in the village? The only ones of any use? The old fellows can't do anything. They can't march. They can't fight. And the women can't do anything. And the girls can't. So it's up to us! We've got to do something!

Tenyear old: But I'm hungry!

Fourteenyear old: Our army keeps falling back. And the enemy advances, deeper and deeper into our country. Occupies one town after the other, one village after the other. We've got to stop them!

Elevenyear old: You're right!

Thirteenyear old: How can we stop them? What can we do?

Elevenyear old: I've been counting the bullet holes in these walls. Tirty-seven.

Fourteenyear old: Aren't we behind the enemy? Are we or aren't we? In their rear?

Elevenyear old: Yes of course, we are! The enemy is a good thirty miles in front of us, gone farther!

Fourteenyear old: Then there are a lot of things we can do!

Second Twelveyear old: That must have been some bang when that hole was made. Right through the roof and the ceiling, and the floor!

Tenyear old: The same with our place.

Fourteenyear old (to the Thirteenyear old): Can you climb up a pole?

Tenyear old: Better than you!

Tenyear old: So can I! I can climb better than any of you!

Fourteenyear old: Then one of us will climb up a telegraph pole and cut the wire.

Elevenyear old: I can climb like a cat!

Thirteenyear old: You're the hero! You go and do it!

Fourteenyear old: We'll do it together. Three of us. Four of us. That's why I want you to help me!

Thirteenyear old: There's a soldier with a rifle standing guard at every telegraph pole.

Fourteenyear old (producing a knife from under his jacket): This will take care of him. (All stare at the knife).

Elevenyear old: We've also got a big kitchen knife.

Fourteenyear old: You'll each of you get a knife. And at night, when it's pitch black, we'll crawl on our bellies up to where the sentry stands on watch, and we'll stick the knife into him. Then we'll climb up the pole and cut the wire.

Elevenyear old (jumping up excitedly): Yes, that's what we'll do! A knife at his throat. And then we'll climb the pole (making cat-climbing motions).

Tenyear old: And there'll be some bread in the dead soldier's pockets.

Thirteenyear old: Suppose the soldier sees us coming, and shoots before we get to him?

Fourteenyear old: We don't let him! We'll get there first.

Elevenyear old: He won't see us! We'll get there very quietly, very quickly!

Tenyear old: Yes, I know! Nobody can hear me when I crawl on my belly. Only I'm so hungry! The soldier is sure to have some bread on him.

Fourteenyear old: And then we can go on to another one. We can kill a lot of sentries, and cut a lot of telegraph wires.

Elevenyear old: And when the telegraph wires are cut the enemy commanders won't be able to pass on their orders. Their army will be in a mess. And then our side will win.

Tenyear old: And then we'll have a lot of bread to eat.

Second Twelveyear old: The enemy army carries a lot of bread with it. Have you seen their food wagons? I've counted them. Forty four! And their field kitchen!

Fourteenyear old (excited): There are lots of other things we can do. There's an army officer living in the Squire's house. He's got all the strategic plans and dispatches there. We can get in during the night and steal them. We could kill him while he's sleeping. That would finish off the enemy!

Elevenyear old: That's a great idea!

First Twelveyear old (full of enthusiasm): We'll kill the commander! And then our army will walk over them!

Thirteenyear old (scornfully): How do you think you're going to get at their commander? He's got a bodyguard round him. We've got no chance!

Fourteenyear old: But we'll try!

Thirteenyear old: We'll try the first idea first! Let's see you kill one of their sentries and cut the telegraph wire!

Fourteenyear old: Yes, I'll do it!

Elevenyear old: We'll all do it!

Thirteenyear old: The sentry will shoot us dead before we get to him.

Fourteenyear old: You're a frightened little coward boy!

Thirteenyear old: I'm hungry! I want something to eat!

Fourteenyear old: I'm also hungry! We're all hungry!

Second Twelveyear old: My mother fainted to-day because she's had nothing to eat. If she gets a bit of bread somewhere she gives it to us children. She doesn't eat it. Oh, I'm so hungry!

Elevenyear old: I'm also hungry! Terribly hungry! But I don't keep talking about it!

Tenyear old: I want something to eat!

Fourteenyear old: We're all hungry. But that mustn't stop us from what we've got to do.

Thirteenyear old: I'm starving! I'll die if I don't get something to eat.

Second Twelveyear old: My mother is dying of hunger. For all I know she's dead already (sobs).

First Twelveyear old: I'm going mad with hunger! I can't stand it any longer! (He breaks into tears. And so do all the others, except the Fourteenyear old).

Fourteenyear old: Look at you! A lot of cry babies, that's what you are! How can I do anything with you! Stop crying! Stop crying! (Waves his knife about, then throws it on the floor and sinks helplessly on to the second chair).

MOISHE BRODERSON

Shylock Laughs

Dressing room of the great English tragedian Edmund Kean. He is made up
as Shylock, ready to go on stage for the Trial Scene. His friend, the Prompter,
adjusting his robe. Kean is tense, on edge. The big dressing room is white-
washed, so that the back wall, as soon as the lights are out, becomes a screen
on which appear as shadows the Shylock figures to which Kean delivers his
monologue.

Prompter: I am afraid, Master!
Kean: What makes you afraid, old fool? Be much better if you opened a
   window in here. It's so stuffy. There's a load of despair in the air!
Prompter: That's what makes me afraid! That's why!
Kean: Why? What? What are you afraid of?
Prompter: The blasted Trial Scene in that damned Jew-Play!
Kean: It isn't a Jew-Play, my friend. It isn't a Jew-Play.

It's a Christian comedium.
A contribution to old William's Evangelium!
Besides, consider all these people in the play.
Shylock is perhaps the only one that we can say,
He is honest and upright in his rage,
Out of all these whom Shakespeare put on the stage.

Do open the window!

Prompter opens a window. The wind rushes in and puts out the lights. The
stage is dark. Kean's Shylock monologue is continually interrupted by lightning and thunder, and the impatient clapping of the waiting audience. The
Shylock shapes appear on the wall.

Prompter: (backing away) I'm going to get a light. Light!
Kean: All right, go! Go to the devil, the lot of you!

(Thunder and lightning) What have you come here for? What do you want?

Why do you plague me? By what devil were you sent?
Go, all of you, bring your light, your fire!
You want to burn me! You have already laid the pyre,

With fuel of lies and hate.
For centuries your injustices have been our fate!
You speak of love, of money prate.
Of the quality of mercy, how it can mitigate
Your savagery.
What do you mean to do with me?
The Jew must be merciful, you say.
But for the Jew, you leave only one way—
To put him down, to slay and slay.
And all in the name of your Christian faith.
In the name of mercy you deal out hate and death!

(Thunder and lightning)

Your God had to make his way to you,
Through storm and mud, blundering through.
And you cut him up, so that each of you
Would have a bit of heaven, as your own to show.
And you think because you speak in his name,
You will escape hell's flame.
You have a crooked soul.
And your road is foul.
But in your folly
You call it Holy.

(Thunder and lightning, Shylock's shadows move across the wall.)

Yet, I Shylock, what wrong have I done?
What have I taken that is not my own?
Have I driven one of you from your home,
Sent you homeless across the world to roam?
Have I betrayed you to your foes?
Do I refuse to obey your laws?
Do I not love Venice as much as you,
Because I love her as a Jew?
But you, you stole away my only child,
My daughter Jessica! I would rather she were killed!
And you have robbed me of all my gold,
All that I had against your thieving world,
All that I had to buy myself a place,

Where you would let me live a little space.
You have stripped me of my possessions and my pride.
You left me naked, to mock me and deride.
Am I not a man as all men are,
That when you hurt me I should cry out, like you should dare!

(Lightning and thunder)

O great Doge of Venice, I can see
How the laws of Venice allow you this liberty,
To take from me all that I possess,
Even my daughter, my Jessica, my Jess!
A foolish girl by a fop misled.
May my curse come upon his head!
What excuse have you, what excuse,
Except that you may do anything with Jews!

As for Portia—
I bow before her, with deep respect,
Before a high-born aristocrat.
She is shrewd, she is ingenious.
How those two maids dressed up and deceived all of us,
And became my Judges!
She knows the value of pledges.
She says, whatever you bring,
She will accept nothing but the ring.
And they condemn me because I too
Demand my pledge, owing from you.
Your Law is blind; it will not see
The Justice that is due to me.
This knife was made to slay, and slay it must,
Slay both the unjust and the just.
But mostly the just.

Prompter, wearing a little Shakespeare beard, enters hastily with a lighted candle.

Kean: Who is that?
    That you, Mr. Shakespeare!
Prompter: Master!

206

I am your friend, the Prompter!
Kean: You back again?
   The devil sent you here!
   Get out! Get out, you and your Light!
   I don't need your prompting!

The wind blows out the light. Pause.

Kean: I need no prompting!
   I know what to say!
   Out with you! Out with your Light!
   Get out, I say! (Laughs)
   I like the idea, Miss Portia!
   And my daughter, as well.
   I like the way you covered up Justice's eyes
   With a spider-web veil.
   You said that I may have my bond,
   My pound of heart-flesh.
   But no jot of blood.
   You say that Venice Law allows it!
   Is that understood?
   Then let me try the experiment.
   Let me see if I can get my pound
   Without drawing blood from the wound.
   Nor must I cut less or more
   Than a just pound,
   The pound you have awarded me.
   I'll try it! Let me see!

He rushes towards Antonio's image, with the knife, and cuts.

   You see!
   Don't you see!
   I said he has no heart in him for me.
   Stupid Portia! Stupid Jessica!
   Come, my daughter, come and see—
   He has no heart, but I have a heart in me!

He plunges the knife into his breast, and falls. Prompter runs out, crying: 'Is there a doctor here?'

Curtain falls. Prompter appears before the curtain.

Prompter: Dear audience,
  A terrible thing has happened. I mean,
  Has happened to our great Master, Edmund Kean.
  He has gone clean out of his mind.
  And this play is now at an end.

'Shylock Laughs' was dedicated by Broderson to the famous Yiddish Actor Abraham Morevski, who played Kean at its first production in Lodz, with Abraham Kurtz playing the Prompter.

ITZIK MANGER

Scene Seven From "The Hotzmach Play"

A Big Store.

Salesmen (singing):
   Customers, come here, come quickly!
   We have bargains for your choosing.
   Come quickly! Quickly! Quickly!
   Don't wait till we're closing!
   If you've got the money
   What we sell is worth double.
   If you have no money,
   Don't waste time and give us trouble!
                              (Snap their fingers)

Enter Three Hotzmachs (not seeing each other, they rush in different directions, bumping into one another):

All Three Hotzmachs Together: Look where you're going!
First Hotzmach: Sure as my name is Hotzmach!
Second Hotzmach: Your name isn't Hotzmach! Because my name is Hotzmach. Who told you your name was Hotzmach?
Third Hotzmach: Yes, who told you your name is Hotzmach?
Second Hotzmach: Another Hotzmach! Look at him! Ha! Ha! Ha! Says he's Hotzmach! What do you say to that?
Third Hotzmach: What are you laughing at? What's so funny about it? Where's the joke?
Second Hotzmach: You saying you're Hotzmach. When actually I'm Hotzmach.
First Hotzmach: Thieves and liars! A man is no longer safe with his own name! I'm Hotzmach!
Second Hotzmach: Whom are you calling a thief? I'm Hotzmach.
Third Hotzmach: No, you're not! I'm Hotzmach. You people must be mad!
First Hotzmach: I'm not mad! I'm Hotzmach! Look, here's my proof. Hotzmach's got a little goatee beard. Look!
Second and Third Hotzmachs (tugging at identical goatee beards): Correct! Hotzmach has a little goatee beard. Look!

First Hotzmach: And Hotzmach has a yellow patch on his right sleeve.

Second and Third Hotzmachs: Correct! Perfectly right! Look! Here's the yellow patch on my right sleeve.

First Hotzmach: More proof. Hotzmach has three grown-up daughters. One hasn't any shoes. Another hasn't got a dress. And the third wants a young man to get married.

Second and Third Hotzmachs: Sure! That's absolutely right! Three grown-up daughters. One who has no shoes. One who has no dress. And the third wants a young man to get married.

First Hotzmach: And they sit at home all day, plucking goose feathers.

Second and Third Hotzmachs: Yes, that's true! They sit all day plucking goose feathers. How do you know what's going on in my house?

First Hotzmach: I'm Hotzmach! Why shouldn't I know what's going on in my own house?

Second and Third Hotzmachs: My house!

First Hotzmach: And for further proof—I can't make a living! (pointing to himself).

Second and Third Hotzmachs (each pointing to himself): I can't make a living!

First Hotzmach: Then we're all Hotzmachs!

Second and Third Hotzmachs: That's right! We're all Hotzmachs! (they sing):

First Hotzmach:
  I have the honour
  To introduce
  Hotzmach, a dealer
  In anything you choose—
  Strings of beads, collar studs and laces,
  Sealing wax, soap and braces,
  Also mirrors, looking glasses
  For young girls with pretty faces.

Refrain. All Three:
  We're all of us Hotzmachs.
  Some older, some younger,
  We're all of us Hotzmachs.
  And we're all dying of hunger.
  We peddle,
  We meddle,

We rush and we fly.
Isn't there anything
You'd like to buy?

Second Hotzmach:
I have the honour
To bring you greeting.
I'm Hotzmach, a dealer
In things good for eating.
I have figs and raisins.
I have old hats and new suspenders.
And only in my dreams
I have money, like the big spenders.

Refrain. All Three: We're all of us Hotzmachs, etc.

Third Hotzmach:
I have the honour—
I'm sure everyone knows,
That I'm Hotzmach, a dealer
In chocolates and old clothes,
Stale bread and rolls,
Purim rattles and soap bubbles.
And from it all
I get nothing but troubles.

Refrain: We're all of us Hotzmachs, etc.
Salesmen: What can we do for you, gentlemen?
All Three Hotzmachs Together: We want some goods.
Salesmen: What sort of goods?
The Three Hotzmachs: Linen.
Salesmen: How many metres?
The Three Hotzmachs: The more the better.
Salesmen: You will pay cash?
The Three Hotzmachs: Cash? No! God forbid!
First Salesman: Then you don't get a single metre!
First Hotzmach: What did you say? What did you say? I'm going straight to
the river to drown myself!
Second Hotzmach: I'll give you a promissory note.
Second Salesman: Who'll guarantee it?

First and Third Hotzmachs (each pointing to himself): Me! I will!
Salesmen (laughing aloud): Ha! Ha! Ha!
All Three Hotzmachs: What are you laughing at?
First Salesman: We don't give credit just like that!
Second Salesman: Come back to-morrow!
Third Salesman: Yes, try again to-morrow.

(The three Hotzmachs go running round the store, looking very down in the mouth).

First Hotzmach (stops short, and beats his forehead): I have a Plan!
Second Hotzmach (also stopping short): I have a Plan!
Third Hotzmach (jumps in the air): I have a Plan! A Plan! A Plan!

(All three rush to the counter).

First Hotzmach: Show me your linen. What's it like? Let me have a sample!
Second Hotzmach: Me too! Let me have a sample as well!
Third Hotzmach: And me! If my customer likes it I'll give you an order right away!

(The three salesmen cut off three strips of linen. All three Hotzmachs run around happily with the linen samples in their hands).

First Hotzmach: Aren't I clever? I've got the linen! Now I can go out and sell it!
Second Hotzmach: And I've got linen too! I'm going straight to the market now to sell my linen.
Third Hotzmach: I'm going to sell my linen. Very good linen. Better than raisins and almonds.
First Hotzmach: I'm going to the market here.
Second Hotzmach: I'll go to the market in Pauperburg.
Third Hotzmach: And I'll go to Mendicant town!
First Hotzmach: Anything goes! This way or that! So long as we don't under-cut. No competition!
Second and Third Hotzmachs: No competition! God forbid!

(All three Hotzmachs sing) 'We're all of us Hotzmachs.'

(They dance, holding up their pieces of linen. The salesmen stand laughing at them).

Curtain

POEMS

HALPER LEIVICK	MOSHE KULBAK
AARON ZEITLIN	A. VOGLER
ZALMAN SHNEOUR	ITZIK MANGER
LEYELESS	LEON FEINBERG
ABRAHAM SUTZKEVER	MELECH RAVITCH
JACOB GLATSTEIN	CHAIM GRADE
ISAAC KATZNELSON	JOSEPH RUBINSTEIN
HIRSH GLICK	BINEM HELLER
MORDECAI GEBIRTIG	PERETZ MARKISH
KADIA MOLODOVSKY	ISSY CHARIK
ROCHEL KORN	MOSHE BRODERSON
ELIEZER GREENBERG	SAMUEL HALKIN
EPHRAIM AUERBACH	ITZIK FEFFER
URI ZVI GREENBERG	A. N. STENZEL
MANI LEIB	

I Was Not in Treblinka

I was not in Treblinka,
And in Maidanek I was not.
But I stand on their threshold,
Very near the spot.

Jews into the gas-chamber!
Forests mourn, are sad
Over the hills and valleys
Winds dance like mad.

The sun burns in heaven,
As it rises higher,
Sending out tongues of flame
From Maidanek's furnace fire.

And I stand waiting my turn,
In Treblinka's fires to burn.

I Should Have Died with You

I should have died with you,
But I found dying too hard.
Now I do everything to hide with colour
The convulsions of my body and word.

Neither grief nor anger can drown
The guilt of my living on,
My guilt because the flames of Treblinka
Didn't consume me flesh and bone.

All words now become smooth masks,
To hide the world's brand of Cain,

To disguise our bankruptcy—
That we can't pay for one child slain.

When I gird sackcloth on my loins,
And on my head ashes spread,
The slayer comes again to slay,
And chops off another head.

Shame grips my heart, when day
Begins at my window to sing.
My knife and fork recall stabbed bodies.
Each gulp is a noose tightening.

I try to hide in the folds of hope.
But now I have understood
That all the vessels in the world are broken.
And God has no place left where to store Abel's blood.

Edgar Allan Poe's Raven

The black crow
Of Edgar Allan Poe
Tapped at my window to-day.
All round black darkness lay.
Who is there? said I.
Doves—came the reply.

It was late at night, there was storm and rain,
And hail beat on my window-pane.
I opened the window wide,
And the poor lost vagrants took inside.

I did not think anyone might
Come to fool me late at night.
I took my visitors at their word,
I took it they were doves, as I had heard,
And I prepared for them a bed.
Sleep in peace, doves, I said.

216

I am always glad when I have done
A kindness to anyone.
Sleep doves, in your quiet bed,
To my visitors I said.

The rain poured down in torrents in the street,
And on my roof like hammers beat.
I pulled the blankets over my head,
And tried to fall asleep in my bed.

But suddenly I
Was roused from my sleep by a terrible cry,
A cry from a mouth that curses and swears.
I rose from my bed,
And my heart and my head
Were filled with horror and fears.

But no sooner had I
Put my foot on the floor
Than vicious beaks and claws
At my face and body tore.

They were carrion crows
Who scratched and tore,
And left me bruised and bleeding
On the floor.

This is no dream story. It is true.
The pit opens wider for me and for you.
Poe lived in the days of nevermore,
And we live in days of outrage and terror.

Halper Leivick

Song About Myself

I have seen flogged bodies,
Seen the blood flow.
When I became a writer
I wrote songs about snow.

People liked those songs,
Because they were white like snow.
But I began to hate them,
Because they hid the blood below.

So the years passed by,
And increased my hate.
But I had become a writer,
And the blood under the snow had to wait.

Then one day I took a pen,
And scraped the snow away.
And all shrank back from the blood
That on the ground lay.

The blood was still warm,
As if freshly bled.
'Why does he torment us with blood?'
People angrily said.

And they cursed my poems,
Poured venom on my tongue,
And my heart fell fainting
Beside my wounded song.

My songs still cried aloud
Their anguish and woe,
They remained lying on the ground,
But no longer covered with snow.

Now I am always a writer,
But this is my truth and my aim,
That in the blood of flogged bodies
Lies also my tormented fame.

So it is also with my songs.
Let them lie so.
I may cover them up again
When I have some fresh snow.

On Your Earth, Jerusalem

On your earth, Jerusalem,
I can be silent for ages.
I open for my words
All their cages.

I let them all
Go out free,
With thanks and with praise
For their loyalty.

I release them—'Go,
Over all the mountains,' I say.
'Over all the hills of Jerusalem,
My dear ones, fly away.
Choose the holiest places—
They are all your own.
Go, rest there, rest.
Leave me here, alone,
With the dream that I dream,
To be for one minute, at least
With myself at peace.'

'On your earth, Jerusalem,
The silence goldens by day.
The silence blues at night.
I stop, and I suddenly say:
"Was it here Isaiah trod?
Was it really here?'

The night-silence answers:
'Yes, it was here he stood.'
Baffled, I call to my words,
I call them back like birds:
'Return, my dear ones, from your places.
Help me in silence to rejoice,
That here where Isaiah trod,
My foot now paces.'

AARON ZEITLIN

A Dream After Maidanek

This too will be forgotten, this too.
They have burned my people,
And it will be forgotten, this too.
Where the Nalevkis roared
The wind blows among the grass.
Wind and grass.

Rechov Zeitlin in Tel Aviv

I walk in the street which bears my father's name,
And tremble in my shoe.
Soon he will rise up there,
A tall prophetic Jew,
In that corner of the street,
His beard like a stormwind in front of him flies,
And behind follow balconies,
All Tel Aviv, every street.
And all the doors that to Messiah lead
Rushing on, with wild holy speed.

No, the street is still.
A child laughs.
And there is sunshine on a window-sill.

One Summer

In post-Maidanek godless years,
I see the past mirrors, like a dreamer.
One summer we went to Plotzk,

Aaron Zeitlin

Down the Vistula by steamer.
To Plotzk down the Vistula by steamer.

A single cloud was floating by.
How comes a Vistula-fish to be on high?
The cloud flowed, and the Vistula flowed,
A cloud that looked like a dove,
A fish floating happily above.

And I, on the steamer's deck, with her,
The loveliest of Warsaw's daughters.
God spread the blue wedding canopy over us,
And broke the sun like a plate in the waters,
The sun in the Vistula waters!

Good luck! Over bits of broken sun
Our ship goes sailing on.

ZALMAN SHNEOUR

The Last Words of Don Henriquez

These words spake Don Henriquez
As he burned in the auto-da-fé,
And the banner with the image of the Saviour
Fluttered before his eyes:

Jesus of Nazareth,
Son of man, and my brother,
Your robe, stained with suffering,
Has darkened the light of the sun.

Your pierced feet redden
All the rivers of Spain.
There is none holy save you,
None that is tormented in the name of God
Save Jesus the Jew,
Who was crucified on Calvary.

On the spires of the temples
You have fixed your cross.
It is hung in the bedchambers,
And from the necks of women and children.

You are worshipped on your cross,
Your wounds are kissed on your marble image,
And Jews and heretics are slain
As an offering to you this day.

Do not trust these strangers, Jesus!
Wandering through the centuries
I have learned their ways and language,
I have learned to know them now.
Like straw in the mouth of a tiger
Is to them the taste of your compassion.
Moloch still reigns in their houses of worship,
And the beast of prey is in their blood.

Since the wild beasts have gone from the forests,
And the forests are thinned and cleared,
They now hunt men in the cities,
With prayer and with organ chant.

In your name, in the name of grace and salvation,
In God's name, on with the hunt!

Do not believe these strangers, Jesus.
The day will come, it is not far off,
When they will hunt you too from their churches,
From their steeples and their domes,
From the throats of their wives and children.

Like a withered branch you will fall
Down from their noble cathedrals,
That are built to mount to the sky,
Coptic, Byzantine and Gothic,
For the glorification of your name.

And kings will kneel down,
And princes beat their breast,
And nations will be ashamed
Because they had worshipped a Jew,
Worshipped him all these centuries
That we have been dispersed.

'Out with you!' they will cry,
Just as they cry to us,
Only to you they will also add—
'Huckster with love and meekness,
You have cheated us, you Jew,
For a wooden cross you exchanged
Zeus's hero-deeds and Odin's.
To the stake with you, to the stake, Marrano!'

It is the fate of us both,
Henriquez to-day, and Jesus next.

And they will break open the graves,
And bring out the dust of their ancestors,

For their honour will massacre children,
They will mate in the sun like cattle,
That their seed may be increased,
And then they will send these children
To death on the field of honour.

Thus the One will be disrupted,
The Creator severed from His world,
And man from the Law.
And each nation will serve a different idol,
And when a nation is vanquished in battle
Its god too will be vanquished,
And will become an object of scorn
To his former worshippers.

You will be deserted, Jesus,
Forsaken on your breaking cross,
With your outstretched arms—
And on your bleeding feet you will limp,
As we do, along strange roads,
And the hem of your garment
Will sweep up the filth of the nations and lands
That you will pass on your flight.

And out of each town and land,
Out of cathedrals and museums
They will hurl with execration
Your image and your name,

Paintings and statues
Hewed in stone and in marble,
Crowned with haloes and thorns,
A multitude of the tormented,
A hundred times the number of those
Who went out from Egypt.

Dripping red from their wounds,
And with tears frozen in their eyes,
A procession growing in number,
Winding across the highlands and streaming down

Zalman Shneour

Like a waterfall into the valleys,
Broadening out and narrowing again—

The last crusade
To the distant hills of Judea.

And mothers and daughters and sisters,
All the pure daughters of Israel,
Dressed in white and in black
Will stand on both sides of the roadways,
A guard of honour for the hunted,

And they will recognise in you and your effigies,
And in the thousands of ikons,
Each mother her son who was tortured with glowing pincers,
And each wife her husband whose tongue was torn out in the market place,
Each sister will find her brother who was massacred,
Each orphan her murdered father,
All who were falsely accused of ritual murder and of poisoning wells,
Who perished in the crusades, and during the black plague,
And me too, my wife and daughters will recognise.

And each Jewish woman will press to her heart
A picture, a statue, the image of her lost one,
Tormented and crucified,
And each will be a Madonna weeping for her dead.
Oh, what a vast number of Pietas,
All the way from Europe to the hills of Zion!

And you, noble martyr, who will head the procession,
A new Sanhedrin will welcome you.
They come, to lead you to the banks of the Jordan,
To bathe in the holy water,
To heal your wounds,
Till your tear-stained eyes light up and shine,
And you will be cleansed from the taint
Of the dead they have slaughtered,
And the Scrolls of the Law they have burned in the market place,
Whose smoke has blackened your forehead.

226

And being clean as Naaman when he was healed of his leprosy
They will receive you with new psalms,
With open arms and with hearts full of love,
As to-day we receive a Marrano
Who returns to his faith.

No Pilate will be able to judge you by Roman law,
Nor any zealot or pharisee to denounce you,
For ours will be the land,
And the courts of law will be ours.
No stranger will interfere in a dispute between brothers.

Jesus of Nazareth,
My breath fails me,
My word is being carried to heaven by horses of fire,
The stake has become like the throne of Solomon,
I am clad in purple,
And my burning hair is my crown.

I shall not cry out as you did, Jesus,
'My God, why hast Thou forsaken me!'
I have been favoured by the God of Jacob
Far beyond the lot of other mortals,
And therefore I will glorify God's Name,
That He has found me worthy to be a torch for the erring,
Burning with my blood and flesh,
And pointing in the dark and the mist
The way to eternity to my brothers.

The fire is near my heart,
The wet cloths steam and my tongue roasts between my teeth,
Strengthen me, God of Jacob, for one more moment,
That I may cry even as I die,
'Hear me all peoples!
Hear oh Israel',
And you too, Jesus, cry with me—
'The Lord our God is One God!'

A. LEYELESS

To the Jewish People

Another foe, another foe—you are too experienced and wise,
Another vein cut, some of your blood drawn off again,
Another dazzling vision in the new darkness dies;
You are experienced and know that none the cup of fate can utterly drain.

You do not need my weeping over your disaster, no redeemer you need,
You know yourself and know man too well—that noble creature man,
You realised long ago punishment is futile and futile is reward and meed,
All is wind and vanity—both tears and wrath as futile ban.

You run, fall, rise, run again, get heated and shout till your very coat
Perspires and is thrown out of shape, so that fine folk sneer,
But presently you find your breath, yet something sticks in your throat,
And in your eye the sadness of the whole rotten earthly sphere.

Then your eye peers omnisciently through all disaster and dismay,
All creatures' shame and anguish struck terribly dumb in your sight,
Then you are you, are mighty, glorious like the bridge of the milky way
That links the dark infinitudes with little dots of light.

At such times I love you, people of thoroughly tanned hide,
With a love that a son for his father has never known yet,
You, the riddle, inventor of answers pretty and self-satisfied,
You who deny the second great riddle—death.

The new huntsmen and encirclers you will survive them as well.
You need no redeemers, you know each saviour's futile end,
Your Moseses are stammerers, your Davids stumbled and sinned and fell.
And your strength is contempt for the strength of those who seek to destroy
    and to rend.

228

A. Leyeless

Homer and Isaiah

The beauty of Homer is unsurpassed—it is Homer.
His simple nobility, heroic grandeur,
The manly strength, the straight childlike desire.
But more wonderful is Isaiah.

A flowing, limpid stream is Homer.
He bathes in the sun on the shores of Achaia,
And sings to the moon with a silver voice.
But the water of life—is Isaiah.

A bright field, a fragrant forest is Homer,
With princely stags, and singing birds,
And skipping lambs, that never tire.
But eyes turned to heaven—that is Isaiah.

With laughing nymphs disporting on the hills—is Homer.
His man is a noble savage, full of lustful fire.
But 'drive out the ram and the bear'—
That said Isaiah.

Homer brought together many gods—the gods of Homer.
To the sins of both he added more—the heap of sins rose higher.
But that God is good, and to fight for the good to the death—
That was the word of Isaiah.

Hector was thrown to the wild dogs by Homer.
Achilles refused him his funeral pyre.
But that a kingdom is destroyed because of an orphan's tear—
That was proclaimed by Isaiah.

Wonderful is the gold and green of Homer.
His world is transparent, blue and trusty.
But the world will be bright only when we aspire
To make equal the native-born and the stranger—
The vision of Isaiah.

A. Leyeless

Sutzkever

Father Jacob, Patriarch of all the Tribes,
Had twelve hearty sons. My father had four.
I loved my brothers. It is pulse and breath,
It is the call of roots, the way of the world, a man's inner core.
Only today the postman delivered to my door
A letter from my brother Moses in London.
The pages in my hand sound like our cradle song.
A world looms up on the paper, a world that has gone.

But any man can have brothers in blood.
Memory spins without knowing its thread.
I had in my innermost heartland embedded here,
A longing for a brother, in spirit near,
Turning towards him, back and forth,
As a southern bird is drawn to the north.
That is how atoms for atoms long.
How word longs for word till it becomes song.

Twenty-five years have grown to age, since he sent me
From Vilna his first young batch of poetry,
With an orchestra of words, a brother's call.
Now I have met him in Montreal.
My arteries played a serenade with my blood,
As I travelled to him on the Canadian road.

Through all the years Sutzkever's voice made itself heard,
Over continents, over seas to me came his word.
Not songs, letters—ships passed and greeted each other.
Brother recognised brother.
In quiet times, in dangerous days,
Through ghetto and underground, Moscow, Lodz and Warsaw,
Nuremberg and Rome—a brother's ways.

The whole long stretch of letters and poems
That moment in my memory stirred,
When I kissed the son of the Young Vilna idea,
Then gripped the hand of the ripe Sinai bard.

230

We had never deceived each other,
So we could now look into each other's eyes straight.
The long road we had travelled was a rainbow
Of truth-bond that had known how to hold on, to wait.

Was I to him Joseph? He Benjamin to me?
Bible! Bible! Don't read Book of Books only—
Read also Book of Brothers. Call name after name,
And see how your brother's blood like a flame
Into history's hungry open lap ran.

I fall prostrate before the angel of amnesia.
I sing a new song of brothers in poetry,
The song of the Tree of Life in the House of Man.

ABRAHAM SUTZKEVER

Jewish Street

You have not vanished. Your emptiness is full
Full with your people, as my mother fills my eye.
Somewhere a Synagogue still proudly lifts its head.
The flames had no power over it, passed it by.

You are a melody that fine musicians
Played generations ago.
The music turned into a street.

Only to the poor and lowly you seem poor and low.
But those who have vision see how you are bright.
Their arms are heaped full with your light.

Can the whole measure of five hundred years
Grow less because of our bit of now?
Who says you have vanished? No, you live!
Else how could I walk through you, in the way I do?

Does not the music live, when the composer
Is long lying dead in his place?
I can hear you singing in eternity,
High above time and space.

Like Groping Fingers

Like groping fingers through gratings,
To catch the bright air of free openness,
We reached through the night to take the plates,
The plates of Rom's printing press.
We dreamers must now become soldiers,
Melting words into bullets of lead.

We unsealed the imprint that opened the entrance
Down to a deep, eternal mine.
Armoured in shadow, by the light of a lamp,
We poured molten type line by line,
As our forefathers once in the Temple
Poured into golden menorahs oil.

The lead glowed in our casting of bullets.
Thoughts melted line after line—
A line from Babylon, a line from Poland
Flowed into one bullet, became one sign.
Jewish force buried till now in words,
Now must blow up the world!

Those who saw in the Ghetto
Jews with bullets and cannon balls,
Saw Jerusalem struggling,
Saw the fall of the granite walls.
They grasped the sense of words molten in lead.

A Cartload of Shoes

The wheels turn, keep turning.
Whose cart is it, whose?
It carries a cartload
Of quivering shoes.

The cart looks like a wedding
In the evening light.
All these shoes together,
Like people packed tight.

Is it a wedding party?
What has dazzled my eyes?
The shoes are familiar.
I know them, recognise.

The heels go tapping,
With a clatter and a din;
From our old Vilna streets,
They drive us to Berlin.

I should not ask questions.
But my heart misses a beat.
Here are the shoes,
But where are the feet?

Among this heap of shoes,
Are those my mother used to wear?
She kept them only for Sabbath days.
Her favourite pair.

The heels go tapping,
With a clatter and a din;
From our old Vilna streets,
They drive us to Berlin.

Peretz Markish

On the steps of Pushkin's Monument
We said our goodbyes.
Moscow had too long rained red stars
On us out of her skies.

As we released each other,
And quivering lips made a 'Keep well' sound,
You saw Alexander in bronze
Hide a burning wound.

Then your hand again in mine,
And horror in your eye—
'I don't want to become a gypsy!'
I heard your twisted lips cry.

Poet! You wander in eternity,
Where our dust catches flame,
And over you, Alexander
Hid in bronze his shame.

I said—a black wedding canopy,
Spun of death is my town.
We are texts to your story
That to the scaffold leads down.

Yes, the snow is my own.
And it will never melt.
It will always lie at my head,
A Jewish soft stone.

Suddenly the trumpets
Were extinguished in the square.
And I saw your tear in chains—
Home went your tear.

Where are you? Sing the truth!
Sing freely from the grave:
I gave you, my country, poems.
And to me a bullet you gave!

From Babylon

I was in Lydda, with a lot of others,
Watching among the incoming stars, watching with them
For the one that was bringing out weary brothers,
To taste of the grapes of Jerusalem.
With a heavenly whirr the star approached; and the unloading started.

There was a twitter of prayer, as once in my hometown, I heard
In the bird-market the twitter of every bird.
In all the seventy tongues of the globe
Met a people, who were clad in bird-like robes.
A people that never from its destiny parted.

235

Then an old man, in his Tallith enfolded,
Fell to the ground and kissed the ground he beholded.
And with the kiss his heart cracked. It could no more be mended,
Though they tried hard. His life was ended.
The wind from the scented fields sent his hair flying.

As he died, his face was suddenly illuminated.
He twittered a few words, which being translated,
Were for his grandson, who stood at his side,
A black swan, like the sea deep-eyed.
And this is the prayer he breathed as he lay dying:

'Now that I am blessed to lie where Isaiah is lying,
Where my bones will sing praises, and there is no need to mourn,
Let my grandson respect the wish of a man who is dying,
And place in my grave three pebbles from Babylon.'
He had brought them with him in his silken abayah.

The Glory of Sinai

Almighty God, how have I deserved this greatest of deservings,
That I, up to my neck stuck in Goshen,
Should come where there sounds the echo of 'I Am'.
Where there is still the rushing of Your wings!

Here manna still falls in the morning,
And the bright branches are sunny.
A shepherd lad gathers it in his basket.
It still has the taste of a bun with honey.

Here still lives a language that needs no lips.
Here is a rock giving water where you have struck.
And I have come to link myself with this—
To quench my call with water from this rock.

Fled Jewish words, in the ancient
Hebrew footprint: In the caves where you dwell.

One day a Prophet may come here to hide.
And he will hear what these caves have to tell.

Then suddenly the stars over Mount Sinai appear—
Wandered in from exile, just as we have done.
Caught in the light, we see and hear,
And with the planets become one.
Up on the Mount a young man makes a stand,
And anoints the hero who so bravely strove.
He takes it, takes it up above.
Whoever saw a Sinai night,
Him Sinai will remember, his name and sight.
Whoever saw Sinai glory,
Can for a thousand years say Amen to the story.

JACOB GLATSTEIN

The Dead Do Not Praise God

We received the Torah at Sinai.
And in Lublin we gave it back.
The dead do not praise God.
The Torah was given for the living.
And as surely as we all stood together
At the Law Giving,
So surely we all died in Lublin.

The ruffled head, the innocent eyes,
The quivering mouth of a small Jewish child,
I shall conjure them into such an awesome tale,
I shall fill a Jewish sky for him with stars,
And say to him this:
The Jewish People is a flaming sun,
From beginning, to beginning, to beginning.
Learn this, little boy, dear Jewish boy—
From beginning, to beginning, to beginning.

Our whole dream-evoked People
Stood at Mount Sinai,
And received the Torah,
The dead, the living, the yet unborn.
All the Jewish souls responded:
We will obey and hear.
You, the saddest Jewish boy in all the generations,
You too stood at Mount Sinai.
Your nostrils caught
The raisin-almond taste of each word in the Torah.
It was Shevuoth, the Festival of Green.
Like a songbird you sang with them—
I will obey and hear, hear and obey.
From beginning, to beginning, to beginning.

Little Jewish boy, your life is mapped out
In the starry Jewish sky.

You were never missing.
You never dared to be missing.
We had hoped and prayed you to be there.
Always when we were there you were there also.
And when we were no longer there,
You were gone, with us.

And so, together, as we all together
Stood at the Law Giving,
So surely we all died in Lublin.
From everywhere dear Jewish souls came flying,
Full-lived, young-died,
Tortured, tried and tested in all the fires,
Not yet born.
All the Jews who have died, from Grandfather Abraham onward,
They were all in Lublin for the holocaust.
All who had stood at Mount Sinai
And received the Torah,
Took on themselves these sacred deaths—
'We want to die with the whole People!
We want again to be dead!'
So these souls cried.
Mother Sarah, Mother Rachel,
Miriam and the Prophetess Deborah
Went to their death, singing prayers and songs.
And Moses, who had so wanted not to die
When his time came,
Now died again.
And his brother Aaron,
And King David,
And Maimonides and the Vilna Gaon,
And Maharam and Maharshal,
The Seer, and Abraham Eiger.
And with every holy soul
That perished in torment,
Hundreds of souls
Of dear dead Jews died with them.

And you, nice little boy, you were there too.
You, marked out in the starry Jewish sky,

You were there too, and you died there.
Sweet as a dove you offered your throat.
And you sang with the Patriarchs and the Matriarchs,
From beginning, to beginning, to beginning.

Close your eyes, dear Jewish child,
And remember how the Baal Shem rocked you
In his arms,
When the whole dream-evoked People
Perished in the gas chambers of Lublin.

Over the gas chambers,
And over the sacred dead souls
Rose the smoke of a deserted, extinct Sinai.
Little boy with the ruffled hair,
And innocent eyes and quivering mouth,
You were there then,
When the Torah was given back.
You stood on Mount Sinai and wept.
Wept to a dead world.
From beginning, to beginning, to beginning.

And this is what you said when you wept:
We received the Torah at Sinai,
And in Lublin we gave it back.
The dead do not praise God.
The Torah was given for the living.

Holy Name

If I had now been Abraham, Terah's son,
I would bow down to all sorts of idols,
And I would not bow down to His dear, great Name.

I would think that the machine-gun is God,
That the global death,
Annihilator of whole nations
Is God.

And at the edge of the undecided day
I would prostrate myself, a bewildered lad.
I would bow down to the least blade of grass,
And pray:
Dear, pure, holy name,
Reveal your dear awe to Abraham.

But I am Abraham, Isaac's son,
And I know that over all the dead
Blues a clouded Truth.
But I fear to look for it
Among the graves of millions.

Perplexed I shall leave
This world of chaos,
Where the seed of my people has been cut off,
Without a Voice from heaven, on a blood-drenched way.

Let my children's children
Unravel this tangle,
And I will lie among my own,
An unrecognised one.

No matter how much the scales justify,
They will never exonerate for us the heavens.

And no matter how many weeping generations will howl over us,
They will still hear our dead lips mutter.
For we shall be always demanding,
'Dear, beloved, Holy Name,
It was always beyond our understanding.'

Souls of Jewish Towns

Souls of Jewish towns,
Hidden in the parchments of eternity.
Will they rise from the valley of death?
Will there come to them living breath?

Only You, my God, know how strong they were,
For You built them with Your power.
Only You, my God, knew how they were weak,
Before they went up in smoke.

The souls of the Jewish towns
Wept before God's Mercy Seat.
See, Lord God,
How our ruin is complete.
You created us in Your image,
So part of You they destroyed.
Like idol-bells now ring
The names of Jewish towns, Warsaw, Vilna, Chelm, Lublin.

The day I rebuild my House,
I shall not forget the Jewish towns,
Else let my tongue forget
To utter sounds.
Even now my tongue must be silent,
And sad the hand that builds
God's House on the hills,
On foundations of so much forgotten suffering.

Without flesh and bones, only spirit,
Prophesy, son of man, if you can,
In the Valley of Destruction,
That the spirit will rise again,
From the ashes and pain,
Song will join to song,
Smoke to smoke, and what we long for to that for which we long,
Holiness to Holiness.

And Jewish towns will once more
Rise where the destruction was before.
Prophesy, prophesy, prophesy son of man,
Till your last breath, if you can!

But don't think it can be forgiven,
Don't think the best rebuilding
Can make the evil forgotten.

See how the face of the world
Is distorted and apelike.
Hear how they no longer understand
The other's language.
Hear them building
Higher and higher
The Tower of Destruction.
See if the face of the world
Has one trace of gentle Jewishness.
Read the books and marvel
How all the letters of Mercy
Have been erased,
All the letters of the Book.

Back to the Ghetto

Good night, big world,
Great big stinking world.
Not you, but I bang the door and break off the latch.
With a long gaberdine,
With a flaming yellow patch,
With proud step and mien,
At my own command I go
Back to the ghetto.
All apostate traces I stamp out, obliterate,
In your dust and mire I sprawl,
Praise, praise, praise,
Crippled Jewish life.
I bar your unclean cultures, world, I erect against them a wall.
Though you are waste and desolate,
I make myself dusty with your dust,
Miserable Jewish life.

Good night, world, you may keep for all it matters to me,
My liberators of humanity,
My Christs and Marxes and all they would do,
Keep the baptised blood they gave to you.

Jacob Glatstein

I have hope though he delay
Our redeemer will come one day,
And there will be
Fresh leaves upon our ancient tree.
I want no comforting, no pity,
I go back to my own city,
From Wagner's heathen music to my own Biblical chant.

Sad Jewish life, I kiss you,
I weep with the joy of coming back to you.

ISAAC KATZNELSON

The End

From *The Song of the Slaughtered Jewish People*

The end! Heaven blazes each night, smoke by day and night fire!
Like in the wilderness, at our first beginning, a pillar of smoke by day and
    a pillar of fire by night!
My people that was full of strength and faith is ended!
They have slaughtered us, old and young, with their devilish might!

The German who stopped us in the street, and put us behind barbed wire,
He was the devil, the black fiend, straight from hell-fire.
He was a German, Hitler, Himmler, Rosenberg, all Germans in one,
The whole murderous nation, the unspeakable Hun!

That German who stopped us in the Gelanska Street,
Had I shot him dead, you might still have lived, my sweet wife, my sweet!

Among the Poles they sought those who fought for freedom,
Those they suspected were their foes,
Those who were loyal to their nation;
And Russians too, the partisans, they killed all those.

But they killed all Jews without exception.
They murdered babies in their cots.
They led us to the death chambers of Treblinka,
Old men and women, and tiny tots.

How could we fight? We had no weapons in our hands.
Yet an axe too is made of iron.
And bullets dig no deeper in the flesh than do sharp nails.
We did not let them slaughter us like lambs!

On January 18th. I saw five thousand Jews led to their death.
And I saw twelve Germans killed before their victims died.
Only twelve. But the Germans were strongly armed.
'The Jews resist!' those armed cowards cried!

I had friends in the Ghetto, dear friends, writers, men of learning and song.
They were all killed! I saw Hillel Zeitlin dragged along,
Wearing his prayer-shawl. So they shot him dead.
And Israel Stern and Gilbert, gems in the crown on our head,
Warshawsky, Levy, Davidowitch, dead, all dead.

Yes, among the Poles they sought only the freedom-fighters, those who
    were true
To their country. They killed many more Russians. Russia bled!
But with us, they murdered us all, even babes in their cots!
We were all taken to Treblinka, and before they killed us they said:

'Undress! Leave your clothes here! Your shoes there!
Go to the bath-house, you need a bath after your long journey.'
And they packed us in, a thousand at a time, a mass, massed,
Jews from Warsaw and Paris, from Salonika and Prague—a thousand at a
    time they gassed!

Why? All ask—why? Why? Why did they do it?

Every Jewish home stands empty, and the murderer slays and slays.
But homes don't stand empty long. Others are moving in,
People with a different tongue and with different ways.

The sun rising over Poland and Lithuania will no longer find a Jew
Sitting by a light in the window saying Psalms, or at dawn on his way
To Synagogue. Peasants with their carts will still come to the town,
But there will be no Jews there to deal with them on market day.

And there will be no more Jewish children, to wake in the early morning
To go to Chedar, to listen to the birds, to play with their playmates.
Oh, lovely Jewish children, with shining eyes,
Lovely Jewish girls, with your braided plaits.

You are no more! You across the ocean, don't ask where they are!
Don't ask what has happened to Kasrilevka, to Yehupetz, don't look
For Tevya, for Menachem Mendel, for Shlomo Naggid and Mottke Thief.
They are with the Prophets of the Bible, with Isaiah and Jeremiah!
They are in Bialik's songs and in the pages of a Sholom Aleichem and a
    Sholem Asch book.

The voice of Torah will no longer be heard from the Yeshivah.
The young boys are no longer at their Gemarrah, studying God's lore.
The Rabbis and the teachers, the Gaonim and the scholars,
They are all murdered, they are no more!

Jews will no longer die! There are no Jews left to die!
And no Jews will be born, for there are no Jews left to give them birth.
There will be no more poems written by Jewish poets.
Jewish life is dead, with all its joy and sorrow, with all it was worth.

How you used to fight with each other—the bitter struggles of your parties
    and your movements!
I watched you quarrelling, and because of it my heart was grieved.
But I would gladly see you quarrelling again,
If only you lived!

There was a Jewish people, and it is no more!
It is a tale that began with the Bible, and went on till to-day.
It is the story again of Amalek, of the Germans who are much worse than
    Amalek!
It is the story of the Germans, who slay and slay!

O, great heaven, O vast seas,
Do not gather together in one destroying ball,
To wipe out the evil ones from the earth.
Leave them to destroy themselves, all of them, all!

Shlomo Jelichovski

Sing, earth and heaven, sing God, sing Jews,
Sing all below and above, sing,
Sing all worlds, sing the name Shlomo Jelichovski.
He ennobled man and the earth, he ennobled everything.

Rise, Homer, great blind singer,
And David, son of Jesse, too,
Take your harps, and play a song of praise
To Shlomo Jelichovski, the Zdunska Vola Jew.

Zdunska Vola is astir, there is a bustle,
It is the eve of Shevuoth, the feast of the Giving of the Law.
The Ghetto has been opened to non-Jews all around.
Even the Germans are preparing to celebrate this day of awe.

They have flung wide open the gates of the Ghetto.
There is going to be something grand
For the sightseers who come.
In the market place ten gibbets stand.

The Jews have been chased out of their homes into the market place.
The Germans have come into the fenced-off Ghetto-town.
They are reading from a list ten names,
The names of ten hostages, chosen and marked down.

Shlomo Jelichovski!—the name rings out,
The name of this Jew, in every German ear,
And one of the ten lifts his head, in answer.
This is the man! You cannot mistake him for any other here!

Shlomo Jelichovski of Zdunska Vola!
It is the name of a hero! Like one of the heroes of old!
A heroic Jew, whose face shines with courage,
Self-sacrificing, defiant, bold.

Shlomo Jelichovski! It sounds like the beginning of a song,
Like the opening words of a Psalm, a song of praise!
Here he is, standing ready at the gibbet,
As though he were the Cantor at the Synagogue dais.

Shlomo Jelichovski, the Jew, with everything about him Jewish!
Through the Zdunska Vola market place this Jewish name goes ringing!
Give him a cup of wine, for he is making Kiddush,
He is singing the Sanctification—at death's gate he is singing!

He is not singing alone! Together with him
All Israel is singing, every Jew in the world sings!
From his throat sing all the Jewish generations!
And over his head beat seraphim wings!

No! He was wrong! Nobody else is singing!
Even these Jews at the gibbet are dumb.
'Why are you silent! Lift up your voices,
Lift up your heads, come, sing with me, come!

'Why are you sad, why are you disheartened?
Why do you stand here lost, in despair?
Summon up courage! Strengthen your faith!
There must be no melancholy here!

'It is Erev Shevuoth, Jews! To-morrow
We shall receive our holy old Torah again!
Let us rejoice, we who will not live to see it,
We more than all others, before we are slain!

'Let us rejoice! To die thus is a privilege!
We should be proud they chose us to be hung
For Kiddush Hashem, for the Sanctification!
Lift up your voices, Jews! Let's have a song!'

Then he raised his noble head to heaven,
High above the Germans, ignoring them,
And in the market place of Zdunska Vola
He sang the song of Jerusalem!

'When I remember, O God, how every city
Rises on its hill in state,
And how our holy city
Lies desolate!

'My heart faints,
And my eyes grow dim.
Yet however they prosper with their lies,
To God alone we turn our eyes!'

So he sang, with his head held high,
This Jerusalem psalm.
And to the Jews in the market place of Zdunska Vola
His voice was balm.

They lifted up their heads.
Their hearts grew strong.
And God Himself smiled happily
When He heard Shlomo Jelichovski's song.

'This is a man after My heart,'
Said God. 'When the world began,
I had him in My mind,
When I created man.'

Sing, Shlomo Jelichovski, sing!
As you sing, you grow!
All the Jews of Zdunska Vola
Envy you now.

They wish they had been chosen,
Like these ten to hang,
To have the privilege of being martyrs,
Like this man who at death's door sang.

A German wild beast with a face like lard,
Walks up to Shlomo Jelichovski with measured tread,
And as he is singing his song of Jerusalem,
Hits him over the head.

But Shlomo Jelichovski sings on.
He does not feel the blow.
His eyes are turned to heaven.
He does not see this beast below.

He sings on, and the other nine hostages sing,
Ecstatically, on only their singing intent,
Among them an apostate, and a former Bundist.
'Forgive us, God,' they pray, penitent.

Now the hangman has dropped the nooses
Over the ten necks.
And they stand firm like ten strong pillars,
Like rocks.

'Rejoice!' cries Shlomo Jelichovski, 'Be glad, Jews!
It is Erev Shevuoth, and we are going to die,
We are going singing to God,
Dancing up to the sky!'

He flung out his arms in exaltation.
And so did the nine other Jews.
And as they stood there with arms and eyes uplifted,
The German hangman drew round each the noose.

Sing, earth and heaven, sing God, sing Jews,
Sing all below and above, sing,
Sing all worlds, sing the name Shlomo Jelichovski.
He ennobled man and the earth, he ennobled everything.

Sing to him a song of praise,
Sing to him a high song under the sun,
For such a man as Shlomo Jelichovski,
Do you know like him anyone?

Sing his praise, land and sea,
Forest, river, hill,
God Himself sings his praise.
He has done God's will.

Sun and moon and stars all sing.
The light sings his praises—whose?
The praise of Shlomo Jelichovski,
The hero of the Jews.

He never destroyed a town,
This heroic Jew.
He never bombed defenceless folk,
No sword from its scabbard drew.

Sing to him, this hero of a poor small town,
Who went singing to God,
The hero of Zdunska Vola,
Where the ten gibbets stood.

HIRSH GLICK

Partisan Song

Never say, this is the last road, the end of the way.
Though leaden skies now hide the light of day,
The hour we long for will at last appear.
Our tread will fall like thunder—we are here!

From the land of palms to the distant land of snow,
We come with our sorrow and our woe.
Wherever a drop of our blood was shed,
There our courage will lift its head.

The morning sun again will gild our day.
The past will with the enemy fade away.
Yet should the sun delay, and spring be late,
This song for generations will reverberate.

This song is written not with ink, but blood.
It is not the song of a free bird in the wood.
This song a people sang between collapsing walls.
This song to future generations calls.

So never say, this is the last road we have gone,
This is the last time that the sun has shone.
The day will dawn, the sun will reappear.
Our tread will fall like thunder—we are here!

MORDECAI GEBIRTIG

In the Ghetto

Like the steps of footsore armies,
Through sandy desert ways,
In the Ghetto drag our sleepless nights,
And our weary days.

The hours are heavier than lead.
The minutes are filled with fear.
We pray the day should end,
And the night should disappear.

We do not sleep. We listen.
Dreadful thoughts pass through our head.
Who will be picked upon tonight,
And tomorrow will be dead?

We lie awake and shudder
At the sound of a creaking door.
And the heart goes cold when a hungry mouse
Scurries across the floor.

So we lie awake all night and think
Full of dread and fright.
Thus we pass our weary day,
And our sleepless night.

KADIE MALADOVSKY

God of Mercy

God of Mercy, choose
Someone else than the Jews.
We are weary of dying,
Of suffering and tears,
We have no more blood,
And we have no more prayers,
Our homes are a wilderness,
We have no more graves for our dead,
We have no more dirges to sing,
For our blood that was shed.

God of Mercy, Most High,
Choose another Holy Land,
A different mountain sanctify.
We have left our bones
In all fields, on all stones.
We have paid bitterly to every rogue
For each letter in Your Decalogue.
God of Mercy, Lift Your eyes,
Look down from the skies—
There are so many nations here.
Give them Your Prophets and Your Sacred Year,
Sabbaths and feast days and fasts.
They all repeat Your words in their creeds.
Teach them to do Your deeds!

God of Mercy,
Give us the simple dress
Of the shepherd and the shepherdess,
Make us farmers in the field,
Blacksmiths who heavy hammers wield,
Make us unlettered, low and base,
Teach us to keep our lowly place,
And take away from us Your Light,
That makes us great!

Kadie Maladovsky

Boots

Quick, feet, into these leather boots,
Once more I have no home.
And I have no money for the train.
So get into these accustomed leather boots,
And we'll set out on the road again.

It has happened—
Upon you rests the hope of thousand-league boots,
Forgive me, my feet,
But we must go, and the road is familiar as our own street.

It isn't a pleasant road—
Full of insults and pogroms,
And all go barefoot as I do.
Get into the old leather boots, feet,
A little shoe-polish will soon make them shine like new.

So many languages I have taught my tongue.
My spirit is strange and cold to them.
I bear a language as I bear a life
Under a storm of insult and hate.

And though my heart is now a little weaker,
Still strong like stone are my feet.
I shall have so much to relate.
How all the rivers are bitter,
How all the rivers want to be sweet.

ROCHEL H. KORN

East

In this direction my father turned his face,
With his prayer shawl over his head.
Here are the fields and forests
He walked with firm tread.

My father's murmuring prayer,
That like autumn leaves fell,
Could take my wild blood,
My fierce passions quell.

Now I walk here alone,
The last of my race.
My grandfathers with their prayers
Made this a holy place.

And they and their grandfathers, too,
With their prayers and with their plough,
Dug themselves into this soil.
And the bond still holds now.

Under Poland's poplar trees
They dreamed of the Holy Land,
They planted here the mountains of Gilboa.
Here their Jordan ran.

We are coming back from far places,
From ghettoes, bunkers, crematorium fire,
The heirs of six million graves,
And we shall rise high, if not higher.

Arthur Ziegelboim

When was it sealed, when was it decreed,
Your great, your wonderful deathless deed?
Did it come to you like a child in your dream?
Or did a dark messenger bring you the tale,
In your London exile?

Did the messenger come to your door, and knock,
A woman heavily shrouded in black—
'I come from the Warsaw Ghetto, where the earth is on fire!'
Her clothes in rags, a tattered shroud,
And her lips red with blood.

Then you knocked at doors, and found hearts that were closed.
You tried to rouse them, but they wouldn't be roused.
What people were those who refused to listen,
When children were gassed and flung on the mound?
And no one raised a hand!

You carried round stacks of papers to show.
'You may be right,' they said, 'but how can we know?
We want to believe you. But these are not facts.
And we are bound by conventions and acts.'

You brought out a list of the dead.
'How can you prove they are dead?' they said.
So to convince them, you added your name to the list.
You always gave proofs, like a realist.

One May night, when the orchards ripened in the land,
And Spring walked around with stars, hand in hand,
One window in a London street showed a light.
That was you, sitting down alone, to write.

You wrote your last letters, and your last Testament,
For the dawn to read, before the night was spent.

Then a shot rang out, a single shot
To wipe out the shame of which you wrote.
You died to make the world listen to the cry
From the Warsaw Ghetto, across the sky.

ELIEZER GREENBERG

Peretz and Bontche Shweig in the Warsaw Ghetto

No one knows from where but in streets
Full of dead silence a footstep nears.
Peretz glides past, and in his pale face
Two eyes shining like two stars.

The same black hat with the broad brim
Sits on his leonine head crowned with snow.
He has come from a far away world
To see his home, the suffering and woe.

He sees only heaps of ashes and rubble,
Broken down house and wall.
Synagogue and Poorhouse, and sadness.
And desolation over all.

Here would have been Twarda, Krochmalna and the Park
Where he used to take his walk each day.
Here and there a sad wild flower is dying.
And the earth sobs as he goes his way.

Then a crowd of Jews rushes past,
With yellow patches and mute eyes.
How much sorrow hangs down from their heads!
How much agony on their shoulders lies!

They rush past, a herd of dumb cattle,
Their eyes filled with bewilderment and fright.
A man who wears no yellow patch is a stranger!
They rush past and are swallowed up in the night.

Peretz tries to solve the riddle of place and time.
And he suddenly wonders—where have they gone—
Asch and Nomberg and Reisin? And where
Is now good Dinesohn?

We all dreamed a great dream here.
We hammered out a golden chain.
Now I am alone in this valley of tears,
And everything seems in vain.

What century is this? In what land am I?
Pharaoh, Titus? Torquemada? Chmelnicki?
The wind is tearing at Peretz's cloak.
And a gorged crow caws as it flies by.

Peretz goes further, on his way to the Kehillah,
Where he had worked for years as a Registrar.
And on a mound of ashes, with a voice that quivers,
Reading Psalms is Bontche Shweig.

Bontche recognises his creator.
Offers his hand with a respectful stare.
And two eyes answer what two eyes ask.
Bontche silent as always, yet Peretz and the night hear.

Murder. Mass slaughter. Gas ovens. Death Camps.
And over it all the Swastika flag unfurled.
Peretz and Bontche both shiver with cold—
The Jew burns on all the bonfires of the world.

Bontche walks on and Peretz follows.
Heaven is black. Only a lone
White cloud like a boat sails a sea of horror.
And Bontche stops at Ceglana Street Number one.

Of that house only one stone remains.
Bontche drops down on that stone.
The night keeps up an endless sobbing,
And Peretz accompanies it with a moan.

That is where you lived, says Bontche,
Where you hammered out your golden chain,
Where you created me. This is your reward.
I want to give it to you all back again.

I want to scream out now all my years of silence.
Give me a tongue and words, anguished and pained.
Because of my silence even the beasts avoided me.
That is why I have remained

To be a witness—how the world—and God—were silent
When our people were crushed between iron jaws.
You who created me, call the world to judgment.
Let me—who was always silent till now—plead their cause.

Let me open my sealed lips,
Closed with silence all my years.
And my heart, that all my life
Wept in silence, behind locks and bars.

His lament rose to a wild howling.
His voice like wolf-and-dove cried,
Till morning came with feverish madness.
Peretz sobbing, Bontche sobbing. And a whole sobbing world outside.

Now the city sits solitary,
The city that was the joy of the earth is bereft.
Two Jews stand in the shine of the moon at its setting.
In all this city only Peretz and Bontche are left.

Our Small Group

Smaller, lesser grows our little group,
Through all the devastated lands,
In every corner of the earth
Where a tent of ours still stands.

Storms tear at our roofs and walls,
Our foundations are broken away.
No one puts his lips now to the Kiddush cup,
Unopened the Pentateuchs stay.

We Yiddish writers, we spinners of dreams,
Who is lonelier in such a world than we?
We cherished our words, to sow them as seeds,
But all fields now lie desolately.

In the Babel of tongues our tongue is drowned,
We are told that our Yiddish is dead.
Our youth, our renewing Spring, turns away,
And leaves our books unread.

Our well-springs lie open, but Jews won't come
To drink out of our well.
Even Bialik would not scold them now.
What use scolding those who in Sodom dwell?

What use scolding people who live always in fear,
A thorn in the world's eyes?
Our little group should comfort them now,
In their tents under despairing skies.

EPHRAIM AUERBACH

My Yiddish

Maize Yiddish, mine,
Acidy wine with a tang on the lip
With the Moldavian, the Turk and the Gipsy
Now and then you took a sip.

Over the naked steppes you rode.
The winds ruffled your note.
Swaying stalks are the notation
Of both your rhythm and your thought.

You wound together your cotton
With the Baal Shem's silken thread.
And you hung up on the tree tops
Our Prophetic tread.

From the lamb's gentle eyes
You took a text in Holy tongue.
You warmed the high roads with the Pentateuch,
And with a Midrash brought the goat along.

My Yiddish, my Bessarabian Yiddish,
You were raised by the Jew
Who on this black earth
With his Hebrew speech grew.

Early morning snow is blue.
Silence is a frightened lamb.
I have heard the Jewish Wallach song
Sounding like a flame.

Trees, hollow and frosty,
Flame with white fire.
White and pure is my Yiddish,
A sacrifice on the altar pyre.

Ephraim Auerbach

My Son

They are growing, with powerful legs,
With eyes like precious stones.
They are bond, they are severance.
They are our New York sons.

His lithe form cleaves the air.
His bronzed body quivers as it fell.
My son in his youth went riding to-day.
With muscles like cords twisted out of steel.

The breath spurts from his nostrils, sparks from his eyes.
His thick tangle of hair tumbles wild.
Joy for a father to sit here and see
The generation he raised, his grown child.

He leaps a hundred yards, like a panther springs.
The water breaks under him like glass.
He swims, as if swinging on a rope,
And beats the water with a lion's paws.

Hey, young man, I can't high dive as you do.
But I can cleave the water just the same.
I once twisted the Dniester into rings.
I bent the waves, made them tame.

The river plunges. Silently we both swim.
The shore vanishes like smoke under the midday sun.
Who has flung a noose round my neck?
Like savage hounds the waves towards me run,

They drag me down, my legs and arms lose strength.
And you swim towards the storm far away.
I hammered out so many songs in my life,
Joyfully, my son, this last painful song for you to-day.

Beauty

The spring of a cat I have seen,
At a bird in song to devour its prey.
Eyes diamonds, in the burning sun green.
The fur on its back velvet, glistening grey.

Bones full of quiver, ears spread,
Claws playful, like fingers on piano-board keys.
Wisdom in the mouth corners, the poise of the head,
Warmed as on a soft pillow's ease.

A watchful dog on the threshold lies,
Seeming asleep, breath kept in.
But ripples are running over his skin.
Sparks fly from the slits of his eyes.

Head sways to a quiet rhythmic beat,
Distended nostrils sniff the air,
Each nerve tingling, to pounce and eat.
The devouring fangs bare.

A watchful eye, a flash, a spring.
Gleaming teeth, a flutter like a wing.
The rabbit's hot blood on his tongue and teeth.
The warm life under his paws is now death.

Destruction, consuming, the end.
So much beauty in the destroyer's pounce and rend.
The killer is as wearily wise
As the slain victim who wearily dies.

URI ZVI GREENBERG

A Jew Stands at the Gates of Tears

I

For our sins in singing the world, merely singing,
For our sins in setting our hearts aflame for seventy golden birds,
For neglecting our own doves and swallows in the tents of Jacob,
Our plaited Sabbath loaves and our Jewish holy words.

For our sins in running after Baal Peor in Europe,
For stretching out our arms to the nations at their dance,
For trying to ride their lyric horses, even if they kick you,
For going crazy over their coloured peacocks and white swans.

For wanting to exchange Kinnereth and Jordan
For foreign waters, and obscenity.
Therefore the three-knived hooked cross grew over us,
And under our feet rolled a subterranean lava sea.

Today we who survived stand at the gates of tears, impoverished,
Mourners, with Yorzeit lights burning to remind us.
At the high gates of tears Jews can recognise each other,
Jews without beards and earlocks, deluded from top to toe, all our hopes of
    mankind behind us.

At the high gates of tears our gentle Mother-the-Shechina tells us—
Hold on to our own oaks, on our hard rocks find foothold to keep steady.
Those who do not listen to the Shechina forest-call,
Are numbered with the dried branches already.

2

Where are the lustful sisters with apple-and-pear-fragrance?
Like a flourishing land was the altar where their blood was shed.
Where are the heavens with stars of which they were robbed at nightfall,
Accompanied with music by all the Levites who are dead?

How can we who survived weep over the beauties of the landscape,
Sing of precious and lovely things, and the seven-formed graces,

The sounds and colours, and the softness of eyes and hair,
When the Shechina and all the love were ringed round with Gentile hate,
    knocked flat on their faces?

We shall not again be enraptured with sweet music
That was played while we were being slain.
We shall no longer lift our eyes to the golden moon,
Save at full moontime, at the sight of our mother's anguish and pain.

3

On Slav fields, Lettish and Lithuanian,
The soil and the stones and the houses should ring with loud cries.
From Slav forests, Lettish and Lithuanian, filled with horror,
God and Christian folk should listen how we agonise.

Woe! Woe! What has happened to us!
Woe! Woe! What they did to us there!
Where are the holy Gentile people,
Who kept their doors open when we came running to them in despair,
When we jumped from the trains taking us to the death camps,
In Cross-governed Europe, and we pleaded in vain?
Everywhere death met us. And now
There is autumn in these lands, and there is rain!

4

There is autumn approaching in Israel, and my dead rustle the trees.
How unusually I hear human-Yiddish voices crying—
Woe! Woe! In the night when the crows are silent,
And Jews sleep in their houses, in the night, before the rains, when the winds
    are flying.

Who protects these sleeping Jews, who is their shield and guardian?
Generations of heretics, without God, and without angels in the skies,
Without pious father and mother, and grandparents, without prayer,
Their graveyards ploughed up, in the world of only Gentiles, of slaughtered
    Jewish communities.

By the waters of the Bug, was written of Bilkomin,

Surrounded with forests of pine and oak stretching all the way to Brod,
With orchards and God-blessed cornfields and fat grazing lands,
There the house where my mother was born and where I was born stood.
O, Bilkomin, further than the farthest planets now,
Much further than the distance is the time that has passed,
Nest of my birth, house where my mother was born,
By wild Gentiles laid waste.

5

I had a father, I had a mother.
Gentiles flung them on the fire.
They became ashes scattered on the wind,
Over the Gentile fields, where the grass now grows higher.

Belrzyc is the name of the place.
Let God spit on it as He spat on Sodom, that it may never be renewed.
From vast Russia to the four corners of Europe let the fires spread
Over the fields and forest where behind barbed wire their slaughter camps
    stood.

The skies are blue, or clouds pass over them.
We have summer rains, or we have winter snows.
By the Babylonian rivers stand my willows.
Great are my fears, and deep my woes.

There is no grave, not even a grave for my father and mother,
Where I can go with my memories.
There is no tombstone over their bones.
It is as if they were sunk in the seven seas.

6

Don't lose courage, Jews who survived the German slaughter.
Despair is worse than the enemy's fire and sword.
To clench your teeth, and wait for the day of reckoning and wrath,
Must as in olden days be our guiding word.

To-day we curse Edom as we cursed him in the past.
The sea lies at the foot of the barbed wire—go to meet it!

Like weeds thought sprouts and grows and spreads.
You drink it in the camps with water, and with bread you eat it.

The Gentiles can't see you among all the dead.
They must see you! They don't understand miracles. They must see!
Let them see you, who have conquered death,
Have overcome mortality!

They, the always-here, everywhere-belonging,
And you, the never-here. Let them try what you have been through,
And see if they can survive it, if they with their States and their weapons,
Can live through it like you!

They have weapons and they have their State,
And armoured ships and ports of steel.
So they can sit and watch you, and play cards.
Let what we had come upon them, and see how they will feel!

They, and their fathers and mothers, and brothers and sisters, and children.
O, how they will run, with the fire and the wind before them and behind!
When they laugh at you, tell them—you can't know how it is bitter,
Till it comes to you, as it will come to you, as you soon will find.

We shall leave our Egypts. We have known these things before.
But you will go into exile. And we shall see it come,
How Assyria and Babylon, Rome and Greece
Will destroy each other—we shall witness your doom.

7

The Gentiles thought that we were finished,
No longer among the living, not a living Jew.
They praised their Cross, and went to their Churches,
When our Synagogues were burned. And us they slew.

They ploughed up our graveyards,
And joined Naboth's field to their fields.
They used our tombstones for their buildings.
How much marble and granite a Jewish graveyard yields!

Uri Zvi Greenberg

It's a lovely world, Gentiles, without any Jews in it!
It's a lovely Jewless Gentile world.
Now what will you do with your murdering lust, and your deadly weapons?
What will you do with the victorious flags you have unfurled?

As there are no more Jews, you will kill Gentiles.
You must make use of your murderous tools.
You will destroy each other from the face of the earth,
According to your latest codes and rules.

And we Jews who have survived, because God said so,
We shall look on from afar.
We shall watch Europe burning without Jews in it,
In Christendom's exterminating Armageddon war.

Therefore Jews, let us all be together,
In our own land, in Zion, God-promised and God-given,
On our own God-blessed soil,
Under God's heaven.

8

I strain my eyes watching and waiting for you to come.
Now I have lost my own, you are my own,
You are my holy father and mother, my lovely sisters,
And their small children who were murdered before they were grown.

I strain my eyes watching and waiting for you to come.
I yearn for many Jews. And you are these.
My yearnings coo like doves, and my griefs roar and buzz,
Now like caged lions, now like honey-gathering stinging bees.

The spaces here yearn for you to come.
Desert and mountains and valleys. Though they have no voice,
Happy is the man who hears them calling.
He will be glad all his days; his heart will rejoice.

He will conquer the sea and Edom's imperial armed might.
He will reach Mount Zion, Mother Jerusalem on her seven hills,
He will kiss her at the Western Wall. Then go to Tiberias,
Along the shore of Kinnereth, to the Jordan, where the Jewish farmer tills

In the golden fields of Daganiah.
And think—if a Jew must be killed,
Let it be crossing the Jordan,
On the battlefield.

The smell of our own land is like the smell of our strong wine.
Our slaughtered dead children come here to rest and play,
Near to us, face to face with us,
Cooling their faces, no longer wandering homeless.

They

They were, O God, they were so many there—
So full of life and song,
Such dignified, bearded men.
And they had a wonderful tongue.

Under every roof they sang,
Such lovely cheerful melodies,
About the golden peacock,
About the Bible histories.

But over their heads hung cold murder,
The knife of the slayer.
It descended on them without pity.
No one listened to their prayer.

Now all that is left are these—
Of a forest felled, a few trees.

Abraham Liesin and I

In streets New Yorkian, with traders and dust,
In Jewish streets, with Jewish junk and rust,
We saunter, with eternal sun over us high,
Two Yiddish poets, Liesin and I.

He, manly, defiant, a lion from the den,
I, boyish, and lithe, like a young twig, green.
He, Lithuanian wisdom, his face scarred
With song and Torah, from his fathers acquired.
And I, on my shoulders bear my dress,
The song of Ukrainian black-earth happiness.

My older brother, he walks at my side,
And fevers with vision, through time and wide.
He fevers with song, and in the songs comes on
The hero and the martyr shaped in stone.

And here in the streets, with traders and dust,
In Jewish streets, with Jewish junk and rust,
Martyrs and heroes, form on form,
Out of the hard asphalt they grow and swarm.

His younger brother, I walk at his side,
Chattering foolishly, open-eyed,
Of beauty that I in dream had seen,
That had in reality not yet been.

And here in the streets, with traders and dust,
In Jewish streets, with Jewish junk and rust,
Beauty in seventeen colours shines and wings,
And out of the hard, deaf asphalt sings.

In streets New Yorkian, with traders and dust,
In Jewish streets, with Jewish junk and rust,
We saunter, with eternal sun over us high,
Two Yiddish poets, Liesin and I.

Seven Brothers

We are seven brothers,
With eyes blue and grey.
Three brothers are like poplars,
Tall and slim are they.
Three brothers are like sugar-canes,
The sweet roots on the ground.
And the singer of this song—me,
I am a wind-swept green willow-tree.

Our father has died, alack!

It turned our whole world black.
He was like a slender oak on thin earth.
Then we, his seven sons, on that rainy day,
When mist and grief all round us lay,
With weeping hands, as when a father dies,
We laid black shards on his eyes.

Then we shovelled earth and red clay
On his grave in Long Island that rainy day,
And at the head of his grave we set
A wooden board with his name on it.
And like a young forest when the storm
Rages through and does it harm,
We seven brothers with one voice began to call:
Yisgadal!

And that rainy day,
We seven brothers each went a different way,
With grief in our blue eyes and our grey eyes.
At the gate of New York we said our good-byes.

And each brother of the seven brothers,
On that rainy day,
Down a different avenue of the seven avenues
Went his separate way.

The Song of Love

First came the plain song of bread.
Then came the bright song of gold.
Last came the hushed song of the dead.
But always our song of love over everything rolled.

Yoked like the oxen, with heavy tread
These pull the plough over the rich black land.
The black land that groans under their hard hand
Will feed them and their kinsfolk with bread.

But here the song of love
Sadly sighed,
Like doves cooing by the window
At eventide.

And those dig yellow gold, like slaves.
Then they come to the slave towns as liberators.
With gold they set the towns alight,
And dance like apes round a fire all night.

But here the song of love
Rose with alarm and grief,
Like cats weeping for love
At night on a black roof

Death is eternal and everywhere, in fields and towns,
On all roads. Fortunate he who dies of old age,
With his son, his own blood, by his bed,
Taking over his heritage.

But here rings out the song of love,
Full of fear and fret,
Like young hearts in love
Lost in a pit.

My Grandmother

When my grandmother died
The birds sang.
The whole world with her kind deeds
And her good heart rang.

When they lifted my grandmother from the bed,
And laid her on the floor,
Everybody wept, because
The kind old lady was no more.

My grandfather walked up and down the room,
With anger in his eye,
Because he had promised grandmother,
He would be first to die.

When they bore her into the town,
All the Christian folk cried,
And the Greek Catholic Priest lamented,
That such a good woman had died.

Only when the Shamash took his knife,
To cut in their clothes the mourning slash,
My uncles and my father cried aloud,
Like prisoners under the lash.

My Grandfather

My grandfather in Kobilnik is a plain man,
A peasant, with a furskin coat, an axe and a horse,
And my sixteen uncles, and their brother, my father,
Are plain folk, like clods of earth, lumpish and coarse.

They float rafts on the river, haul timber from the forests,
Toil hard like beasts of burden all day,
They eat supper together, all out of one basin.
Then fall into bed, and sleep like lumps of clay.

My grandfather can hardly manage to crawl
To his corner on the stove; he falls asleep there.
His legs carry him on their own to the stove.
They know the way, this many a year.

Grandfather Dies

My grandfather came home at night from the field,
Made his bed, and said the Prayer of those about to die.
He stared hard at the world around him,
Saying to all his last goodbye.

My uncles and my father, his sons, stood silent,
Their hearts were heavy; they couldn't speak.
Grandfather sat up in his bed, slowly,
And addressed them in a voice trembling and weak.

And this is what grandfather said to his sons,
The big, burly fellows, the sturdy ones:
You, Ortche, my eldest, you are the prop of the family,
The first in the field, and the last to come home.
The earth knows the feel of your plough.
Like in rich soil may your seed grow.

Rachmiel, who can compare with you in the meadow?
Your scythe works like fire in the corn.
The snakes know you in the swamps, and the birds in their nests.
May you be blessed in stable and barn.

You, Samuel, man of the river,
Always with a net and fish in your hand,
You have the smell of the fisherman about you.
Be blessed on the water, and on the land.

Moshe Kulback

Night was falling, the sunset glow
Came through the window. No one stirred.
My uncles and my father stood dumbly,
Listening to my grandfather's last word.

Then my grandfather drew his knees together,
And lay down in the bed.
And closed his eyes for ever.
Not one tear my father and my uncles shed.

A bird sang in the forest.
The sunset glow went out.
And my father and my uncles stood there,
With their heavy heads bowed.

A. VOGLER

Break of Day

I shall not sing of my cherry-trees any longer.
The woodman cut them down in my native land.
I shall forge a sword from the raging Niemen,
And watch my star-orchard, sword in hand.

I shall not sing of my wheat fields any longer.
The devil has trodden them down in my home.
I shall chase on the east wind after my brown shadow,
Along the Milky Way, to the day when redemption will come.

I shall not sing of my herds of fat cattle.
The butcher out of my song has cut them away.
I shall waken them, and prostrate myself before them,
From their golden horns trumpet forth the day.

My grey swallows will not light my love ways any longer.
The bloody axe came, and they are all slain.
Eternity cannot hush her birds in the abyss.
But in my hymns to her, in my songs they live again.

I shall not sing of my birch and pine forests any longer.
My mind is full of the lines of graves on my native earth.
I shall be the coffin of my murdered cornfields,
And their cradle when they come again to birth.

My home town will light no candles on Friday evening.
The grave digger took her eyes out with a knife.
And I, her singing conscience, bless the sun,
And call for judgement for the Sabbath he robbed of its life.

I shall not sing of my golden cornfields any longer.
The incendiaries burned them with hate and scorn.
My great grandfathers have wakened from their sleep.
They have learned what death means in the ashes of their holy corn.

*   *   *   *   *

I went from my home with the setting sun.
With my long youth-knife on the White Russian trail.
I stride back to my plum orchards, where my brother was hung
He calls me, with his echo, a nightingale.

My homeless land sits mourning for her children on their grave.
I hear her wailing, and I hear the dogs howl.
The smell of my brother's mop of hair
Follows the track of the criminals who murdered his soul.

Brother, sing from the grave your flowing song.
I sit by your grave, on a felled willow tree.
With the east-rising song of the world's liberation
I destroy the scaffold, and set you free.

Your scaffold is the hangman's harp, and the rope his harp-string.
But your life will be the cornfield, and in your song rivers run.
Sing on the earth the song of the green gardeners,
And your rose-longing for the star-orchard and the sun.

Brother field, grow for me a red cherry tree.
Shelter me from rain, on my way to victory and peace.
I drink your tears, which call to me not to forgive
Your hangman, till he is dead and his evil deeds cease.

Brother, forgive my tread, which limps with weeping,
The sin of our separation forgive.
Your cut-off life will be the rising sun of our generation,
Sowing with martyrs the road where our joy will live.

My generation pours out pain and steel,
And blood and tears that mark our road of woe.
Let me be a dewdrop on the grass over your head,
And on your body the white shirt of snow.

I Am a Pitcher

I am a pitcher dropped from God's Hand into this vale.
At every festive table I sit glum and dour.
Creator, come to me one nightfall! It is my constant wail,
And drink from it your wine that has turned sour.

See, each nerve in me burns with the sunset in the skies.
My body across a thousand miles is strewed.
In every pious little stone over the globe I recognise
A bit of shine that has my similitude.

O God, in the hour of song forgive my prayer.
My breast lies like the earth drenched in its own blood.
And the supplications that on my open lip I bear
Rush through the silent nights like rivers in flood.

At once with shining fingers knead my limbs, until
I feel your breath is stirring there,
And the Angel of grey sentences will
Lock fast the doorways of my prayer.

At nightfall when the sun sets in wound and flame,
I write the pages of my book with tears and bitterness.
Forgive my pain, my scorn, my shame.
Forgive me all my foolishness.

The Lovers of Israel in the Death Camp Belshitz

Reb Moshe Leib of Sossov points to the heaps of ash.
(The storm had just been blowing through.)
His beard trembles, and his body and life are bitter.
'Look at this, dear God, I'm asking You!'

Reb Wolf of Zbarzh murmurs—'Listen, friends, listen to me!'
(His voice is weary like an evening fiddle's sound.)
'God above has not guarded His vineyard.
Here is proof of it, the heaps of ash on the ground.'

Reb Meir of Przemysl leaning on his heavy stick,
Waits, feverish with pain:
'Friends, let us all lift our voices, and repeat in refrain:

' "Creator of the worlds, You are mighty and terrible beyond all doubt.
But from the circle of true lovers of Israel, we Galicians,
For ever shut You out!" '

The Ruins of Poland

Under the ruins of Poland
There is a blonde head—you.
Both the head and the ruins,
Both, my dear, are true.
Dearest, oh my dearest.

The little Polish lady
For her sins has died.
She will from her sleep, no doubt,
Rise up purified.
Dearest, oh my dearest.

Over the ruins of Poland
Falls the falling snow.
The blonde head of my dearest
Makes me die of woe.
Dearest, oh my dearest.

My woe sits at my writing desk,
And writes a letter to you.
The tear in my eye, my dearest,
Is deep as it is true.
Dearest, oh my dearest.

Over the ruins of Poland
A bird flies about,
A big bird of sorrow,
Its wings so devout.
Dearest, oh my dearest.

The big bird of sorrow
Is myself, my dear.
It bears on its wing this song for you.
Under the ruins, can you hear?
Dearest, oh my dearest.

Epitaph

Here lies the sorry weary singing-bird
For the first time in his own bed,
The tailor-lad, the vagabond-poet,
From whom no more songs will be heard.

Don't pluck the weeds that grow over this house.
And in winter sweep not away the snow.
Nothing will now hurt him who sleeps below.
He lives at peace with the worm and the mouse.

Scatter no flowers upon this mound.
Put back nothing the storm hurls to the ground.
And do not drive the owl from the tombstone.

Let the wasp and the bee undisturbed hum.
Let the sexton's goat to these pastures come.
And leave me lying here alone.

A Song of the Dean of St. Patrick Dr. Jonathan Swift and the Yiddish Rhymster Itzik Manger

Extinguish the stars on my window.
Let it be quiet here.
Shut the mouth of the cricket,
And stop the flowing tear.

I have the Dean of St. Patrick
Sitting at my side.
He missed the train back to Lilliput,
So here for a while he must bide.

He is crunching a baby's breast-bone,
With green mustard in a cup,
And puffing at a big cigar,
Because his pipe is blocked up.

Friend Jonathan, I say to him,
You know our pal, Old Nick
Has changed his name and got a new girl,
And he's getting married quick.

The Dean fills up his glass again,
And says, Here's how! Chin, chin!
And nibbling at a Chelsea bun,
Goes on with a grin:

I'll send him Stella's golden brooch,
She won't mind, I am sure.

She'll manage well enough, I know,
Without that golden lure.

And to his bride, Vanessa's tear
As a wedding gift I'll send.
What more indeed can a bride need?
What more have we, my friend?

In the railway station across the road
The Lilliput train I hear.
The Dean puts on his black broad-brimmed hat,
And his shawl of thick cashmere.

And as he goes, Itzik, he says,
The September moon rides high
Over your neighbour's roof, and sneers
At you. So do I.

Light up the stars on my window.
It is too quiet here.
Open the mouth of the cricket,
And liberate the tear.

LEON FEINBERG

Bialik and Mendele

I remember one evening in Bialik's home,
When he was holding forth.
His words were a fresh spring of water to me,
Words of rich worth.

'They crowned me Prophet,' he said, 'and words
Of flame from me demand.
But I am only the tablet of wax,
Graven by my people's hand.

'They ask how I come to write Yiddish.
It's the language of Exile, it's wrong!
You who have given us poems
In the Bible tongue.'

'Language,' I say, 'is not only words.
It is the mother's milk you drink,
It is the face of your loved one,
It is all that you feel and think.

'Hebrew and Yiddish are the two stone tables,
God's, Israel's bond, the twain.
Each equally precious.
A link in the golden chain.

'Hebrew, the stern father,
Who scolds and wields the rod,
The first of the two partners to the bond
Between Jew and God.

'And Yiddish is the sweet mother,
Who shields the child from father's wrathful awe,
Heals bruises with balsam—
Mercy against law.

'Hebrew is the High Priest in the Temple,
Levites singing in the choir,
The atonement at the altar,
The sacrificial fire.

'Yiddish—Synagogue, Beth Hamedrash,
Jews praying with bowed head.
'Dear God, Father in Heaven,
Give us our daily bread.'

'Hebrew—the holy, the eternal tongue.
Yiddish—the holy language of the folk.
On the lips of our people both are living,
As father and mother talk.

'Hebrew—the language of Isaiah.
Yiddish—our gay and our grim.
Sisters, both equally dear.
There is no clash between them.

'Forgive me, young man, I'm not trying
To teach you what to do.
I like your song. But it hurts me
To see on foreign roads a Jew.'

* * * * *

The evening is full of brightness.
The red lights shine on the snow.
Bialik is taking me to visit—
To my first meeting with Mendele we go.

We enter through the courtyard.
'Mendele lives here, look!'
I am taking to Mendele
My first Russian book.

Mendele peers from behind his glasses.
His eyes burn and glow.
And little shivers of happiness
Through my whole body go.

The room, I think, is beginning,
Like his eyes, to burn and glow.
'I have brought you,' says Bialik,
'A young poet I want you to know.

'He is a branch that has gone astray,
From an old wonderful tree.
He is descended from Baal Shem.
But he writes poems in Russian, you see.'

Mendele looks at me hard.
Looks at me hard and long.
'The language, Bialik,' he says, 'doesn't matter.
What matters, young man, is the song.'

Yiddish

In the grey night of the middle ages,
Amid the flames of autos-da-fé,
Along roads chill and stormy
A people wended its way.

As a heart craves for joy that is quenched,
As parched throats for water long,
The dumb people sought a language,
Yearned with a chattering tongue,

Borrowed the yeast from the French,
From the Bible a measure of honey,
That after the fermenting and rising
There should some sweetness be.

A little corn from the Slavs,
A deep bowl from Germany,
And motherly hands kneaded the dough
From which Yiddish came to be.

From words simple as small copper coins,
Plain speech from heart and head,
Yiddish mother-tongue emerged
Like good new crisp home-made bread.

In villages crooked and hunched,
In hovels miserably poor,
On all the dungheaps that lay
In the mean streets at the door,

From South Ukraine and Lithuania,
From Russia, Poland, Volhyn,
Came youthful sages
With backs twisted, hunched and thin.

First, old Mendele the Bookseller,
With his story books in his hand,
Leading his wise old mare
Through the rutted roads of the land.

After him, with his thirst for knowledge,
Unprepared for the effort and strain,
Came Peretz, struggling helplessly,
A lion—the vestibule on a chain.

Then with reproachful smile on his lips,
His face furrowed with suffering,
Sholem Aleichem with his Tevya's
Common plebeian pleasuring.

In his triumphal chariot
With his three-in-hand onward sped
Sholem Asch, wearing his crown
Jauntily on his head.

And here in this land of pedlars and business,
Orchard Street, Rivington Street, round there all along,
There has risen like corn-flour cake
In narrow basins our song.

And here in the land of toil and sweat-shop,
Here in this new alien land,
Vintchevsky fought for freedom,
And Rosenfeld made his stand.

Now a generation of poets
Strides through hunger and want and strife,
And weaves the bright red thread
Of our bubbling times and life.

By the Hudson, Vistula, Dniester,
The Dnieper, the Bug and Niem,
How many wonderful names,
With flaming heads among them!

We rise up on all the tracts,
Young and fresh go singing along,
And gushing out in a thousand strains
Everywhere is heard our song.

Over the heights and the deeps,
Fearless of danger we tread.
And the song of our Mother-Yiddish
Rises like new crisp home-made bread.

MELECH RAVITCH

Song on the Seas to My Mother-Tongue

Despised mother of mine, tongue of the common folk
Everywhere the same, poor-sanctified in all the five continents,
Tired head in your lap, lips scorched by world-winds and world-sufferings
    and discontents.
I sit at your feet, your son, let me kiss your old gnarled hands and weather-
    beaten cheeks.
Light the candles in your potato-candlesticks, it is always Sabbath with you
    all through the long weeks,
But I have nothing but weekdays, every day the same.
I have myself smashed all my gods, and all my faiths the world has pierced
    with swords and burnt with flame.

Despised mother of mine, you who comfort our common folk
Your couch is rags, and your food for a couple of borrowed pence bread.
In all the attics and cellars from Warsaw to New York you lay your head,
You come like an old mother, wearing an old apron, into the homes of your
    daughters,
And they are ashamed of you, and your grandchildren greet you with
    scoffing laughter,
And often enough one of your sons has lost his temper at the sight of you,
And kicked you out of his rich home at the point of his elegant shoe.

Despised mother of mine, you who are the leader of our common folk.
You have risen like a prophetess in one day from your rags, from the dust,
You are the only one who still believes there is justice in the world, though
    there is no one anywhere who is just.
You alone, mother of mine, have arisen from your poverty and your shame,
And with youthful fervour you have raised over Vilna, your capital, a
    banner of flame,
And have hurled it under the rotten foundations of the old world and set it
    ablaze.
And then the drunken executioner gagged you, and now strips the flesh
    from you like rags, skins you and flays.

Despised mother of mine, saint of the common folk,

Melech Ravitch

To you all come with feelings of love, to tell you their griefs, to weep and
    to moan,
All complain to you, but you never complain to anyone.
The daughter of the people in the days of your youthful bloom,
In your age the mother of all you have now become.
And only once I saw on your furrowed face a sardonic smile appear,
When your sons prepared a grave to bury you there.

Despised mother of mine, our mother,
Of lonely Yiddish poets who were suckled at your breast,
The sea-wind runs shrieking from the east to the west,
Lightning, like deer with antlers of fire,
And heavy thunders pursuing clatter by with wild hunters' desire.
The storm leaps into the water from the sky,
And then out of the water back on high.
The foam-zigzag of the sea-serpent, look,
It is caught, the monster, like a fish on a hook,
On the steel screw of the ship,
Then it plunges, breaks loose and is lost in the deep.
I stand on deck alone,
Wet through from the rain and the waves over me have gone.

The hours pass, great vast hours,
The thunders have ceased and the showers,
But the lightning like fiery albatrosses still flash by.
It is now night on sea and sky.

Then suddenly I see you come to me,
From all the corners of the earth, across every sea,
Mother of mine, mother dear.
And all the winds are singing your lullabies, I hear.

A Song About Songs of Today and Timeless Songs

I too would like once in a while to write a song about snow
In winter, when snowfields stretch, stretch far away,
Far away past my window. And sometimes also a song about flowers
In Spring. And about green trees and fields where the harvests grow.

I too would sometimes like to write an old-fashioned song
About the pleasures of life, on some ordinary day, bright with sun.
My heart also is full of all kinds of longings,
Full of all kinds of sentimental fancies of my own.

I would even, in my old age, sure as I am a Jew,
Like to write a song about old times, about a Sabbath night,
About my grandmother saying the God of Abraham prayer, and about the
    three stars,
Week-a-day stars in a heaven of Sabbath blue.

But no sooner I sit down to write such a song, with wrinkled brow,
Pen in my hand, the first rhyme in my head, and I start to write,
Than a pack of wild dogs beset my table.
And my song runs off terrified, and the dogs pursue.

And an iron fist crashes down on my table.
And there opens in front of me an iron maw,
And cries: Don't come to the world with your slobbering song.
This is my world. I am Esau.

Then I rise from my table,
From my unwritten song,
And trembling with fear I stammer a few words:
'Forgive your brother Jacob!' I stutter and babble.

'Forgive him, let him rest in his corner,
A Yiddish poet's corner.
And he will stop longing for worlds, past and over.
From now on he will be cold and sober.

'Forgive him for blundering into your world, a world foreign and strange.
These worlds are not his, nor these his times.
Forgive him, let him dream, the old fool!
Dream that the times and the worlds will change.

'Forgive the old fool for believing in people.
His tearful song still wanders and strays—
His song of yesterday, his song of tomorrow.
Esau, he blundered into your everlasting todays.'

Melech Ravitch

Three Old-Time Friends

I think and dream, as though I flew on wings.
Out of the mist come two men, each from a different end.
I hear them speak to my comrade-son,
And he answering these two, to him unknown men.

They stand in the light of a lantern. I see them plain.
One looks as Apollo would look, grown old and white.
The other, lanky and bony,
Looks like Don Quixote, that noble, dreaming Knight.

We have recognized each other, through the years and the seas of blood,
Through the worlds of thought and belief that divide us. We embraced each
  other.
Uri Zvi Greenberg, as of old, stretched his heavily-veined hands to me.
And Peretz Markish slapped me on the back, like an old friend and a dear
  brother.

But Markish was silent, and Uri Zvi spoke for both:
'Still wandering? Not reached anywhere? Still on the way?'
'How can I come?' I said, embracing my two friends,
'If I never went away? My land is Jew, my yesterday-tomorrow is forever
  my today.

'The borders of my land are where stands the farthest lighthouse
Of Jew and world, where a last Jew still carries the week-day Sinai load.
No Sabbath-festival Jews are mine, no Psalm and prayer-Jews,
No rest-and-Sabbath is my world, but always weekday, and unrest is my
  road.

'My world grows and shrinks as grows and shrinks
The sum of Jew in the world. I tremble and say—my frontier is eleven, at
  this hour—

The sum of my people's millions—because our farthest border has been torn
By howling hyenas, crocodiles weeping tears, and wolves out to kill and
  devour.'

Triumph flashes in Greenberg's green eyes. Markish is sadly silent.
And I—I put my hand over my eyes, and say—
'What land? There is no safe land. For such things are beyond man's power.
You see, Markish, you lived on a rock, and now you are a cosmopolitan,
    with no home where you can stay.'

As we talk, from the dark heaven-island in the cloud-houses sea comes a
    book,
A book without beginning or end, which like Time was never young and
    will never age,
The book which is a pillar of fire when its people need fire at night, and
    by day is a pillar of smoke,
The book which never changes its soul, though it always moved forward,
    from stage to stage.

I turn back the pages, through Jewish history.
How clearly now I know what I want, as I let the parchment leaves go by.
I have reached Judges, Moses' death, the years in the wilderness,
And now I am at the beginning, the first Jewish beginning since Creation,
    at Sinai.

Our people wandered in the desert, seeking a bit of soil where to rest.
It came to Sinai, and hoped that a milk and honey land from the milky way
    would fall;
But what fell was God's yoke on Israel's stiff-neck.
And eternally this people, which wanted to be like all other peoples, is in
    its thrall.

It was the great moment, when once only a people was fated
To say, first—'We hear,' and then, 'We shall do,' and the whole world still
    marvels to see
What was and will be to the end of time.
But this people and no other people will remain yoke-crowned eternally.

'My friends, from this fate, however hard it may be, we can never escape.
You, Uri Zvi, think the crown on the tree is all, and the chief thing in a
    fire is the flame.
You, Markish, thought the branch can be more than the crown,
Because the best fruits grow on the branches, but I always knew that the
    basis of all is the seed from which we came.

Melech Ravitch

'You see, Markish, how your fate led you to your source, to the sacrifice,
    you yourself Isaac, yourself Abraham.
From being the word-stormiest you are now silent, like a sacrificial lamb.

CHAIM GRADE

Poem About the Soviet Yiddish Writers

I weep for you with all the letters of the Aleph Bet,
That you for singing spirited songs into service took.
I knew your illusory hopes, and I know that
Your hearts were torn like an old prayer book.
I stayed the night in your house on my wanderer's road.
And in your house I heard the rustling sound
Of resurrected shades in a time of forced conversion to the mode.
I well remember the hospitality among you found,
As I remember the Russian who gave me bread at his door,
As I remember his homeland that with his blood was running out,
The broad steppes and the narrowness of a prison cell,
Songs on the Volga, and bending under the knout.
I always tried to find some excuse that would in your favour tell.
Not because you are dead have I come to speak of you well.
While you still lived in the land of Russian superabundance, of rich over-
    flows,
I knew that deep in your hearts you were Marranos.

I saw how you in silence shuddered and shook,
Yiddish poets of Minsk, Moscow and Kiev,
When the survivors, spared by fate, came and made you believe
Tales of horror, like those the messengers brought Job in the Holy Book,
I saw you quiver with anger and fear,
When your faith in the 'Friendship of Peoples' lay dead in Babi Yar.
David Bergelson came to me one night.
'Are you sleeping? I can't sleep,' he said.
'There are nails, Chaim, nails all over my bed.
We hoped for the New Educated Man.
I have lived to see him, now I am old.
I have seen the New Man!'
I see him with the noose hanging down heavily like lead.
I see his brown eyes of a clever tiger,
How he bites his knot of thoughts with his crooked teeth, and his fingers on
    the trigger.

Kushnirov fought in the Civil War.
And the Communist in him fought against his disillusion more.
The demolished Vilna Synagogue after the great victory
Shook him, the grey-haired captain out of his complacency.
His son fell in battle; and he sobbed to me:
'My son was your age, so it should hardly be
Surprising that I speak to you as if you were he.
But what I mean to say is, on the other hand,
Teach me the Bible, and in Yiddish, that I should understand.'
David Hofstein played a Jewish violin.
So did David Bergelson, and often both played in.
Both Davids shrouded me in grief, and made me sad
That no violins played when they were on the altar laid.
Hofstein was there when they built Tel Aviv.
But he did not stay there, to live.
The immense Russian plain
Lured him back to his homeland again.
And when his homeland sentenced him as a traitor, to die,
He laughed from the grave with his mad eye.

Mikhoels, the tragedian of Tevye and King Lear!
You played the dairyman's trust in good, and the King's wild despair!
And with you too Fate played a mad game.
Moscow put on you a crown,
And called you 'Wise Solomon.'
But I kept away from the actor Mikhoels and his fame.
I did not trust him that he could feel
With pain, Israel's Song of Songs, and the laments of Israel.
But one night of frost and driving snow,
When Moscow celebrated the New Year so,
We both staggered through the blizzard drunk as can be.
And he groaned, what came out of his blood's agony:
'I play the King with my hands and Suskin the fool with his feet,
Because the audience doesn't know the Yiddish in which we create.'
His death shook even that land where no one is safe,
Where there is no law to protect an innocent life.

I sat on the springs of an old chair,
And leaning on his stick Dobrushin stood there,
With dishevelled grey hair,

The room cold, and cobwebs all over.
Dust on faded plush, and on every book cover.
He stood in the middle of the room like a Prophet between
The two mountains, Mount Ebal and Mount Gerizim.
'The world is cursed. It is a Hitler world,' he complained.
'Blessings on this Soviet State. We are building Socialism in this land!'
Only The Nistor warned me, 'Run away!'
But he could only get as far as where death waited for its prey.
Leib Quitko drank brandy all night with me,
The last night I was allowed with my friends in Moscow to stay.
He had the smell of the village, the steppe, the smell of milk and bread.
'Don't tell lies about Russia!' as he kissed me when I left, he said.
'Don't tell lies about Russia!' he cried after me on the stairs.
Poor murdered Poet, what would you say after what happened during these
    years!

Quitko smelled of summer and of food.
He had a gentle smile, and winning childish ways.
But Bergelson grunted angrily, 'You'll be sorry, Chaim, for the rest of your
    days
For running away from Moscow.
What you're throwing away is good ground.'
And Feffer, with his arm raised, swore
'The days of the purges will be no more.'
We enthused over paintings on a wall, and forgot
The cellar wall against which people were shot.
The day of his trial—I won't speak of it!
Thank God I was not there, or my head would split
With the bullet aimed coldly at the head
Of Colonel Itzik Feffer, when they shot him dead.
To speak of him is hard, and to be silent is the same.
Yet I must say a word in defence of his name.
Ani ha-gever. I saw his silent tear,
How he responded Amen to our Kaddish prayer.

Poets murdered without a blood avenger.
You too have been changed to ghosts.
And there is no guard, no fence, no frontier
To keep you out; so you flit at night past my window posts,
Sometimes you come to me,

As the wind and the mist blowing in from the sea.
Sometimes you are only shades. Sometimes a flock of doves.
Sometimes you scorch my face with burning ash.
I see you in the rain and the thunder crash.
Your song of faith in the coming Educated Man,
Your belief in the Brotherhood of Peoples, with all mankind one clan,
Is fallen leaves rotting on the ground.
Though you were no song-birds that sing just so,
You are after your death destined as birds to fly around.
Because your blood has had no avenger.
Because you are still loaded up with tears and anger.

Peretz Markish burst like thunder into my room,
Like a flash of lightning out of my mirror he fled,
As though he had grown gigantic in the tomb,
And his arms like open wings were spread.
I loved you and your shape and form,
Dear Poet of the storm.
Yet I must speak the truth, though it is bitter hard.
A huge bird flew about while you spoke. And I heard
Its wings. I heard the rustle of your great forest of words.
There was a rushing of birds.
'Don't worry!' you sang, happily, glad.
Where is your singing now, where the hidden woe
Of those sent to die in the Siberian snow?
You called out to me: 'I am free! I am free! I am free!'
And the lock of hair over your forehead was like your songs, dishevelled,
    wild,
And even as you spoke to me,
The bullet that struck your head was waiting, ready.

I weep for your beauty that rots in the ground.
You were as beautiful as Adam on the day of his creation.
A god carved your arms and your lips and your features.
When I saw you I gaped, awe-struck with admiration.
You were the loveliest of all creatures.
As David mourned for Jonathan, the Prince who fell
In that great battle on Gilboa hill,
So I mourn for you, Peretz Markish. There is no healing for my wound.
And no one knows where in the Soviet land they buried you.

And my brother poets whom Stalin slew.
Even after your death they condemned you to shame,
So that people should trample on your tongue as they trample on your name.
Then let my song be a monument, be your last resting place.
In each verse, as in a casket I hid your body and your face,
That you should not like tired birds go astray, fly past,
Searching in a dead sea for a boat with a black mast.

Peace to your dust, victims of my Yiddish tongue!
To the Father of Nations, that pock-marked wicked man,
In scores of languages celebrated in song,
One survivor of the evil generation before Noah's Flood,
Did you have to sing to him songs that praise and laud?
I was in that Hell, and I know the cause.
You were happy that in the choir that sang they allowed also Jews.
And because fear can bring love also to one's breast.
You had heard of antisemitism raging in the west.
And you had only one choice—to die or to sing.
So you sang. You sang: 'We too will have a good time coming!'
And at night you trembled, lest there is a ring at the door.
Don't judge your Slav neighbour. He is hard pressed as well.
But those who knew your pain and told me not to tell,
When I came into the world again out of that Hell!
That red rabble will fall away,
Like rotten branches from our tree.

How sad that spectres should prove me right,
With their wandering, silent, shamefaced smile,
Your feverish dreaming night after night,
All that remains of it is the beauty of a ruined pile.
In your song you were like a river
Reflecting the true world; but upside down.
A young generation is left, but asks about you never.
Nor about me. Nor about our generations of mourning and moan.
For your lives cut down darkly, murderously,
Your widows have blood money now.
But your language, that the hangman throttled, silenced,
Stays dumb in the land where poets still sing forever.
So I am left with your language; like the dress of one that is drowned in
the river.

JOSEPH RUBINSTEIN

A Jew in Stockholm

There is a Jew sitting in Stockholm at night.
Through his window the northern stars shine bright.
He keeps the door leading outward open wide,
To hear his voice from far away echo inside.

What is he doing here? How has he come here?
Through holocaust, fires and seas,
To hear with unwept tears
His own voice, smelling of fires and incendiaries.

His own voice, trying with hot argument
To tell strangers here of the holocaust days.
And he carries around through strangers' indifference
The pale flame of his scorched face.

What is he doing here? How has he come here
In the shine of the cold northern stars,
To hear with windy ears
His own voice smelling of smoke and tears?

Footsteps

Footsteps.
Heavy jackboots
Stomping up the stairs.
Whom are they going to?
Everyone lies awake and listens, hears.
To whom do they go?

My hearing is still clear.
Since those days and nights of fear
My ear

Listens to the steps on the stair.
I want to know—
To whom do they go?

Every sound,
Every stir
Makes me shiver with fear.
One step more—
They are outside my door!
They are coming for me!
No, not for me!
They have gone past my door.
But I shiver with fear
At every sound, every stir.

Now it is quiet here.
Nobody coming here.
They are over there!
In the land of murder and fear.
And I am not there!
I am here!

The quiet sends me off to sleep.
But in my sleep I hear
Those steps coming up my stair.
Heavy jackboots stomping up my stair.
No! They are not coming here!
It is only my fear,
My fright.
It is happening over there.
Not now, but some other night!

Some other night, some other man.
They are coming for him according to plan.
And he lies in his bed and shivers with fright.
My friend, a Yiddish poet, is being arrested tonight!
And I hear it all—
The Red Land is on the other side of my wall!

I lie in my bed, and tremble with fear;
I hear footsteps coming up my stair.

BINEM HELLER

The Poet's Death

For Peretz Markish

They led the singer to his death,
With his eyes bandaged-blind.
His hands with ropes were pinioned.
He dropped down in the pit behind.

He wanted to ask a question.
For worse than death was not knowing why this wrong.
But this earth was to him now a stranger.
It refused to understand his Yiddish tongue.

So he stood with bandaged eyes,
Facing the execution squad.
They levelled at him their rifles,
And he fell dead, in his blood.

A shudder went right through me.
It was more than I could bear.
In the shots I heard him singing.
His song rang through the air.

Perhaps

Perhaps part of the blame falls on me,
Because I kept silent, uttered no cry.
Fear froze my heart and confused my mind.
And I did not resist the lie.

My clear voice was choked and dumb.
And I allowed them, without protest,
To outrage and to violate
What was dearest to me, holiest.

Cowardice came down and walked the earth.
We hid our true feelings one from another.
We did not hear the cry of a friend.
And our own cry we often had to smother.

Black suspicion, like the plague,
Murdered faith, and left hearts cold.
Courage was branded treason,
Betrayal was called heroic, bold.

The courts were ordered what verdicts to give.
Trials were secret, the result never in doubt.
Light hung its head in shame,
Waiting that at least one man should cry out:

'No!' But no one cried.
Before he formed the word, could articulate,
His head was broken, and his tongue torn out.
Only one thing was left—the patience to wait,

To wait that justice might prevail one day.
Perhaps that was part of my blame,
That I kept silent, did not speak,
As though I had nothing to say.

PERETZ MARKISH

Mikhoels

The wounds on your face are covered by the snow,
So that the black Satan shall not touch you.
But your dead eyes blaze with woe,
And your heart they trampled on cries out against the murderous crew:

'I shall come to your defiled threshold, eternity,
With murder marks on my face, and blasphemy,
So that you see how my people live in this five-sixths of the earth,
With hate and the hangman in the land of their birth.

'Read the marks, cut them into your memory,
And let remembering never stop
For every mark the murderers left on me,
A mother and her child escaped the hangman's rope.'

You were not deafened by the murderer's hand.
The snow does not hide the marks you bear.
The sufferings in your bruised eyes demand,
And from under your brows to heaven tear.

Sleep quietly, sleep! No sorrow touches you now.
Yet one watches you as you lie there dead.
The light of the star of righteousness is on you shed.
And Rabbi Levi Yitzchok sings through you.

Is love extinguished because we mourn?
Can snow cover up our anger and scorn?
Like two lighted Sabbath candles
Your hands out of your coffin shine.

You loved to close your eyes in thought,
When you were thinking, to see clearer.
Now you hold under lock and key your woe,
So that it should not out of your coffin overflow.

306

So much light round you, and mirrors,
As when you were making up for a first-night.
Your lips seem about to open,
To say goodbye, as you set out for the stars on their height.

Your face-lineaments are transformed back into stuff,
Death is already at his destructive work.
Absorb music for the last time—the last time heard—
The music from your beloved play 'Benjamin the Third.'

Under its sounds, soaked with tears and light,
Go into eternity, with unpainted colours.
Don't feel ashamed of your ancient bruised face, full
Of holes through your kingly skull.

This is your word and blood, your best make-up,
In which in death you live on the stage.
Go into eternity! Your name still draws!
The stars will welcome you with applause!

Somewhere in heaven, between the wandering shine,
A star lights up in honour of your name.
Don't feel ashamed of the holes in you, and your pain!
Let eternity feel the shame!

At Night

A lamb comes to me at night.
It is sorrow—new and newer.
We both search the room to see if I am here.
The windows grow blue and bluer.

The room is big, and crammed full.
I walk barefoot, so
That I myself can't hear how I go.
I open my eyes suddenly,
And stick bits of night over them, not to see.

Peretz Markish

And, Sorrow, I say to the lamb, I swear
I am not here!

I cower in a corner, against the wall,
Hiding my hands; and all
The time the lamb keeps looking for me,
Searching for me soundlessly,
Till it finds me, till it finds my face,
And holds me tight in its embrace,
It drops its head on my breast.
It drops its head on my breast.
It wants to suckle from my breast.
I rise, and bent in two,
I press against the wall, I do.
And, Sorrow, I say, I swear
I am not here.

ISSY CHARIK

My Heart-Wrung Cry

Fling more burdens on my back!
I shall clench my teeth more tight.
Load all you can on me. I will say, more!
I will say it still is too light.

No matter how heavy it is, I still
Will say it is not enough.
Everything comes to me easily.
I take it all with a laugh.

If I want to sing, I stand and I sing,
And the Milky Way answers me.
I could go a whole lifetime about on the earth,
With the fresh dew of youth on my lips.

And when things grow hard—how can they grow hard
When young strength drifts and drips?
Everyone gets enough and more,
According to his strength and belief.

Let who will weep silently,
If he has a silent floor.
And I—I have a heart with summery panes.
Let none dare to quench my joy!

When I find happiness in my track,
Let none dare to quench my joy
With words autumnal, with words that are black.
I won't have it! I won't! No! No!

Rather dash my head against a stone
Than break the windows of my heart.
Do you hear me, earth? I shall stride about on you, still young,
When the snow on my head will lie.
Do you hear me, earth? I shall stride about on you, still young,
Till my last blood-drenched heart-wrung cry.

Issy Charik

A Town of Starving Jews

It is hard to die with the town
Where you lived yourself once.
Who will save us here?
Who will give us another chance?

I stared—these people are dead!
Just beards, dead beards!
Enough, I said, earth to earth!
Enough empty words!

The town cried out in a fever.
Each step I take is a hit!
Why did a town of Jews
Call me antisemite!

My tread falls heavily
In this empty street.
This morning a town of Jews
Called me 'Antisemite!'

All in rags, they pointed
Their fingers at me.
'We know him! One of us
Who has turned enemy!

'We'd like to go up to him,
And say—'Brother, things are so bad!
If you could kill the lot of us,
We'd be glad!' '

Night

I can't at my table sit still.
I take down book after book,
Turn the pages without thought, without will,
And replace each in its nook.
I pace up and down the room.
I can't write a word in this gloom.

Who has ever heard
The sobs of paper unwritten on,
When songs want to come, yet no word
Can get written down?
I can't write a word of my song.
Devil knows what has gone wrong!

But the world comes even at night.
You hear the snow in the air.
And behind that wall, sleeping light,
Your neighbour the hero lies there.
He is building our future. He
Knows what is modesty.

You want to knock at his wall.
But it's past midnight now.
Your neighbour sleeps or wakes, and all
The land stands by his pillow
So a broad hand to him I give
Through all the walls where we live.

He sleeps. He breathes easily.
The night becomes friendly, intimate.
And over our high roof I see
The stars shine, scintillate.
I sit at my table quietly.
And calm is waiting there for me.

Gone is my restless night.
My mind is unclouded, it's clear.

Issy Charik

I sit at my table and write
The song you are reading here.
And the paper sings gratefully
A song of thankfulness to me.

MOISHE BRODERSON

Where Shall I Flee?

After seven years in a Soviet prison

I want to open my mouth.
There is something I have to say.
I want to flee from the horror,
Anywhere, by any way—

But my mouth twists into a grimace.
The words freeze and die.
I howl like a wolf in the forest
Up to the stars in the sky.

I want to open my mouth.
There is something I have to say.
I want to flee from the horror,
Anywhere, by any way—

Every wild wind carries me off,
Whirls me round here and there.
The earth, poor devil that I am,
Finds me too much to bear.

I want to open my mouth.
There is something I have to say.
I want to flee from the horror,
Anywhere, by any way—

But the word freezes on my tongue.
It dies in dismay.
Where shall I flee from my anguish?
From myself run away!

Moishe Broderson

Jew

A.

Don't ask of a People a different outlook.
Don't ask the nomad to be proudly shod.
Don't ask it of the People wandering for centuries,
Forever seeking justice from man and God.

Don't ask it of those whose home is the desert,
Whose own mirages lead them astray,
Of those whose harps have been hung everywhere,
For every vagrant wind to play.

Don't ask equality from a People bent
By all the storms of Time since memory.
Have you ever looked deep in the eyes of the Jew?
Have you like them longed for redemption insatiably?

Don't ask for dancing steps from feet that are broken,
From feet dust-laden from the way,
From feet bruised with marching onward to victory,
To bring down Messiah in our day.

B.

I too had a hand in building the Tower of Babel,
Your idolatrous edifice, doomed from the start to fall.
I too sowed high beauty on the wind.
I too served in the ranks with you all.

I brought to the building like you bricks and mortar.
I too like you was smitten with the unknown.
In the end lock and bolt were shut against me.
Each time I appeared I was met by a strange stone.

I too had a hand in building the Tower of Babel,
Vying with you in the contest for eternity,
And all my torments and afflictions and sufferings
I babbled them out in seventy languages foolishly.

314

The seventy languages crush me, my body and my life.
They darken, they blacken my day and night.
The Tower of Babel gave me seventy alien tongues,
And treated my own with contempt and spite.

C.

Gate and door in her bright Palace always stand open.
So every impudent scamp befouls the entrance in.
And then I find her, as to-day,
With weeping ill and worn and thin.

Every nobody passes judgement,
Says her days are numbered, any day she will die.
But none of them know her or understand her—
These false prophets with their false prophecy.

And when I see and hear it, bowed with pain,
Or winged with joy and hope of brighter days,
She dries her tears and the grief of generations,
And waits like a young maid for my caress and praise.

Then I lay her sweet head upon my breast.
And she is beautiful, full of charm, and young.
And I murmur, My dear, my beloved,
My Yiddish, my Yiddish word, my Yiddish song!

D.

I am guilty, you say. I know I am guilty.
And all the measures of sin are full in me.
My first sin was that I was patient.
That was, that is my greatest sin undoubtedly.

I was long silent, dumb to all the wrongs you did.
I clenched my teeth. My pain burned and glowed, tempered into steel.
I was too long the suffering bearer of your burdens,
And in the flames of the auto-da-fe I cried 'Hear O Israel!'

315

I waited too long, and may be too soon,
When the Prophet in his woe revealed himself to me.
I tried to rouse you before time—no wiser by events—
To an understanding of God, and to sympathy.

That frightens you most—for it is hidden from you.
Not only from your soul, from your body too.
The resistance I met from you nearly murdered me.
Yet still I cry—Murder you must not do!

    E.

The earth is everywhere hot under my feet,
And everywhere the sky above me is on fire.
It's all heaven and earth and that damned Jew!
It's all dirt and slime and mud and mire.

I stare at myself—just a crazy riddle.
I wonder wildly about this lunacy.
Am I so big or am I so little,
I—the riddle of this mad century?

In number small, everywhere lost to sight.
Am I the leaven that ferments the dull?
Do blockheads rise through me to importance?
Have I made a lot of empty vessels full?

Am I the ferment of hellish affliction,
Because I forget myself, and forget my own name,
I who beat at the gates of mercy with unblooded hands,
I who stand at the door of redemption bowed with shame!

    F.

There isn't a day I don't say my death-bed confession.
Not a day when I do not confess my sin.
The fear of death dwells in my every limb, weeping.
It besieges me like a conqueror within.

Is it any wonder that every meal I take is poison,
That I am racked with pain, regret, dismay?
Hear me, God, wherever you are! It is true!
I have sinned! I have sinned! But not more than they!

It is true we all sin, we all sorely sin,
Knowingly and unknowingly—all of us, great and small,
Openly and in secret we sinned against the light.
And mostly against ourselves, against ourselves most of all.

But they—they let their empty heroism shine in the sun,
As if on parade puffing out their chest.
While we—we sense things differently—and we confessed our sin.
We say our death-bed confession, and we beat our breast.

G.

When we say Jew we should say grace as for loaf of bread.
For it is like the corn in the field, plain honest worth.
And when we say Jew we don't mean the mob, the dregs,
The apostates and near-apostates, scum of the earth.

When we say Jew we don't mean trimmers and turncoats,
Opportunists feigning foreign dress and guise,
Nor those who roll in the dust of scholarship,
And to all the outside world close their hearts and their eyes.

And when we say Jew we don't mean the closen people,
For there is no pride in being a Jew.
Being a Jew means always remembering and reminding.
Being a Jew means keeping the Prometheus fire burning true.

And when we say Jew, we should be to life responsive.
We should open gate and doors to the human view.
As with bread and salt we should say a blessing
For standing near to that reality called Jew.

H.

Crushed by the millstones of the centuries,
Sifted through thousand-year-old sieves,

317

Moishe Broderson

I strove towards God, hopelessly in love
With what the round of the generations achieves.

I love the world, I am in love with life.
Stronger than death I love them more and more.
And though the Angel of Death stands always near me,
My word is for life, with whisper and roar.

Alas, we overlook so many wonders.
We let miracles unnoticed pass.
And for love of life the coward triumphs,
And the cutthroat leads men to war, alas!

They can all trample on me with their jackboots,
And entangle me in their senseless strife,
I who towards God was striving,
I who am hopelessly in love with life!

I.

Not on a white ass on the Bethlehem roads,
Not heralded by shofar or a bell going before,
Not with hymns, and not with blasphemies,
Not through senseless Gog-and-Magog war—

Not through Torahs intricate and spent,
Not through despair and a sunken head,
Not through slaying false prophets, and not
Through rolling underground when you are dead,

Not through hair-splitting about guiltless or guilt,
Not through foolish self-martyrdom.
A new light rises over the whole world.
A new sun is coming, a new life will come!

And he will be there in every man's mind—
With pure and blessed sanctitude.
He will be smiling on every face.
The miracle of God and man understood.

SAMUEL HALKIN

When Will Day Come?

Between wall and wall, my hand
On the cold pillow lies.
My head is on my hand,
And I can't close my eyes.

The night drags without end—
A cold sleepless night
From evening till morning.
Will it never be light?

Every song till I die
Will never be ended.
I have a thousand worries
That will never be mended.

I lie and I wonder
Will it ever be day?
I lie in the dark, thinking
What my conscience will say.

When I was mourning my father
Did I betray a dear friend?
Will the day never come?
Will this night never end?

A brother disappeared.
Another was slain.
And I was too busy
Writing poems again.

I was busy with my poems.
Wondering what was the right way.
My God, will it ever be morning?
What has my conscience to say?

Samuel Halkin

I Am His Wife

I need no comforters, I ask no sympathy.
With all my bitterness I will despise you
If any one of you will think of a way
To make my grief more easy for me.

I am his wife—isn't that enough?
I need no stranger's sympathy.
No matter where ill-fate may take him,
He is always one with me.

I am his wife. Consider these words!
Have you any idea what they signify?
My grief, my festive day turned to sorrow—
I wouldn't change it for any joy!

I am his wife. Let me lean on those
Who have suffered the same fate as I.
And for him, may all that good people wish him,
And I with them become his recompense, indemnify.

I am his wife. His nearest kin.
Sometimes I tear my flesh not to scream.
But let no one among you dare to think that I
Will ever mention his name.

For how can I divide my dear one from his friends,
From all his friends who suffer the same as he,
Trudging along those desolate roads,
Exiled in a land of pain and misery!

And if you want the whole truth from me,
Forgive me the harsh words that I use.
If to be banished and in prison is the noblest fate now for a man,
Then that, my dear, is your place, where you must be.

ITZIK FEFFER

I Am a Jew

I am a Jew.
The wine of enduring generations
Strengthened me on my wanderer's way.
The evil sword of pain and lamentations
Nothing that I hold dear could slay—
My people, my faith, and my head unbowed.
It could not stop me being free and true.
Under the sword I cried aloud:
'I am a Jew!'

Pharoah and Titus, Haman made their aim
To slay me in their times and lands,
Eternity still bears my name
Upon its hands.
And I survived in Spain the rack,
The Inquisition Fires too.
My horn sounded this message back:
'I am a Jew!'

When Egypt walled my body round,
I felt agonies.
But I sowed my pain upon the ground,
And saw the sunrise.
Under the sun a road lay spread,
Where thorns and prickles grew,
And as they pierced my eyes, I said:
'I am a Jew!'

My forty years of wandering
In the wilderness,
Gave me in age the hardening
To bear pain and distress.
Through all my sufferings and my fears,
Bar Kochba's call came to my ears,
Through every sound and view

I cried: 'I am a Jew!'

Samson's hair that Delilah shore
Shone brighter than gold could do.
Always one cry was at my core:
'I am a Jew!'

Rabbi Akiba's sagacity,
And wise Isaiah's word,
Kept alive my love in me,
Till my hatred stirred,
And I felt the blood of the Maccabees,
Whom the tyrants slew—
I cried from all the gallows-trees:
'I am a Jew!'

Solomon's wisdom guided me
Along my wanderer's road,
And Heine's twisted smile I see
As a scourge and a goad.
Yehuda Halevi's song in my head
Echoes through and through.
I have often faded but never died:
'I am a Jew!'

In the market places of Amsterdam
Spinoza worked undeterred.
On this earth like a bright sun came
Karl Marx and his word.
It filled with fresh red blood my veins,
And made my old heart new,
It healed my sorrows and my pains:
'I am a Jew!'

My eyes are dazzled with the sunset glow
Of a painting by Levitan.
The road that Mendele trod I go,
And meet the bayonet of a Red Armyman.
The sickle shines on the ripe corn.
I am a son of this Soviet land where I was born.

And too
'I am a Jew!'

From Haifa Harbour answeringly,
From London comes the response to me,
From Buenos Aires and New York
Come songs from Jews who fight and work.
And even from the burning hell
Comes a shuddering I know well.
In them all one word runs through:
'I am a Jew!'

I am a Jew who has drunk up
Happiness from Stalin's cup.
To those who would let Moscow go
Under the ground, I call out—'No.'
The Slavs are my brothers, too,
'I am a Jew!'

I am a ship against both shores.
Into eternity my blood pours.
On my pride in Sverdlov I depend,
And on Kaganovitch, Stalin's friend.
My young go speeding over the snows.
My heart bombs and dynamite throws.
And everywhere the call comes through:
'I am a Jew!'

I am not alone! My strength is growing.
Battle is now my daily bread.
I send the storm raging and blowing,
And the brown enemy falls dead.
Gorelik and Papernik, too,
Cry from under the earth:
'I am a Jew!'

Despite the foe who comes destroying
Under the Red Flag I shall live,
I shall plant vineyards for my enjoying,
And on this soil I will thrive.

Itzik Feffer

Whatever the enemy may do
The liberty of the world we shall save.
I shall dance on Hitler's grave.
'I am a Jew!'

A. N. STENZEL

After Treblinka

From Treblinka and Maidanek,
From Oswiecim we came.
And Peretz came with us,
A miraculous flame.

From flame rises a phoenix.
You rose an eagle from our poor hearth.
Though we can hardly keep our fire burning,
Your wings span the earth.

Winston Churchill

Not a flag in the wind is a leader,
But one who gathers in his folds all the gales.
He holds them in his grip, strongly,
And so to safe anchorage sails.

Like the wake of the ship his thoughts run,
Like the spray alongside,
Running all the time, wider and wider,
However strong the tide.

His face smiles, but his teeth are clenched.
His heart is steel, but his tongue sings.
With his cigar he forges
For our strong anchor the rings.

Not a flag in the wind is a leader,
To turn to all sides his head.
He is the proud mast on which the canvas
Against the storm-winds spread.

A. N. Stenzel

The Levites' Song of Praise

And if you cut down the tree,
The root in the earth will remain.
And if you tear out the roots,
A seed will spring up again.

We bear heaven and earth in ourselves.
Our dream is the growing germ.
Body, broken by griefs and pain,
Swelling soil ploughed up and firm.

By the Nile, the Jordan, Euphrates,
A singing harp is each tree.
Everywhere is the sun, man, and you,
One dream that forever will be.

And if you cut down the tree,
We shall say nothing, but bend low.
Our hearts, sheep caught
In the tangle of each bough.

Biographical Notes

SHOLEM ASCH b. 1880 in Kutno, Poland. d. London 1957. Outstanding Yiddish novelist. Widely translated into English and other languages. His 'Shtetl' (Township) published in 1904 lifted him to fame. Works include 'Three Cities', 'Salvation', 'The Nazarene', 'God of Vengeance'.

ZALMAN SHNEOUR b. 1887 in Shklov, White Russia. d. New York 1959. Famous as poet and novelist in both Hebrew and Yiddish. His novel 'Noah Pandre', running to several volumes picturing Jewish life in White Russia won acclaim in English, German and other translations. A direct descendant of the Chassidic Rabbi Shneour Zalman, the founder of Chabad and the Lubavitcher dynasty, his many-volumed novel 'The Emperor and the Rabbi', centres round his great ancestor and his times, his imprisonment by Czar Paul and his death during Napoleon's invasion of Russia.

DAVID PINSKI b. 1872 in Mohilev, White Russia. d. Haifa, Israel, 1960. Played important part in the early days of the Jewish Socialist and Socialist Zionist movement. Was one of the organisers of the meetings of Friends of Yiddish held in Basle immediately after the First Zionist Congress held there in 1897. Was invited in 1899 to settle in New York. Former President Yiddish PEN Centre. Editor of New York Yiddish daily 'Zeit'. Spent his last years in Israel. His play 'The Treasure', translated into English by Ludwig Lewisohn was highly praised.

DAVID BERGELSON b. 1884 in Uman, Ukraine. Victim of the Soviet purge of Yiddish literature in 1948. In 1908 while studying at Kiev University he wrote his novel 'Around the Railway Station', which won him immediate recognition. His novels 'After All', and 'By the Dnieper' are ranked among the chief works of Soviet Yiddish literature. Numbered with Sholem Asch and Zalman Shneour as the outstanding trio of the generation subsequent to Mendele, Peretz and Sholem Aleichem.

THE NISTOR. Pen-name of Pinchas Kahanovitch. b. 1884 in Berditchev, in the Ukraine. Victim of the Soviet purge of Yiddish literature in 1948. Wrote many poems, ballads, children's stories. Translated Hans Andersen into Yiddish. Regarded with David Bergelson as the chief representatives of Soviet Yiddish literature. Used Yiddish folk-motifs very largely, with a simple naive style, and often a somewhat twisted syntax.

MOISHE KULBAK b. 1896, in Smorgan, Vilna. Victim of a Soviet purge in the 30's. His father worked in the forests; his mother came of a peasant family. His first poems were in Hebrew and he was for a time a follower of Achad Ha'am. Went to Berlin in 1920 as a prompter with the Vilna Troupe. Returned in 1923 to Vilna, teaching Yiddish literature in the Yiddish High School. Went to Soviet Russia in 1928.

ISAAC BASHEVIS SINGER b. Bilgoray, Poland 1904. Since 1935 resident in the U.S.A. Most of his novels have appeared in English translation: 'The Family Moskat', 'Satan in Goray', 'The Magician of Lublin', 'Gimpel the Fool', 'The Spinoza of Market Street'.

ITZIK MANGER b. Jassy, Roumania, 1901. d. Israel 1969. Poet, playwright, essayist. Lived in London 1941-51, then in New York till he settled in Israel in the last year of his life.

MENDEL MANN b. 1911 in Warsaw. Novelist and short story writer and Editor of Yiddish daily 'Unser Vort', in Paris. Was in Russia during the Second World War as an officer in the Red Army. Was in the march into Berlin. His Trilogy 'At the Gates of Moscow' pictures the fighting on the Eastern fronts. Lived in Israel for several years after the war.

EPHRAIM AUERBACH b. 1892 in Bessarabia. His first poem appeared in 1909 in a Yiddish magazine in Vilna. Went to Palestine in 1913, working as an agricultural labourer. When Turkey entered the war in 1915 he was expelled like all other aliens, and went to Egypt where he joined the Zion Mule Corps serving the British Army at the Dardanelles. Invalided out, he went to America where he continued to live, working as a Yiddish journalist. Published several volumes of poetry and essays. Former President Yiddish PEN Centre in New York. Died in Israel in 1973.

SHLOMO BIRNBAUM b. 1891 in Vienna. Son of Nathan Birnbaum, organiser and President of the First Yiddish Conference held in Czernovitz in 1908.

Yiddish philologist and Orientalist. Till the Hitler regime was Lecturer in Yiddish at Hamburg University. Later Lecturer in Yiddish Studies and research lecturer in Hebrew Palaeography, London University. Now resident in Toronto, Canada.

AARON ZEITLIN b. 1889, in White Russia. Brought up in Vilna, then from 1907 till 1939 lived in Warsaw. Since 1939 in New York. Poet, playwright, essayist. Son of Hillel Zeitlin, Yiddish and Hebrew religious-philosophical writer, murdered in a Nazi death camp in 1942. Died in New York in 1973.

HALPER LEIVICK b. 1888 in White Russia. d. New York 1962. Was arrested in 1906 for political activity against the Czarist regime, and spent four years in prison in Warsaw. In 1912 sent to Siberia for life, but escaped a year later and made his way to New York where he remained. His name was Leivick Halper; he reversed it to avoid confusion with the New York Yiddish poet Moishe Leib Halpern. Former President Yiddish PEN Centre in New York.

ABRAHAM GOLOMB b. 1888 in Lithuania. Yiddish essayist, scholar, pedagogue. Lived in Vilna, Palestine, South America, Canada. Now resident in Los Angeles.

CHAIM GRADE b. 1910 in Vilna. Studied in several Yeshivas. First poems published in 1934. One of the leaders of the 'Young Vilna' group of Yiddish writers. Spent the years of the Second World War in Russia. After the war settled in New York.

MELECH RAVITCH. Pen-name of Zachariah Berger. Poet and Essayist. b. 1893, in Galicia. Has travelled round the globe. Lived in Vienna and Warsaw, then for some years in Australia, then in Israel. Now resident in Montreal, Canada.

SHLOMO BICKEL b. 1896 in Roumania. d. New York 1969. Doctor of Law Czernovitz University. Practised in Bucharest. Resident in America since 1939. Essayist and literary critic.

ZALMAN SHAZAR, President of the State of Israel 1963-73. b. 1889 in Mir, Russia. Minister of Education in Israel 1949-51. Editor Israel Hebrew daily 'Davar' 1925-1949. Hebrew and Yiddish scholar. Essayist and poet.

MOISHE DLUZNOVSKY b. 1906 in Poland. Yiddish novelist and essayist. Lived for years in France till the Second World War. Escaped from occupied

France to North Africa. Resident since the end of the war in New York. His novel 'The Potter's Daughter' has appeared in English translation.

MOISHE BRODERSON b. 1890 in Moscow. His family moved to Lodz in Poland, where he grew up. Returned to Moscow in the First World War; was there during the Revolution. Returned to Lodz in 1918. Was the leading figure in the Lodz group of Yiddish writers. Active in the Yiddish Theatre. Founded Yiddish Marionette Theatre and Ararat Yiddish Art Theatre. His play 'David and Bathsheba' was produced in Warsaw in 1924. Translated into Yiddish Alexander Blok's 'Twelve' and Pushkin and other Russian poets. Was in Moscow during the Second World War. Imprisoned in a Siberian slave camp during the Soviet purge of Yiddish literature. Was released after Stalin's death and went back to Poland a sick man; died there soon after his return, in 1956.

LEYELESS. Pen-name of Aaron Glanz. b. 1889 in Wloclawek, Poland. d. 1966 New York. Grew up in Lodz. Went to London in 1905, and studied in London University. Settled in New York in 1909. His first book of poems appeared in 1918. Leader of the group of Introspectivists in Yiddish poetry in America. Served several terms as President of Yiddish PEN in New York.

ABRAHAM SUTZKEVER b. 1913 in Smargon, near Vilna. When the Cossacks burned down Smargon in 1915 the family wandered to Omsk in Siberia. His father died there and the family returned in 1922 to Vilna. He was first interested in Yiddish poetry by the work of Moishe Leib Halpern, Leivick and Kulbak. Then strongly under the influence of Leyeless and the American Yiddish Introspectivist poets. One of the leaders of the 'Young Vilan' group. In the German invasion of Poland he was in the Vilna Ghetto. He broke out and fought with the Partisans in the woods round Vilna. Decorated by the Russians for bravery. Settled after the war in Israel, where he edits the Yiddish literary magazine 'Goldene Keit'.

JACOB GLATSTEIN b. 1896 in Lublin, Poland. d. 1971 in New York. Emigrated to America in 1914. Began writing poetry in Yiddish in 1919. Together with Leyeless and Minkoff founded the group of Introspectivists.

ISAAC KATZNELSON b. 1886 in Minsk Province, Russia. Came to Warsaw as a boy to work on the Hebrew paper 'Hazefirah'. Was known as a Hebrew writer, but when the Germans occupied Poland and drove the Jews into ghettoes and death camp Katznelson, who was himself in the Ghetto and was killed there, took to writing Yiddish. His 'Song of the Slaughtered Jewish

People' roused wide attention when it was found after the war. Was translated and published in several languages, including German.

HIRSH GLICK b. 1920 in Vilna. Member of the 'Young Vilna' group. Fought as a partisan in the Vilna woods, and was killed in battle in 1944. His 'Partisan Song' became the anthem of the Jewish partisans.

MORDECAI GEBIRTIG b. 1877 in Cracow. Worked all his life as a carpenter in Cracow. Abraham Reisen in 1906 encouraged him to write poetry and he became one of the most popular folk balladists. Served in the Austrian army in the First World War from 1914 till 1918. Was put into the Cracow Ghetto and killed there in 1942. His poem 'Our Town is Burning' written in 1938 was taken up as one of the most popular songs in the ghettoes and concentration camps and among the survivors in the D.P. camps.

KADIE MALADOVSKY b. 1893 in Lithuania. Lived till 1938 in Warsaw. Now in New York.

ROCHEL KORN b. 1898 in a village in Galicia. Her first poems were in Polish. Her first printed work, short stories, also in Polish, appeared in 1918. Then took to Yiddish. Spent the Second World War period in Russia. Now in Montreal, Canada.

ELIEZER GREENBERG b. 1897, in Bessarabia. Since 1913 in America. Co-Editor with Irving Howe of 'Treasury of Yiddish Stories' and 'A Treasury of Yiddish Poetry'.

URI ZVI GREENBERG b. 1894, near Zlotchev, Galicia. Joined the Austrian army in the First World War and fought on the Serbian front. Experienced the Lemberg pogrom in which his family was murdered. In 1920 he joined a group of young advanced Yiddish poets, Ravitch, Markish, Broderson and others in publishing magazines containing also prose by I. J. Singer, Opotoshu and art by Marc Chagall. Settled in Israel in 1924. Stopped writing Yiddish and wrote for years only in Hebrew, till 1957 when he published several new poems in Yiddish.

MANI LEIB. Pen-name of Mani Leib Brahinsky. b. 1884 in Tchernigov Province in Russia. Emigrated to London in 1904, and a year later to America. Died in New York in 1953.

A. VOGLER. Pen-name of Elchanah Rozanski. b. 1907 in Vilna. First published poetry in 1925. Member of the 'Young Vilna' group. Spent the war years in the far interior of the Soviet Union. Died in Paris in 1971.

LEIB FEINBERG b. 1897 in Podolia. d. New York 1972. Graduated at Moscow University in literature and philosophy. Started writing Russian poetry as a boy. Won first prize in 1918 All-Russian Poetry Contest. Served three years as an officer in the Red Army. Was captured by Denikin. Escaped in 1920 and made his way to the United States. Died while in office as President of Yiddish PEN Centre in New York.

JOSEPH RUBINSTEIN b. 1904 in Poland. Spent the years of the Second World War wandering in the Soviet interior. After the war he settled in New York. His latest book of poems 'Exodus From Europe', 1970, is dedicated 'To you, America, where my wife and I have after long years found a home'.

BINEM HELLER b. 1908 in Warsaw. Spent the Second World War years in Soviet Russia. Now lives in Israel.

PERETZ MARKISH b. 1895 in Volhynia. Joined the Russian Army in 1916, fighting on the German front. Was wounded. Started writing poetry when 15, in Russian; published his first Yiddish poems in 1917. Victim of the Soviet purge of Yiddish literature in 1948.

ISSY CHARIK b. 1898 in Minsk, White Russia. Was first a factory worker and later became a teacher and librarian. Joined the Red Army in 1919. After his first book was published his regiment ordered him to Moscow to study at the University. Graduated at the Faculty of Yiddish Linguistics and Yiddish Literature. Was Poet Laureate of the Soviet White Russian Republic. Disappeared in 1936.

SAMUEL HALKIN b. 1899 in White Russia. d. Moscow 1960. Wrote his first poetry in Hebrew. Turned to Yiddish in 1921. Translated Shakespeare's 'King Lear' and work by Pushkin and Gorki into Yiddish. Arrested in the purge of Yiddish writers but survived the camps and was released after Stalin's death. In 1958 the Government Publishing House issued a volume of his poems in Russian translation.

ITZIK FEFFER b. 1900 in Shpole, Ukraine, in a working class family. Fought in the Revolutionary war. During the Second World War was a Colonel in the Red Army. Published 15 volumes of poems in Yiddish. Victim of the Soviet purge of Yiddish literature.

A. N. STENZEL b. 1897 near Sosnowice, Poland. Joined a Hehalutz group, because the idea of agricultural work appealed to him. Went in 1919 to Holland, where he worked as a farm labourer. In 1921 he travelled the German countryside, living and working with the peasants. Published his first poems in 1925. Thomas Mann, Arnold Zweig, Elsa Lasker-Schueler and others wrote highly of them. Since 1934 resident in London.

Glossary

ABAYAH   A long Arab surcoat.

ABAYE AND RABBAH   Babylonian Rabbis of the 4th century. Noted as Rabbinical disputants, whose disputations have gone into legend, "Havayot de Abaye ve-Rabbah."

AGADAH   The non-legal part of the Talmud. Largely legends, sagas, fables, parables, proverbs, about God and His relation to humanity and to Israel.

AIN HAROD   A large agricultural settlement (Kibbutz) in the Valley of Jezreel, in Israel, under the shadow of Mount Tabor.

ALEF BETH   The first letters of the Hebrew alphabet (Alpha Bet).

ALIYAHS   Calling congregants up to the Reading of the Law.

AM YISROEL CHAI   "Long live the Jewish People!"

AN-SKY'S "DYBBUK"   A popular play by the Yiddish writer Sh. An-sky, first produced in Hebrew in Moscow by the original Habimah, directed by Vachtangov, Stanislavsky's colleague in the Moscow Art Theatre. Then in Yiddish by the Vilna Troupe, and in English and other translations. A Dybbuk in Jewish folk legend is a departed spirit that has attached itself to a living person, and has to be exorcised. The play centres round a dead young man refusing to leave his living betrothed; and when he is exorcised by the Rabbi, she dies.

THE ARI   Rabbi Isaac Luria, 1534-1572. Mystic. Founder of the modern Caballah.

BAAL SHEM   A great teacher, founder of the sect of Chassidim, born in the Ukraine 1700, died 1760. Martin Buber among others has written much on the Baal Shem and the Chassidic movement.

BETH HAMEDRASH   Literally House of Study, usually attached to a Synagogue, where Jews come to study Hebrew lore, and listen to the discourses of the Rabbi. Some Jews abandoned outside pursuits to devote themselves wholly to study.

BILKOMEN   A Jewish township.

BIMA   Also Almemar. The Reading Desk in the Synagogue, usually in the centre, where the Scrolls of the Law are placed for reading out the appropriate portions.

CHAI ADAM   Code of Jewish Law, compiled by Rabbi Abraham Danziger (1747-1820).

CHASSIDISM   (See note on Baal Shem). A mass movement inspired by the Baal Shem in the 18th century, and still numerous, which taught joyous

334

devotion as more important than learning. "All service to God must be done with the burning glow of enthusiasm." Chassidim are divided in a number of separate but allied followings of different Rabbis. Poland was the great centre of Chassidism and millions were exterminated in the ghettoes and the death camps in the holocaust. The movement is experiencing a revival in America and Israel.

CHEDAR BOYS   Young boys attending Hebrew elementary religion classes.

CHEDAR LAD   A young boy of the age for attending the chedar, the elementary Hebrew religion school.

CHUMASH WITH RASHI   The Pentateuch read together with the commentary by Rashi, born and died in Troyes, in France, 1040-1105. It is the standard accepted Jewish commentary.

CHUPPA POLES   Jewish marriages take place under a canopy, or chuppah, supported by four poles.

CHURBAN   Literally Destruction. The Destruction of the Temple. The Holocaust in the Hitlerist occupation of Eastern Europe.

DREIDLACH ON CHANUKAH   Chanukah, eight day Feast of the Liberation under the Maccabees, related in the Books of the Maccabees. Popular children's festival celebrated in the lighting of candles, and with traditional games, chiefly the dreidel or trendel, a spinning top, with Hebrew lettering on the sides, for the miracle of the cruse of oil in the Temple that lasted eight days.

EUROPEAN MASKILIC CONCEPTION   Haskallah, the movement of the Maskilim, "the Enlightened", who inspired by Moses Mendelssohn (1729-1786) believed the walls of the Ghetto had been broken down, making Jews free to absorb the general European culture. It led largely to assimilation and provoked a counter-movement, back to the traditional Jewish ways, in one direction Chassidism, and later the Mossur movement, and in another direction Zionism.

GALUTH   Also Golus. Literally Exile. The Exile of the Jews from the Holy Land after the Destruction of the Temple. Also used in the sense of the Dispersion or Diaspora, the wide-spread dispersion of the Jews in the world.

GAON   A high Rabbinic title. A great Jewish scholar. Intellectual and religious giant.

GEMARRAH STUDENT   A student of the Gemarrah, the Talmud. The study begins at an early age.

GIBBET   gallows.

GOLDEN MENORAHS   The Menorah was a seven-branched gold candelabrum, burning oil, made by Bezalel for the Tabernacle (Exodus 25). There were menorahs in the Temple. And the menorah is still in use in homes and Synagogues, notably for lighting the candles at Chanukah. The menorah is also used as a Jewish symbol, in the same way as the Shield of David.

GOLUS CLASSIC   (See Galuth). Characteristic, model expression of Jewish life in the Dispersion, as against that of the Bible period.

HALACHA   The Jewish Religious Law. Jewish traditional practice. Also the name given to the legal part of the Talmud.

HAZEFIRAH   Hebrew daily newspaper published in Warsaw. Edited first by its founder Chaim Selig Slonimsky (grandfather of Antoni Slonimsky) and then by Nahum Sokolov.

HIRSCH LEKERT   A young Jewish Socialist in Vilna, who in 1902 outraged by the brutality of the Czarist Governor, General von Wahl, shot at him, but unsuccessfully. He made no attempt to escape and went spiritedly to his execution.

HOTZMACH   A personal name, which has come to stand for a half-pauperised trader, living cheerfully on his wits, with some clowning. From a play by Goldfaden, the "father" of the Yiddish Theatre. Hotz Mach, Have me.

HOUR OF NIELAH   Nielah, the solemn closing service at the end of Yom Kippur. Nielah—concluding, closing. "Before the closing of the gates of Forgiveness."

KIDDUSH HASHEM   "Sanctification of God's Name." Dying for God's Sake. Martyrdom.

KLAUS   A chapel attached to a Synagogue, for withdrawal for prayer and study.

KNOUT   The Russian Lash, used by the Cossacks in Czarist Russia in dispersing demonstrations, or flogging prisoners, especially when taking them in chain-gangs to Siberia.

KOL NIDREI NIGHT   The evening before Yom Kippur, the Day of Atonement, which begins then with the Kol Nidrei service in the Synagogue. Kol Nidrei—the annulment of past vows and prayer for forgiveness for having made them. "It should need no special vow to live the right life."

LADINO   Also Judeo-Spanish, from Ladinar, meaning to translate, in the same way as Yiddish was originally Teitch, also meaning to translate. The language taken by the Jewish exiles from Spain in the expulsion of 1492. As with Yiddish, an amalgam of medieval German with Hebrew, it is an amalgam of old Castilian with Hebrew and other elements, largely Greek, Arabic and Turkish. Still used among Sephardic Jews, Jews of Spanish and Portuguese origin.

LATKES   Pancakes, traditional for Chanukah.

LONG GABERDINES   Long loose overgarments worn distinguishingly by Jews in Eastern Europe. Known also as caftan or chalat.

MACH   Unintelligible part of a word, all that is left of a broken-off signboard after the war bombardments.

MACHZOR   The Jewish Festival Prayer Book, containing the special liturgy for the respective Festivals.

MARRANOS   Jews forcibly converted under the Inquisition who remained secretly practising Jews, and were often imprisoned and burned at the stake when their deviation was discovered. The term is still used for Jews hiding their Jewish identity.

MEGILLOTH ESH   "The Scrolls of Fire", by the great Hebrew poet Bialik (1873-1934). It exists in a Yiddish translation by I. J. Schwartz, published in New York in 1909.

MORDECAI ANILEWICZ   Leader of the Warsaw Ghetto Rising in 1943, killed in the fighting. His memory is preserved in Anilewicz Road in Warsaw, on the site of the battle, where the Warsaw Ghetto Monument stands.

MOSSUR   Also Musar. A movement initiated by Rabbi Israel Salanter (1810-1883) to stress the ethical side of Judaism. Faced with Jewish Emancipation he and his disciples and followers feared a growth of worldliness. "His problems were Jewish living and Jewish character."

NATHAN ROTENSTREICH   Professor of Philosophy at the Hebrew University in Jerusalem. Born Poland 1914.

PODOLIA   A Province in the Ukraine. An area with many forests, where the Baal Shem spent much time in communion with nature and God.

PURIM   A Jewish Festival celebrating the deliverance recounted in the Biblical Book of Esther.

RASHI   (See Chumash with Rashi).

ROSH HASHONAH   Literally Head of the Year. The Jewish New Year, a day of congregational prayer in the Synagogue. Traditionally the anniversary of the Creation, a Day of Judgment—"Who shall Live and who shall Die." The Jewish year is lunar, and New Year's Day usually occurs in September.

SARAH BATH TOVIM   A pious woman of the 18th century, who wrote beautiful poetic prayers in Yiddish for women. She has gone into Jewish legend as a female counterpart of the legendary Prophet Elijah, who goes about the world helping people in need.

SELICHOT TIME   Selichot, forgiveness. The time when the special penitential prayers are said, principally in the Ten Days of Penitence between the New Year (Rosh Hashonah) and the Day of Atonement (Yom Kippur).

SHAMAS   Or Shamash. The officer of the Synagogue, beadle, sacristan, verger, who sees to keeping order, calling congregants to the Reading of the Law, looks after the sacred articles, and attends to Synagogue arrangements generally.

SHECHINA   God's Presence, the Glory of God, Ruach Hakodesh, the Holy Spirit, taken over in the New Testament as the Holy Ghost.

SHEKEL   Ancient Jewish coin in Biblical and Maccabean Palestine. Adopted by the Zionist Organisation as the name of its membership fee.

SHEVUOT   The Festival of Weeks, or Pentecost. The Festival of the First Fruits.

SHLOMO MOLKO   (1501-1532). A Portuguese Marrano, a secret Jew, who avowed himself openly as a Jew, and attached himself to the False Messiah David Reubeni (Max Brod's "Reubeni King of the Jews"). He was hailed as the Forerunner of the Messiah. He was burned by the Inquisition.

SCHMALZ HERRING   Fatty salt herring.

SHOCHET   Ritual slaughterer, qualified to carry out the killing of animals and poultry for food, in accordance with Jewish law.

SHOFAR   Ram's horn, sounded in Biblical times for the advent of Sabbath and Festivals and proclaiming the Jubilee. Sounded now in the Synagogues on the New Year and the Day of Atonement.

SHTETL   Literally, Township. A small town in places of compact Jewish life in Eastern Europe, with a distinctive Jewish way of life. Pictured typically in the town of Kasrilevke, immortalised by Sholem Aleichem.

SHTETL LIOZNE   Liozne was Chagall's birthplace, and is near the big town Vitebsk, where he grew up.

SIMCHAT TORAH   The Festival of the Rejoicing of the Law. The last day of the Festival of Tabernacles, commemorating the Giving of the Law at Sinai.

TALLITHIM   Or Tallism. Prayer shawls of wool or silk, with fringes, worn for public or private prayer, according to Biblical commandment. (Numbers 15.37).

TECHINOTH   Books of prayer and supplication.

TEPHILIN   Two black square leather boxes containing on parchment the Biblical passages in which they are enjoined—to wear "as a sign upon thy hand and between thy eyes." They are so worn at prayer, on the left arm near the heart, and on the forehead.

TEVYE STORIES   A series of stories by Sholem Aleichem, built round Tevye, a village milkman, which were used in the musical, Fiddler on the Roof. Tevye is the type of the Yiddish-speaking folk Jews of the old Eastern Europe, the embodiment of Yiddish folk life of the past generation.

TISHA B'AV   The Ninth of Av. Day of Mourning, commemorating the Destruction of the Temple.

TOSEFOTH   Explanations and glosses on the Talmud, originating from the French and German schools of Talmud of the 12th and 13th centuries. The Tosefoth are printed in the Talmud text, and are discussed with it.

TOSEFOTH YOM TOV   Rabbi Yom Tov Lipman Heller, Polish Rabbi (1579-1654). Author of "Tosefoth Yom Tov."

TRUMPELDOR   Joseph Trumpeldor, Russian army officer. 1880-1920. Distinguished himself at Port Arthur, where he lost his left arm, and was decorated for valour. Afterwards settled in Palestine, founding the Chaluz movement, recruiting young Jews mainly from Russia to do land work in Palestine. Founded and fought with the Zion Mule Corps with the British army in Gallipoli. Was killed beating off an Arab attack on Tel Hai in the north of Palestine.

TZE-ENU U'RENU   The Bible translation into Yiddish for women. The words mean "Come and Behold." It was compiled around 1600 by Rabbi Jacob Janov in Lublin, and includes a rich collection of Aggadic material, stories, legends and commentaries.

VEANI   The passage in Genesis—48.7—beginning with the word Veani, which means "As for me." Jacob remembering Rachel's death on the road, "and I buried her there."

YEHUDA HALEVI   (1086-1145). Spanish poet-philosopher, of the Golden Age of Spanish Jewry. Author of "The Kuzari," a philosophic work on the continuity of Jewish tradition.

YESHIVA STUDENTS   Older students attending a High School of Hebrew religious studies. Some, like Yeshiva College of New York, are on University level.

YISGADAL   The opening word of the Kaddish, the Glorification of God, recited in the Synagogue and also said specially by a mourner for his dead.

Bibliography

ALEXANDER, EDWARD, "Chaim Grade's Quarrel with Hersh Rasseyner," in Judaism, *Quarterly Journal of Jewish Thought*, Fall Issue, 1972.

ALEICHEM, SHOLEM, *The Old Country*, translations by Julius and Frances Butwin. Crown Publishers, New York, 1946; Andre Deutsch, London, 1958; Vallentine Mitchell, London 1973.

——, *The Great Fair*, translated by Tamara Kahana. Vision Press, London 1958.

——, *Mottel the Cantor's Son*, translated by Tamara Kahana. Abelard Schuman, London-New York, 1958; Collier, New York, 1961.

——, *Stories and Satires*, translated by Curt Leviant. Yoseloff, New York, 1959.

——, *Some Laughter Some Tears*, translated by Curt Leviant. Putnam, New York, 1969.

——, *Inside Kasrilevke*, translated by Isidore Goldstick. Schocken, New York, 1948.

——, *Stempenyu*, translated by Hannah Berman. Heinemann, London, 1913.

——, *Jewish Children*, translated by Hannah Berman. Heinemann, London, 1920.

——, *Sholem Aleichem Panorama*, edited by Melech Grafstein. London, Ontario, 1948.

——, *The World of Sholem Aleichem*, by Maurice Samuel. Knopf, New York, 1943; Vallentine Mitchell, London, 1973.

ASCH, SHOLEM, *Children of Abraham*, translated by Maurice Samuel.

——, *The Nazarene*, translated by Maurice Samuel.

——, *The Apostle*, translated by Maurice Samuel.

——, *Moses*, translated by Maurice Samuel.

——, *Passage in the Night*, translated by Maurice Samuel.

——, *Three Cities*, translated by Edwin and Willa Muir.

——, *Salvation*, translated by Edwin and Willa Muir.

——, *Mottke the Thief*, translated by Edwin and Willa Muir.

——, *The Calf of Paper*, translated by Edwin and Willa Muir.

——, *Tales of My People*, translated by Meyer Levin.

——, *Mary*, translated by Leo Steinberg.

——, *The Prophet*, translated by Arthur Super.

——, *Pushcarts and Dreamers*, translated by Max Rosenfeld.

——, *Three Novels*, translated by Elsa Krauch. Routledge, London, 1938.

———, *Song of the Valley*, translated by Elsa Krauch. Routledge, London, 1939.

AUSUBEL, NATHAN and MARYAN, *Treasury of Jewish Poetry*. Crown, New York, 1957.

BECK, EVELYN, *Kafka and the Yiddish Theatre*. University of Wisconsin Press, 1972.

BELLOW, SAUL, editor, *Great Jewish Short Stories*, Dell, New York 1966.

———, translator *Gimpel the Fool*, by Bashevis Singer.

BERMAN, HANNAH, translator: *Stempenyu* by Sholem Aleichem. Heinemann, London, 1913.

———, *Jewish Children*, by Sholem Aleichem. Heinemann, London, 1920.

BILETSKY, ISRAEL, *Essays on Yiddish Writers of the Twentieth Century*. Peretz Publishers, Tel Aviv, 1969.

BIRNBAUM, SOLOMON, "Cultural Structure of East Ashkenazic Jewry," in *Slavonic and East European Review*. London, 1946.

BLUM, ETTA, translator: *Poems by Jacob Glatstein*. Peretz Publishers, Tel Aviv, 1972.

CHAGALL, MARC, Illustrations to *Siberia* by Abraham Sutzkever, Abelard Schuman, New York, 1961, *Unesco Collections of Contemporary Works*.

CHARLES, GERDA, editor *Modern Jewish Stories*. Faber and Faber, London, 1963.

CLARK and LIEBER, editors *Great Short Stories of the World*. Heinemann, London, 1926.

CREEKMORE, HUBERT, editor *Little Treasury of World Poetry*. Scribner's, New York, 1952.

DAWIDOWICZ, LUCY D., *The Golden Tradition*. Holt, New York, 1967.

DLUZNOVSKY, MOSHE, *The Potter's Daughter*. Cooper Books, London, 1959.

Encyclopedia Britannica, Chambers' Encyclopedia, Encyclopedia Judaica, Valentine's Jewish Encyclopedia. Articles on Yiddish Literature.

FEINSILVER, LILIAN, *The Taste of Yiddish*. Yoseloff, New York, 1970.

FRANK, HELENA, translator: *Stories and Pictures. Tales by Peretz*. Jewish Publication Society of America, 1906.

———, *Yiddish Tales*. Jewish Publication Society of America, 1912.

GINSBURG, MIRA, translator *The Spinoza of Market Place*, by Bashevis Singer. Farrar Strauss and Giroux, New York.

GITTLEMAN, SOL, *Sholom Aleichem: A Non-Critical Introduction*. Mouton, The Hague, 1974.

GLATSTEIN, JACOB, *Poems by Jacob Glatstein*, translated by Etta Blum. Tel Aviv, 1972.

——, *Holocaust Literature*, joint editor. Jewish Publication Society of America, 1969.

GLICKSMAN, WILLIAM, *In the Mirror of Literature. Jewish Life in Poland Reflected in Yiddish Literature*. Living Books, New York, 1966.

GOLDBERG, ISAAC, translator *In Polish Woods*, by Joseph Opotoshu. Jewish Publication Society of America, 1938.

——, *A Lithuanian Village*, by Leon Kobrin, 1920.

——, *Temptations*, by David Pinski. Allen and Unwin, London, 1921.

——, *God of Vengeance*, by Sholem Asch. Samuel French, New York, 1932.

——, Editor *Great Yiddish Poetry*. Haldeman Julius, 1923.

GOLDSTICK, ISIDORE, translator *Inside Kasrilevke*. Schocken, New York, 1948.

GRADE, CHAIM, *The Wall*, translated by Ruth Wisse. Jewish Publication Society of America, 1967.

——, *Chaim Grade's Quarrel with Hersh Rasseyner*, by Edward Alexander, in *Judaism*, 1972.

GRAFSTEIN, MELECH, editor *Peretz Memorial Book*. London, Ontario, 1945.

——, *Sholem Aleichem Panorama*. London, Ontario, 1948.

GREENBERG, ELIEZER, joint editor *A Treasury of Yiddish Stories*. Viking, New York, 1954; Andre Deutsch, London, 1955.

——, *A Treasury of Yiddish Poetry*. Holt Rinehart and Winston, New York, 1969.

GROSS, A. H., translator *The Family Moskat*, by Bashevis Singer. Knopf, New York, 1950.

HOWE, IRVING, joint editor *A Treasury of Yiddish Stories*.

——, *A Treasury of Yiddish Poetry*.

IMBER, SAMUEL J., editor *Modern Yiddish Poetry*. East and West Publishers, New York, 1927.

KAHANA, TAMARA, translator *The Great Fair*, by Sholem Aleichem. Vision Press, London, 1958.

——, *Mottel the Cantor's Son*. Abelard Schuman, London, New York, 1958; Collier, New York, 1961.

KNOX, ISRAEL, joint editor *Holocaust Literature*. Jewish Publication Society of America, 1969.

KOBRIN, LEON, *A Lithuanian Village*, New York, 1920.

KREITMAN, MORRIS (CARR), editor *Jewish Short Stories of To-day*. Faber and Faber, London, 1938.

LANDIS, JOSEPH, *The Dybbuk and Other Great Yiddish Plays*. Bantam Books, New York, 1966.

LASK, I. M., translator *Burning Earth*, by Aaron Zeitlin. 1937.

LEFTWICH, JOSEPH, *Yisroel*, Anthology of Short Stories. Yoseloff, New York, 1963; original publication 1933.

——, *The Golden Peacock*, Anthology of Yiddish Poetry. Anscombe, London, 1939; revised edition, Yoseloff, New York, 1961.

——, *The Way We Think*, Anthology of Yiddish Essays (two vols.). Yoseloff, New York, 1970.

——, *The Book of Fire*, Stories by Peretz. Yoseloff, New York, 1960.

——, *Abraham Sutzkever*. Yoseloff, New York, 1971.

LEVIANT, CURT, translator *Stories and Satires*, by Sholem Aleichem. Yoseloff, New York, 1959.

——, *Some Laughter Some Tears*, by Sholem Aleichem. Putnam, New York, 1969.

LEVIN, MEYER, translator *Tales of My People*, by Sholem Asch. Putnam, New York, 1956.

LEWISOHN, LUDWIG, editor *Jewish Short Stories*. Behrman House, New York, 1945.

LIPTZIN, SOL, *A History of Yiddish Literature*. Jonathan David, New York, 1972.

——, *The Flowering of Yiddish Literature*. Yoseloff, New York, 1963.

——, *The Maturing of Yiddish Literature*. Jonathan David, New York, 1968.

——, *Peretz*. Yivo, New York, 1947.

MADISON, CHARLES, *Yiddish Literature Its Scope and Major Writers*. Ungar, New York, 1968.

MANGER, ITZIK, *The Book of Paradise*, translated by Leonard Wolf. Hill and Wang, New York, 1965.

——, "Itzik Manger Wandering Poet," by Joseph Leftwich. *Menorah Journal*, New York, 1952.

MARK, YUDEL, "Yiddish Literature," in *The Jews, Their History, Culture and Religion*. Jewish Publication Society of America, 1949.

MENDELE, *The Nag*, translated by Moshe Spiegel. Yoseloff, New York, 1958.

——, *The Parasite*, translated by Gerald Stillman. Yoseloff, New York, 1958.

——, *The Travels of Benjamin the Third*, translated by Moshe Spiegel. Schocken, New York, 1958.

——, *Fishke the Lame*, translated by Angelo Rappaport. Stanley Paul, London, 1920.

MUIR, EDWIN and WILLA, translators: Sholem Asch *Three Cities; Salvation; Mottke the Thief; The Calf of Paper*.

OPOTOSHU, JOSEPH, *In Polish Woods*, translated by Isaac Goldberg. Jewish Publication Society of America, 1938.

——, *The Last Revolt.* 1952.

——, *A Day in Regensburg.* 1968.

PERETZ, I. L., *Peretz Memorial Book,* editor Melech Grafstein. London, Ontario, 1945.

——, *In This World and the Next.* Stories from Peretz, tranlated by Moshe Spiegel. Yoseloff, New York, 1958.

——, *The Book of Fire.* Stories by Peretz, translated by Joseph Leftwich. Yoseloff, New York, 1960.

——, *Stories and Pictures.* Tales by Peretz, translated by Helena Frank. Jewish Publication Society of America, 1906.

——, *Yiddish Tales,* translated by Helena Frank. Jewish Publication Society of America, 1912.

——, *Bontse the Silent,* translated by Angelo Rappaport, 1927.

PERLOV, YITZCHOK, *The Adventures of One Yitzchok.* Introduction by Bashevis Singer. Award Books, New York, 1967.

PINSKI, DAVID, *Temptations.* Allen and Unwin, London, 1921.

RABOY, ISAAC, *Nine Brothers.* New York, 1968.

RAPPAPORT, ANGELO, translator *Bontse the Silent,* by Peretz.

——, *Fishke the Lame,* by Mendele.

ROBACK, A. A., *The Story of Yiddish Literature.* Yivo, New York, 1940.

——, *Contemporary Yiddish Literature.* World Jewish Congress, London, 1957.

——, *Curiosities of Yiddish Literature.* Sci-Art, Cambridge, Mass., 1933.

——, *Peretz, Psychologist of Literature.* Sci-Art, Cambridge, Mass., 1935.

ROSENFELD, MAX, translator *Pushcarts and Dreamers,* by Sholem Asch, 1967.

ROSTEN, LEO, *The Joys of Yiddish.* McGraw-Hill, New York, 1968.

SAMUEL, MAURICE, *Peretz, Prince of the Ghetto,* 1948.

——, *The World of Sholem Aleichem.* 1943.

——, *In Praise of Yiddish.* 1972.

Translations from Sholem Asch:

——, *Children of Abraham, The Nazarene, The Apostle, Moses, Passage in the Night;*

Translations from I. J. Singer:

——, *The Brothers Ashkenazi, Yoshe Kalb, The River Breaks Up, East of Eden, The Family Carnovsky.*

SHNEOUR, ZALMAN, *Noah Pandre,* translated by Joseph Leftwich. Lovat Dickinson, London, 1936.

——, *Noah Pandre's Village,* translated by Joseph Leftwich. Chatto and Windus, London, 1938.

——, *Noah Pandre.* Lee Furman, New York, 1936.

——, *Song of the Dnieper.* Roy Publishers, New York, 1945.

——, *Restless Spirit*, translated by Moshe Spiegel. Yoseloff, New York, 1958.

SINGER, BASHEVIS, *Gimpel the Fool.* Farrar Strauss and Giroux, New York, 1951.

——, *The Spinoza of Market Place.* Farrar Straus and Giroux, New York,

——, *The Family Moskat.* 1950.

——, *Satan in Goray.* 1955.

——, *The Magician of Lublin.* 1960.

——, *My Father's Court.* 1966.

——, *Mazel and Shlimazel.* 1967.

——, *Short Friday.* 1966.

——, *The Manor.* Secker and Warburg, London, 1968.

——, *When Shlemiel Went to Warsaw.* 1968.

——, *A Friend of Kafka.* Cape, London, 1972.

SINGER, I. J., *The Brothers Ashkenazi.* Knopf, New York, 1933.

——, *Yoshe Kalb.* 1936.

——, *The River Breaks Up.* 1938.

——, *East of Eden.* 1939.

——, *The Family Carnovsky.* 1943.

——, *In a World that is no More.* 1972.

SINGER, JOSEPH, translator *In a World that is no More*, by I. J. Singer, 1972.

SONNTAG, JACOB, translator *Siberia*, Poem by Abraham Sutzkever. Abelard Schuman, New York, 1961.

——, "The Development of Yiddish Literature," in *Literature and Western Civilisation*, London, 1973.

——, *Jewish Quarterly Omnibus*, editor. Yoseloff, New York, 1973.

SPIEGEL, MOSHE, translator *The Travels of Benjamin the Third*, by Mendele. Schocken, New York, 1968.

——, *In This World and the Next.* Stories from Peretz. Yoseloff, 1958.

——, *Restless Spirit*, by Zalman Shneour. Yoseloff, 1958.

——, *The Nag*, by Mendele, 1958.

STEINBERG, LEO, translator *Mary*, by Sholem Asch.

STILLMAN, GERALD, translator *The Parasite*, by Mendele.

SUPER, ARTHUR, translator, *The Prophet*, by Sholem Asch.

SUTZKEVER, ABRAHAM, *Siberia*, Poem, translated by Jacob Sonntag. Abelard Schuman, 1961.

WAXMAN, MEYER, *A History of Jewish Literature.* Bloch Publishing, New York, 1941; Thomas Yoseloff, 1960.

WEINREICH, URIEL, *College Yiddish.* Yivo, New York, 1966.

——, *Yiddish Language and Folklore.* Yivo, New York, 1959.

WHITE, BESSIE, translator, *Nine One Act Plays from the Yiddish*. Crescendo, Boston, 1968.

WISSE, RUTH, translator, *The Well*, by Chaim Grade. Jewish Publication Society of America, 1967.

WOLF, LEONARD, translator, *The Book of Paradise*, by Itzik Manger, 1965.

YAIR, ISH, editor, *Poet*, International Monthly, Jewish Number. Madras, India, April, 1968.

Yiddish: A Quarterly Devoted to Yiddish and Yiddish Literature. Queens College, New York.

ZEITLIN, AARON, *Burning Earth*. 1937.

de proprietatibus litterarum

Dfl.

de proprietatibus litterarum

Dfl.